# BRITISH MISSION
## TO THE JEWS
### IN NINETEENTH-CENTURY PALESTINE

# British Mission
# to the Jews
# in Nineteenth-Century
# Palestine

### Dr Yaron Perry
*University of Haifa*

FRANK CASS
LONDON • PORTLAND, OR

*First published in 2003 in Great Britain by*
FRANK CASS PUBLISHERS
Crown House, 47 Chase Side, Southgate
London N14 5BP

*and in the United States of America by*
FRANK CASS PUBLISHERS
c/o ISBS, 920 NE 58th Avenue, Suite 300
Portland, Oregon, 97213-3786

*Website*: www.frankcass.com

Copyright © 2003 Yaron Perry

British Library Cataloguing in Publication Data

Perry, Yaron
    British mission to the Jews in nineteenth-century Palestine
    1. Jews – Missions – Palestine – History – 19th century
    2. Protestant churches – Missions – Palestine – History –
    19th century
    I. Title  II. Yodim, Elizabeth
    266'.02341'05694

            ISBN 0-7146-5416-7 (cloth)
            ISBN 0-7146-8385-X (paper)


Library of Congress Cataloging-in-Publication Data

Perry, Yaron.
    [Nesi'im ve-ruah ve-geshem ayiun. English]
    British mission to the Jews in nineteenth-century Palestine / Yaron Perry;
    translated from Hebrew by Rebecca Toueg; edited by Elizabeth Yodim.
        p. cm.
    Includes bibliographical references and index.
    ISBN 0-7146-5416-7 (cloth) – ISBN 0-7146-8385-X (paper)
    1. London Society for Promoting Christianity amongst the Jews.
    2. Missions to Jews–Palestine–History–19th century.  3. Judaism–Relations–
    Christianity–History–19th century.  4. Christianity and other religions–
    Judaism–History–19th century. I. Yodim, Elizabeth. II. Title.

BV2619.L63P4713 2003
266'.0234105694–dc21                                        2002041564

Typeset in 11/12.5pt Palatino by Frank Cass Publishers Ltd
Printed in Great Britain by MPG Books Ltd, Victoria Square, Bodmin, Cornwall

To my Professor and friend
Alex Carmel
1931–2002

# Contents

# List of Illustrations

# Preface

This study originated in a random meeting which took place several years ago in the yard of the Anglican Christ Church in Jerusalem between my professor, Alex Carmel, and an English tourist who was particularly interested in the history of that church. During the conversation that developed between the two about the London Society for Promoting Christianity Amongst the Jews, which built the church in mid-nineteenth century, the Englishman wondered how it could be that Carmel, as a Jew and as an Israeli, did not despise such an institute. Carmel replied that he believed that 'every man shall live by his faith', and he went on to cite an array of prominent institutions that were built by the society during the process of the reconstruction of Palestine in the nineteenth century. At the end of the conversation, the Englishman introduced himself as the head of that mission society, and declared that, in view of these sincere statements, Carmel was cordially invited to England to review the society's entire collection of documentation, from its inception at the beginning of the nineteenth century to this day. After scrutinising the material (which no one had ever seen in its entirety before) and realising its massive scope, Carmel promised that the day would come when he would return with a student whom he would deem worthy of the task of writing a doctoral thesis on the basis of this confidential material.

Apart from its rich archives, the London Society has several periodical publications, two of them of particular importance, whose content encompasses its activities around the world and in Palestine in particular. The wealth of information to be found in these periodicals is often perceived by us as one-sided and biased. Support for this perception has also been found in the personal diaries of several figures operating in Palestine during the research period, which are also kept in the society's archives.[1] This study has therefore focused on locating and analysing documents kept in the archives of other institutions operating in Palestine at the time, in Britain and in other European countries. This endeavour included probing the archives of the Foreign Offices in London and in Bonn, the archives of the Anglican Church in London, and in particular, the archives of competing missionary societies in Birmingham, Oxford, Edinburgh and Basle.

Use of Turkish documents has been minimal since the Ottoman regime was not interested in the attempts of one type of 'heretic', in this case the Protestants, to convert other 'heretics', in this case the Jews. The scant Turkish material relevant to this study refers to rent agreements, building permits etc., which were translated by British interested parties. The Arab press at the end of that period was naturally interested in missions active among the Arab population, rather than the London mission, which focused on Jews, and only on Jews.

Several scholars have already dealt with the activities of the London Society in Palestine, and this study does not mean to contend with them. One remark must be made, however, regarding the most prominent of these scholars, Abdul Latif Tibawi, the Palestinian-British scholar who studied the British religious and educational initiatives in the context of British interests in Palestine in 1800–1901. His work discusses the British Foreign Office's policy through its consuls in Jerusalem and the activities of British institutions in the city, primarily the Anglo-Prussian bishopric, the Church Missionary Society, the Palestine Exploration Fund and the Jerusalem and East Mission. The London Society comprises only a small part of Tibawi's pioneering and comprehensive work, covering mainly the issues of faith and education in the city of Jerusalem until the end of the nineteenth century. Tibawi, however, did not, and possibly did not wish to, dwell on the centrality of the 'Jewish factor' in the general network of British interests in Palestine. In any case, he himself has admitted that he did not have the privilege of reviewing the Society's files.[2] Tibawi was thus forced to rely mostly, and then cautiously, on the book written by the official historian of the London Society, who has also presided at its head for many years.[3] This flaw in Tibawi's research has already been discussed by Meir Vereté, who pioneered Israeli research on the subject, in his excellent studies on the history of the British consulate in Jerusalem. Ironically, Vereté, who penned an in-depth study about ideological roots of the society in the years 1790–1840, was not privy to the society's archives either,[4] and this was why Vereté kept imploring Alex Carmel, his student, never to let go of the subject, until it would be possible to unravel the tale of the society's endeavours in Palestine, from beginning to end. The completion of that task eventually fell to my lot, and the result is now presented to the reader. I would like to thank Rebecca Toueg, who translated the text from Hebrew into English; and Elizabeth Yodim, for her editing of the manuscript.

## NOTES

1. See, for instance, *Joseph Barclay, Third Anglican Bishop of Jerusalem: A Missionary Biography* (London: 1883), p. 333. In response to his mother's complaints regarding the paucity of information sent by him from Jerusalem for insertion in the London Society's periodicals, Joseph Barclay (1831–81), third Protestant bishop in Palestine, mentions the regulation according to which critical statements about the Society should not be published. Barclay writes as follows:

   > The reason why I can write so little about Jerusalem is that it is forbidden by special rule of the Society. And as to so little being published that I write, it is accounted for by my position. Being head of the mission here, it would be indeed inconvenient to give to the world my opinions about private persons, and our plans of procedures. I dare say the Jews and Roman Catholics would also be glad to see them in print.

2. Tibawi, A.L. *British Interests in Palestine 1800–1901: A Study of Religious and Educational Enterprise* (Oxford: 1961), pp. 264–5. Tibawi explains that a special permit is required to examine the archival material of the London Society, and that the Society does not maintain an archive 'in the strict sense of the word'.

3. Gidney, W.T. *The History of the London Society for Promoting Christianity Amongst the Jews, from 1809 to 1908* (London: 1908).

4. Vereté, M. 'Why was a British Consulate Established in Jerusalem?' *The English Historical Review*, 85 (1970), pp. 318–19, where Vereté criticises Tibawi regarding the arcane methods of archival search; Vereté, M. 'The Restoration of the Jews in the Protestant Thought in England during the Years 1790–1840', *Zion*, 33 (1968), pp. 145–79 (Hebrew).

# Introduction

POLITICAL AND IDEOLOGICAL BACKGROUND

The process of 'opening up' the Holy Land began with the expedition of Napoleon Bonaparte (1769–1821) to Palestine on the threshold of the nineteenth century. The expedition was not noted in history as being very successful, and this was also the immediate impression it made on the country and its inhabitants. Its main impact on the history of Palestine was the gateway that was opened through which the Western powers and America entered at a later date. Napoleon fired the imagination of the public in those countries, being the first Christian military leader since the Crusades to have managed to take control of parts of the Holy Land, if only for a short time. By doing so he opened an additional fissure in the wall surrounding the Ottoman Empire, and his expedition served as a forerunner of the process termed the 'Crusade by Peaceful Means'[1] which was joined by other Western powers during the course of the nineteenth century.

Three decades passed before it became possible for another military commander to widen this fissure into a real opening. In the summer of 1832, with the assistance of France, Mohammed Ali (1769–1849), the Governor of Egypt, completed his conquest of Palestine and Syria as part of his campaign against Ottoman rule. Only the soldiers of Czar Nicholas I stood in the path that led to Constantinople. The obligation felt by Mohammed Ali and his son, Ibrahim Pasha (1789–1848), towards their ally in Paris and their desire to curry favour with other Western Powers led them to introduce a series of goodwill measures intended mainly for non-Muslim residents and the few foreigners residing in Palestine. These reforms carried the country across the threshold of the modern era and made it possible for the Western powers and their citizens to gain a foothold in Palestine and to alter it completely.

In 1839 Sultan Mahmud II (1785–1839) tried to avenge himself on Mohammed Ali by seeking the assistance of his European neighbours. The Prussians lent him a young officer to organise his army and the British signed a trade agreement with him. In the spring of that year, contrary to the advice of his allies, the Sultan sent his recruits into battle against Mohammed Ali, and by June, after having been soundly defeated, he dropped dead 'with rage in his heart and curses on his lips'.[2] His 16-year-old son and heir, Abdul Magid (1823–61), learnt the lesson of this defeat and was wise enough to enlist additional allies. Unlike the situation at the beginning of the decade, when Russia stood alone in the breach, she was joined this time by Prussia, Austria and most of all by Britain, who wished to see the Egyptian ruler 'withdraw into his original shell'.[3] In November 1840 Acre, 'the key to Syria and Palestine', surrendered and Mohammed Ali was pushed back into Egypt. The period of Egyptian rule was over, and, although the Ottoman Empire resumed control of Palestine, it was forced to respond to the expectations of the Western powers and to continue maintaining the course of political reform initiated by the Egyptians. It was within this framework that the London mission established a foothold in Palestine.

Britain showed very little interest in Palestine during the nineteenth century. In those days it was of prime importance for the British Empire not so much to take over Palestine and to speed the decline of the 'Sick Man on the Bosphorus', as the Ottoman Empire was then called, as to take the necessary steps to prevent other powers from carrying out any actions that might jeopardise British interests in the East. It is probable that the loss of the British Crown Colonies in North America several decades earlier had cast its shadow over British foreign policy, resulting in priority being given to India and the route that led to it. Even when Britain first became actively involved in events in Palestine – when Napoleon's attack upon the walls of Acre was repelled in 1799 by the naval cannons of Sir Sidney Smith (1771–1845) – she was motivated by her evident desire to prevent the French general from conquering India. Britain acted in a similar manner during the crisis of 1840, throughout the nineteenth century and until World War One.

In addition to this policy line, which gave preference to the rule of the Sublime Porte (the title given to the Ottoman ruler) and to securing the route to India rather than allowing the rule of a rival power, we should include the underlying aspects of Protestant England, which showed interest not in the holy sites in Palestine, but rather in the idea of the 'Restoration of the Jews', the principles of which will be described below. The main tenets of faith that had taken hold among the Protestants in the sixteenth century stated that the Second Coming of Jesus Christ was imminent, and his advent would herald the utopian epoch of the millennium. An important factor in this body of faith and a condition for the fulfilment of this apocalyptic vision was the return of the Jews to the land of their fathers and their immediate conversion, or, alternatively, their recognition of the Messianic claims of the Christian Saviour. The turbulence caused by the French Revolution in the minds of Protestants in Europe and the United States raised new hopes among the millions of Christian Protestants yearning for the Second Advent of Christ. Eschatologists, who based their doctrine on biblical prophecies and the New Testament,[4] saw the French Revolution as the first link in a chain of events that would confirm their beliefs and as the first testimony among many others of the imminent approach of the apocalyptic End of Days.

Some men of religious faith who were prompted by a deep sympathy for the Jewish people, which they had derived from the Holy Scriptures, considered the idea of their restoration as a means of atonement for the sins committed by the Church against the Jews. There were also some practical people who considered the Jews a useful tool in the process of hastening the return of the Messiah. In any event, both these groups gave active support to the return of the Jews to their homeland, either by attempting to make Palestine a habitable place, or by promoting the welfare of the Jews living in Palestine in order to attract their Jewish brethren in the Diaspora. Either way, their main purpose was still defined by the desire to bring the Jews closer to Jesus and thereby also to 'redemption'. On the basis of this belief, many societies were established around the world with the aim of spreading the missionary gospel among the Jews. The most prominent among all these is the subject of this study.

Before examining the guiding principles of the Protestant mission in the nineteenth century and the special characteristics of the London Society within its framework, it may be worthwhile to present as well the attitude of the Catholic Church towards everything that concerned missionary activity at that time. Generally speaking, precise distinctions between the various streams of Christian belief demand a wider canvas than the one now being spread out. Since our concern here is with Palestine, we shall deal only with certain central principles and substantial differences between Catholics and Protestants.

The Catholic Church is characterised by an explicit tendency to claim supreme authority over its congregation, either through Church leaders or the rulers of Catholic states, foremost of which is France. They saw it as their duty to initiate, guide and even finance missionary activity under the protective umbrella of the Vatican, and for that reason, the nationality of their delegates was only of secondary importance. In Palestine, for example, at the Carmelite monastery on Mount Carmel, Catholic monks of various nationalities served under the patronage of the King of France, and the tricolour flag was hoisted on the roof of the monastery. This gave the northern sector of the mountain the name 'French Carmel', which is still in use today.

At the beginning of the nineteenth century the Catholic mission reached an unprecedented nadir. The process of decline was already beginning to be evident during the eighteenth century with the decreasing powers of Spain and Portugal – once the banner bearers of Catholic Christendom. But the Catholics suffered their biggest reverse towards the end of that century during the course of the French Revolution and anti-clerical manifestations appeared in France and spread to other countries. Only after the Napoleonic wars had ended, and Europe had won 100 years of relative peace, did the Catholic mission resume its usual activities. Thus began the 'Century of Christian Missions'.

The vacuum left by the Catholics was quickly filled by the Protestant societies, some of which sprang up in the last decade of the eighteenth century, marking the beginning of the modern Protestant mission. The very structure of the Protestant Church, developing out of a community of believers rather than through a single, superior spiritual body, created a variety of national churches. Each of these individually, aside from spreading the gospel, tried to inculcate Western cultural values and the political heritage of its mother country. The Protestant mission occasionally served as an arm of colonial rule in order to realise the political interests of its country of origin, and sometimes contented itself with a certain degree of 'Spiritual Imperialism'. The two churches differed also in the economic sphere. The financial resources of the Catholic mission were derived from the budgets of church and state leaders. The Protestant mission, on the other hand, was supported by the large-scale collection of modest donations from the general community of believers. In certain cases large contributions were donated by wealthy adherents who set up a special fund, the interest from which was used to cover the needs of the societies. The rulers of Protestant states sometimes funded certain missionary enterprises as representatives of their subjects and were not necessarily motivated by foreign policy.

At the centre of Protestant belief stood the concept that the highest level of Christian activity lies in the transmission of the faith from one single individual to another. The Protestants regarded the Catholic idea of working within an entire community in order to convert it as a whole as superficial in effect. Another main characteristic of the Protestant mission was its tendency to work among non-Christian communities and to refrain from devoting too much effort to converting Catholic or Orthodox Christians into Protestant adherents. Such aspects typify most of the national Protestant churches, but not necessarily the Anglican mission, which will be discussed below.[5]

The main tenets of the London Society, derived from its affiliation with the Anglican Church, generally resemble those of the Protestant missions: the society focused upon the individual and did not try to work within whole communities or to 'create' new social groupings; the society was not funded by the church or state authorities, and its system of fundraising was based mainly on the contributions of its numerous adherents. In one area we find a salient difference, which sets the society apart from the general trend of Protestant missions: the society has never served as the political arm of Britain, even though its patrons and leaders were elected from among church leaders and the English aristocracy, if only because Palestine never was a colonial objective for Great Britain. The very opposite was true: in more than a few instances, disputes arose between the heads of the society in Jerusalem and the British consuls in the city concerning the definition of their roles. This indicates a unique phenomenon, which is incompatible with the accepted method for the dissemination of Western culture among the 'natives' by the missionaries.

The first decade of the London Society's activities in Palestine was characterised by the dispatch of missionaries from all ranks of European society on reconnaissance ventures that were doomed to failure. Among those sent from 1820 onwards were: a Swiss missionary who hired out his services to the society; a converted Jew from Bavaria; a well-to-do British jurist; an Irish doctor; and a Danish missionary. Only after the mission station had actually been set up was a fixed standard applied to the qualifications required of those appointed to serve in Palestine. The first choice for manning the senior positions, such as the head of the mission and the medical director was usually given to born Christians, preferably British nationals. On the other hand, most of the routine missionary jobs were deliberately assigned to converted Jews.[6]

It took only a few years of experience for the London Society to realise that converted Jews were able to penetrate Jewish communities with relative ease. Quite naturally, they gave first priority to the employment of emissaries who could speak the language of the local Jewish population and evidently made constant use of them. The relative success of the converted missionaries did not escape the notice of the Jerusalem rabbis, who assembled together to declare that:

> It is no secret matter that the most dangerous among the inciters are the 'apostates' who are of the seed of Jacob. Verily, the best among the propagandists, instigators, and seducers in the Land of Israel and in the East, have been, and still are, the apostates who have become the disciples of missionary institutions in Jerusalem and Safed.[7]

Various means were employed by the missionaries in their attempts to bring the Jews of Palestine closer to the Christian faith. First and foremost, they tried to expose them to the Christian scriptures. They set up a book depot, where texts sacred to Judaism and Christianity were available for sale or distribution. Converted Jews were employed in this repository to read certain chapters from the New Testament to passers-by in their own language. Jewish book lovers often came and discussed the relative merits of the two religions with the missionaries. In time, the missionaries improved their techniques of persuasion. For example, towards the end of the nineteenth century, a Jaffa missionary, taking advantage of the revival of the Hebrew language and the strong desire to obtain texts written in the holy tongue, promised to bestow a Hebrew bible free of charge on every Jew who first took the New Testament, studied the Gospel of Matthew and took a test to prove his proficiency.

Another way to reach the hearts of the Jews was to set up a secular school system with the intention of influencing the children of the community first, and then, through them, reaching their parents. The members of the Society took advantage of the fact that Jewish youngsters received only religious education in their communities, and offered them the acceptable alternative of a free education system. The missionaries also set up schools for Jewish girls, who were not provided with any educational institutions by their communities. In due course the education system of the London Society in Palestine developed further to include boarding facilities attached to the schools for boys and for girls, institutes for technical training, and educational frameworks for those interested in religious conversion, as well as evening courses for adults.

The institutions that proved to be the most successful in religious conversion were the hospitals of the London Society, whose leaders were well aware of the poor standard of health among the Palestinian Jews and of the total lack of any Jewish medical facilities. In the early stages of their missionary activities they already dispatched doctors to their mission stations, and opened both dispensaries for the sale and distribution of medicines and clinics to provide first-aid services. Once the mission stations were well established in Palestine and the real medical needs of the local population were realised, hospitals were built in Jerusalem and Safed. The deep gratitude felt by the Jewish patients towards the missionaries who served in the medical institutions made them far more receptive and willing to become familiar with the Christian scriptures. Occasionally medical treatment was made conditional upon listening to sermons and the study of the New Testament. A description of a typical morning in the Mission Hospital in Jerusalem goes as follows:

> All patients must be there by eight o'clock and, in order that the earliest comers may reap the advantage, each patient receives a metal number showing his order of coming. At eight o'clock the doors are closed and a short service is held in the waiting-room ... with an address in either Hebrew or Judeo-German. [Only] after the service the patients come one by one into the consulting room.[8]

The missionaries also instituted a wide-ranging welfare system intended for the benefit of Jews who had already converted and for the support of those intending to do so. Although they were careful enough to declare publicly that they would not buy the hearts of Jews with the promise of monetary support, they did not always keep their promise and gave economic assistance to converts and potential converts. Members of the society did not feel at ease with this approach and sometimes termed it a 'system of bribery'.[9]

WORLDWIDE ACTIVITIES OF THE LONDON SOCIETY

As stated, the present study deals with the history of the London Society and the contribution of its institutions and members to the development of Palestine in the nineteenth century. However, during the course of the period under research, the society sent out its members to establish branches in all parts of the world. It would therefore be well to take a glance, however brief, at the centres it established around the world in order to comprehend the extent and significance of its activities in Palestine. The activities of the society in its native city, London, are discussed in detail in this study in connection with the history of its founding and the connections of its institutions with events in Palestine. Activities in other parts of the British Isles were concentrated in three administrative areas. In the north, the most important cities were Liverpool and Manchester, the former being a port city through which thousands of Jews passed during the nineteenth century, on their way to the United States. This opportunity immediately caught the imagination of the society's leaders, and in 1838 Liverpool became a mission station second in importance only to the one in London. Jewish converts were appointed to head it, and towards the end of the century a medical wing was added to this mission station. In Manchester, a prominent city in its own right, the same process was repeated: in 1850 the mission station was opened there, to which a medical wing was added in 1897. In the southern part of England, the society established the centre of its activities in the city of Bristol in 1884, and a year later chose Birmingham as a residence for independent missionary representatives for the centre of Britain.

The first bridgehead of the London Society in Europe was established in Holland in 1820 in response to the demands of scores of Jews in Amsterdam. A converted Jew served as a full-time missionary until 1835 and then left to bolster the missionary centre in Poland. In 1844 the society resumed its full-scale activities in Amsterdam and founded another branch in Rotterdam, a port through which many Russian Jews were passing on their way westward.

The countries of Eastern Europe with their millions of Jews were the preferred focus of the London Society's activities. Because of the constantly shifting borders in those areas, and the frequent changes in rule, we shall mention only the main cities in which the society founded a centre. In the summer of 1821 it established its first permanent presence in Warsaw, and very soon set up additional centres in nearby cities which were also manned by chosen missionaries of British origin. In 1825 a permanent representative was nominated in the Posen district, where, within two years, a prominent educational institution was established. The districts of Galicia also received early attention with a mission station being set up in Cracow in 1833 and another one in Lvov in

1867. In Bucharest, one of the society's emissaries stayed for a few months in 1841, and in 1846 a permanent base was established there. In 1851 representatives were sent out to other Jewish centres, the foremost being the city of Jassy. In 1862 the society set foot in Pest (today part of Budapest) and also in Prague in 1869. In both these cities, the Scottish mission was simultaneously active among the Jews, and therefore, after a few years, the London Society elected to leave their Edinburgh colleagues to proceed with their work and to discontinue their own activities there. Towards the end of the nineteenth century the number of Jews living in these areas decreased as a result of growing anti-Semitism and also because of the inviting possibilities of employment in Western and Central Europe, mainly in Berlin. For this reason, the society diverted its attention to the realms of the Ottoman Empire and slightly reduced its presence in Eastern Europe.

In Western and Central Europe the leaders of the London Society recognised Prussia and the other Germanic states as having the greatest potential for missionary activity. In Berlin, which became a prominent centre for the Reform Movement in Judaism, a mission station had already been established in 1822 under the patronage of the King of Prussia. During the course of the nineteenth century, the society set up missionary outposts in about 40 additional cities throughout Germany. Towards the end of the century, it became a generally accepted policy in London to refrain from missionary activity in predominantly Protestant countries, since other missionary societies active there were faithfully performing their task. Correspondingly, the society thought that it was necessary to have the support of a national church in order to persuade the Jews more convincingly to adopt the Christian faith. Therefore, in conformity with its policy, the London Society decided to leave Berlin and the other German cities, and to leave the centre stage to the German Evangelical Church.

The activities in France during the nineteenth century were minor for two main reasons. One was rooted in the anti-religious spirit that spread through post-revolutionary France and affected the Jews living within its borders, who seized upon reformist beliefs more readily than their fellow Jews in other European states, and who, in any case, did not take much interest in religious matters. The second reason for the low level of missionary activity probably lay in the persistent hostility that hung like a dark cloud between France and Britain and may have hampered the ability of the Anglican mission to operate in France. Nevertheless, the first mission station was set up in Strasbourg in 1826 as a regional centre for activities in northern Switzerland, eastern France and the duchy of Baden, with an additional station being established in Paris in 1856. Neither of these stations proved to be successful for missionary work. To complete the picture of its activities in Europe, it is worth mentioning that the London Society also set up stations for various periods of time in Jewish centres in Italy, Austria, Switzerland, Denmark and Sweden, Spain and Portugal, and Greece.

The third focal point of the London Society's missionary activity to engage its considerable attention was the extensive stretches of the Ottoman Empire. The first station was established in Izmir in 1829. This port city contained a large Jewish community and also served as a major trade centre in the East, acting as a magnet for the inhabitants of neighbouring islands such as Rhodes and Crete, among others. The society set up another station in Constantinople in 1835 and added a third one in Salonica in 1847.

The society was quick to seek a foothold even in areas that were distant from the Ottoman capital. Visits had already been made in 1828 to Jewish centres in the cities of North Africa, and the first outposts were established in Tunis in 1834, in Morocco in 1844 and in Algeria in 1845. Baghdad was given a mission station of its own in 1844 after some misgiving about the difficulties that might arise given its considerable distance from transportation routes, the monetary investment needed, the hostile environment and the harsh climate conditions. Aleppo (Halab), which was an important Jewish centre in northern Syria, was adopted by the society in 1845, while a permanent station was set up in Damascus only in 1870. The strained relations between Muslims, Christians and Jews in Damascus made gaining a stable foothold there difficult, but its importance as a mission station induced the society to invest considerable resources in it, and, in 1895, a medical wing was opened to the same model as those in other important cities. Beirut, which from the very first served the society's emissaries as a springboard or rear station on the way to Palestine, was permanently staffed in 1849. A mission station was set up in Cairo in 1847 and the society maintained an intermittent representation in Alexandria from 1871 onwards.

Besides in Britain, the European continent and the Middle East, the society went on to establish mission centres in more distant areas, extending as far as Ethiopia, where it combined its efforts with those of other missions. The London Society, which desired to work among Ethiopian Jews (the *Falasha*, which means 'exiles' in the local language), did not maintain a mission station there but rather sent a few missionaries for limited periods of time during the course of the century. The society was not very successful in converting the Ethiopian Jews, but it certainly contributed its share to the controversy over the Jewishness of some of the Ethiopian immigrants to Israel today. Far-off Persia was already visited by the society's emissaries in the 1820s. However, only in 1889 were three permanent mission stations set up among the Jews of Isfahan, Teheran and Hamdan. Towards the end of the century the society conducted expeditions and activities on a limited scale among Jewish communities as far away as India, China and Canada.[10]

## NOTES

1. Tobler, T. *Nazareth in Palästina* (Berlin: 1868), p. 322.
2. Marriott, J.A.R. *The Eastern Question: An Historical Study in European Diplomacy*, 4th edn (Oxford: 1940), p. 238. Mahmud II died on 30 June 1839 after the defeat near Nessib northeast of Aleppo.
3. Ibid., p. 240.
4. Mainly Daniel 12; Matthew 20.
5. For a thorough analysis of this aspect see for example Latourette, K.S. *A History of the Expansion of Christianity*, Vol. 3: *Three Centuries of Advance* (New York, Evanston and London: 1939), pp. 36–42, 50–1.
6. Archive of the LJS, St Albans: General Instructions to Missionaries, 1850; General Instructions and Regulations for the Guidance of Missionaries and Agents, 1897. These contain a detailed account of the selection process for missionaries and the definition of their assignments. See also, *Jewish Records, Chiefly for the Use of Collectors and Small Subscribers of the London Society for Promoting Christianity Amongst the Jews*, 5 (1820), p. 7.
7. Grajewski, P.B.-Z. *The Struggle of the Jews Against the Mission from 1824 till our Times* (Jerusalem: 1935), n.p.: 'Introduction' (Hebrew).
8. *The Report of the London Society for Promoting Christianity Amongst the Jews*, 86 (March 1894), p. 99.
9. Archive of the LJS at the Bodleian Library, Department of Western Manuscripts, Oxford, Dep. Cmj, d.140: Letter from George Margoliouth to Oswald John Simon, dated 7 January 1887. This is part of a series of exchanges on the nature of missionary activity.
10. Reference sources for this chapter as a whole can be found in Gidney, W.T. *Sites and Scenes: A Description of the Oriental Missions of the London Society for Promoting Christianity Amongst the Jews*, 2nd edn, 2 Vols (London: 1899); *At Home and Abroad: A Description of the English and Continental Missions of the London Society for Promoting Christianity Amongst the Jews* (London: 1900); Gidney, *The History*.

# 1

# 1809–1841

BIRTH OF A SOCIETY

A great deal of ignorance exists in the subject of Mission to Jews. Some persons seem to think that, previous to the commencement of the present [nineteenth] century, no efforts whatever were made since Apostolic days for their Evangelisation. Others are inclined to magnify those efforts, and to give them an importance which they certainly did not possess ... We therefore propose to give a very brief account of what has already been attempted in this direction.[1]

The London Society for Promoting Christianity Amongst the Jews (abbreviated as LJS) emerged from another missionary society – the London Missionary Society – which was founded in London in 1795 and was involved in missionary activity among an extensive public and not specifically among the Jews. After a few years, when this society wished to extend its activities beyond the limits of the British Isles and expand into Africa, the need arose to recruit emissaries who could speak additional languages. The society therefore turned to the seminary for missionary training in Berlin – the Berliner Missionsschule, under the direction of Johannes Jänicke (1748–1827) – with a request for suitably qualified personnel. Jänicke sent three of his students to London in 1801, foremost among them being the converted Jew, Christian Friedrich Frey (1771–1850).[2]

Frey was born in Meinstockheim near Kitzingen in the duchy of Franconia. He changed his name from Joseph Samuel Levy to Christian Friedrich Frey when he was baptised as a Christian in 1798. From London, he was supposed to have been sent to the Cape of Good Hope in order to work at converting the Hottentot tribes, but was forced to wait a few months for a boat to transport him there. Because of his difficulties in understanding the English language, Frey spent his days in the company of the Jewish community in London, and even engaged in missionary work. He was very soon convinced of the need to give this community the full missionary attention it deserved, and submitted a request to

1. Christian Friedrich Frey, founder of the London Jews' Society

the directors of the society to allow him to remain in the city for another year. Frey had in the meantime composed a manual on practical methods for realising his plans to christianise the Jews of London, and submitted it to his superiors. The directors of the London Missionary Society granted his request, and Frey was sent for advanced study at its institution in Gosport (near Portsmouth). When he completed his studies there in May 1805 he was put in charge of missionary work among the Jews in the British capital.[3]

After a few years of work, Frey pleaded with the missionary leaders to apportion a more significant share of their endeavours to activities within the Jewish community, and to provide funds for the establishment of welfare institutions such as workshops so that the Jews could support themselves. In March 1809, after his demands had been rejected, in spite of his repeated attempts to impress his views upon his colleagues in the society, he realised that it would be better to create a separate framework for missionary activities among the Jews, and officially resigned from the London Missionary Society.[4] His resignation aroused the anger of his fellow missionaries, since Frey had become an able missionary in whose training much effort and expenditure had been invested. News of his desertion reached the inner circles of the Jewish community and one of its members even indicated the motive for Frey's resignation: 'A certain foreign convert, who adopted the name of Frey, exerted himself zealously to induce his former brethren to follow his example, like the fox which had lost its tail.'[5] Even before his resignation, Frey had tried to promote his ideas independently, and on 4 August 1808, he announced the establishment of an additional society to be called 'The London Society for the purpose of visiting and relieving the sick and distressed, and instructing the ignorant, especially such as are of the Jewish nation'. On 1 May 1809, when Frey concluded that the new programme was also inadequate, he decided to change the name of the society that he had just recently established to 'The London Society for Promoting Christianity Amongst the Jews'.[6] It was not by chance that stress was laid on the term 'promoting' in the title, implying that the society did not intend to convert the *entire* Jewish people but only to promote Christianity *among* them.

Two ideological trends were formed within the new London Society as soon as it came into being.[7] One of these, which was close to the established church, held the view that the time was not yet ripe for the active conversion of the Jewish people, but that one should provide for their welfare and confine oneself to attempts to bring them closer to the Christian faith. According to the second trend, which comprised those choosing to separate themselves from the established church, the time had come for full-scale conversion. These two trends began simultaneously to carry out their programmes to promote the objectives they had set for themselves, and actually began working among the Jews of London. For this purpose, the London Society rented a church that had just been built, changing its name to the 'Jews' Chapel', where they delivered sermons to hundreds of Jews in the city. In 1813 it also leased a large site which was named 'Palestine Place' and laid the foundation stone for a new church, schools, seminary and dormitory for converts.[8]

These hasty purchases brought the London Society heavily into debt in 1814, and drove it into a severe crisis. This adversity deepened the rift between the two leading trends and sharpened the differences between their ideological outlooks. In undertaking to save the society, Charles Simeon (1759–1836), an ideologist and a prominent clergyman in the Anglican Church, declared that it was mismanagement that had brought the society into this most embarrassing situation and that it was his duty to try to set it upon sounder foundations. The solution prescribed by Simeon to solve the crisis was for the faction closest to the established church to take upon itself the debts of the society and so gain full control over its institutions in the future, while the dissenters would be forced to resign. To assist him, Simeon enlisted Lewis Way (1772–1840) a qualified jurist and extremely wealthy.[9] Simeon and Way drew up a recovery plan that was based mainly on reduced expenditure, and, in exchange for implementing the plan, Lewis Way transferred a huge sum of money to the society to rescue it with one stroke from its deep crisis. Later, in 1821, Way founded a centre for training missionaries on his estate in Stansted.[10]

The solving of this crisis strengthened the bond between the London Society and the established Church, and in March 1815, after its general assembly ratified the decision regarding the change in its statutes, it became in actual fact an integral part of the Anglican Church. A few members of the dissenting faction were obliged to resign, first and foremost Christian Frey himself, who settled in the United States, where he continued his missionary activities. As a result of the resignation of the dissident leaders, conditions became more favourable for the appointment of politicians and prominent personages from the church elite as heads of the society.[11] The position of president of the London Society for Promoting Christianity Amongst the Jews was given to a Member of Parliament, Thomas Baring (1772–1848), and the position of patron of the society was conferred upon a bishop of the Church. In later years, from 1841 onwards, the bearer of this title was the Archbishop of Canterbury, the head of the Anglican Church.[12]

Missionary activity in those days was conducted mainly in London, and the financial supporters of the society thought it was high time to explore additional fields of activity outside the British Isles, mainly in the Mediterranean littoral and in Palestine. Lewis Way, who was passionately concerned with the destiny of the Jewish people and its right to acquire land in Palestine, devoted himself to this task. In 1815 after Napoleon's defeat at Waterloo, Way already tried to include in the framework of the Vienna Congress some mention of this yearning desire and thus to advance the aims of the society. When he did not succeed, he decided to interest the Czar of Russia in the matter, and financed a small delegation, which he himself headed, to conduct a survey of Jewish centres in Holland, Germany and Russia, with the crowning objective of meeting with Czar Alexander I (1777–1825) in January 1818. Nothing resulted from this endeavour either.[13]

In any event, it was then, at the end of the second decade of the nineteenth century, when the London Society was freed from its financial crisis and had resolved its ideological difficulties, that the time had come to put the feasibility of gaining a foothold in Palestine to the test.


EXPLORATORY EXPEDITIONS


> In the first two decades of the Society's existence, the activities of the Mission were minimal and almost nil, apparently because of the lack of financial means and also because it did not receive sufficient political support from any government. It also lacked a 'head' and a 'centre' and therefore could only act on an individual basis, with each missionary making his way according to his own opinion and style. For this reason, the activity of the Mission was ineffective in its early days until the Jewish year 5600 [1840].[14]

Nevertheless, the London Society decided to send out a missionary to determine at first hand the possibility of expanding missionary work in the East and in Palestine. They entrusted this task to the Swiss missionary, Melchior Tschudy (1790–1859), a native of Schwanden in the Canton of Glarus. All that is known of him from the Society's files is that, 'He had already travelled in the East, and was acquainted with the languages for such an undertaking.'[15] Armed with these qualifications, Tschudy left London in May 1820 and reached Malta at the end of July. He spent some time on the island in the company of two missionaries, the Maltese physician, Cleardo Naudi, a member of the Catholic Church in the service of the London Society, and William A. Jowett (1787–1855), a representative of the Church Missionary Society.[16] These two men were supposed to give him guidance and supply him with essential information regarding his destinations. An outbreak of malaria in the East resulting in the temporary closure of the Mediterranean ports forced Tschudy to spend a few more months in Malta. During that period of time Jowett and Naudi put together an itinerary that would take the Swiss missionary to the port of Alexandria and from there to Jerusalem, Safed, Nazareth, Nablus (Shechem), Damascus and Aleppo.

Since the aim of Tschudy's journey was to examine the conditions in the East, great importance was attached to his expected reports. A precise timetable and specific locations were selected in advance for the dispatch of reports and the receipt of ongoing instructions from the society. Jowett and Naudi even recommended that Tschudy should write his reports in German, his mother tongue, so that he would be able to express his feelings freely:

> The translation of them will cost the Society at home a few pounds; the saving will be Mr. Tschudy's time and health, which would be greatly interrupted if, in the midst of his arduous and various pursuits, he had to write in a strange tongue; in which, moreover, he could never adequately express his genuine feelings and opinions.[17]

Tschudy left Alexandria for Palestine at the beginning of 1821, and during the course of his journey managed to convert a few Jews. However, it soon became clear that choosing him was a bad bargain, as he turned out to be a crook, and that among his other double dealings he had offered his services to the Turkish governor as a military strategist. The man

> was evidently a mere speculator. He had already offered the Pasha to drill the Arabs in military tactics in the Desert, provided he was made governor of Arabia and Commander-in-Chief of the troops! He was also a quack, and sold medicines to the ladies, in order that they might be blessed with children; moreover, he pretended to know witchcraft.[18]

Tschudy's deceptions came to the attention of his London superiors in September 1821 and they remained baffled by the situation until April 1822, when they sent a letter to his place of residence in Aleppo stating that the employment contract between him and the Society was signed for a year only, and that, since this period had already elapsed, the Society needed merely to adopt an earlier decision and terminate his employment.[19]

The person who had been informed about Tschudy's fraudulence and reported it to London was Joseph Wolff (1795–1862), an emissary of the society who was in Alexandria at that time. Wolff was the son of David Levy, the rabbi of the Jewish community in the town of Weilersbach near the city of Bamberg in Bavaria. His childhood had been spent with his family in various parts of Germany since his father held temporary positions in several Jewish communities. At the age of 11 he left his home in Württemberg and began wandering through Europe in search of a new faith. In 1812 he was baptised as a Catholic in the Franciscan church in Prague, and adopted the name of Wolff.[20]

In 1819 Wolff arrived in England, contacted the directors of the London Society and went through a two-year training period at various institutions. During the course of his studies he displayed outstanding talent and devotion to the missionary society doctrine. Lewis Way describes him as one

> who passes his days in disputation, and nights in digging the Talmud, to whom a floor of brick is a feather bed, and a box a bolster ... who travels without a guide, speaks without an interpreter, can live without food, and pay without money ... .[21]

In April 1821, before he had completed his training, he decided to set out on a travelling expedition among the Jewish communities in the East. The society thought he should stay on for an additional period in its training institutes, and hindered his departure. Finally, after obtaining monetary support from a wealthy banker and strongly expressing his intentions to act within an independent framework and not according to the limitations of committees and societies, he received the blessings of the London Society for his travel plans.[22]

In August 1821, Wolff left Malta for Alexandria and in March 1822 reached the gates of Jerusalem. For three months he lived among the Armenians in the city and slowly became acquainted with the various Jewish communities in Jerusalem. In the course of his conversations and discussions with the rabbis of the city, especially those of the Ashkenazi community of German and European Jews, he cleverly managed to construct a network of relationships which strongly convinced him that: 'the door is fully open for proclaiming the Gospel in Jerusalem among the Jews'.[23]

Because of local political disturbances in the summer of 1822, Wolff had to leave Jerusalem and spend a period of time in Aleppo and in Alexandria, and left Egypt in November with the intention of returning to England.[24] In Malta, he met two American missionaries, Pliny Fisk (1792–1825) and Jonas King (1792–1869), members of the organisation of American Missions – the American Board of Commissioners for Foreign Missions. This organisation was then taking its first steps in the East, and the emissaries of the American mission often used to join the travelling expeditions of their English colleagues.[25] Wolff was highly impressed by the personalities of his newly acquired friends and gave up his intention of returning to England, choosing instead to guide the two missionaries to Palestine. In January 1823 the three men set out, and in April, after a stay in Egypt, they arrived in Jerusalem. On his second visit, Wolff was received with great warmth by his Jewish friends and even stayed at a residence placed at his disposal on

Mount Zion. The three months they spent in intensive missionary work were summed up by Wolff in his optimistic report to London: 'There is now at Jerusalem, by God's grace, a feeling and a spirit of inquiry excited among the Jews … which never existed among them before.'[26] But the oppressive Jerusalem summer undermined his health, and in July 1823 Wolff had to leave the city. Like many other foreigners, he could not bear the stifling heat and chose to spend the summer months in the mountains of Lebanon before continuing on to the Jewish centres in Eastern Europe.

After a few years Wolff conducted another comprehensive tour among the Jewish communities of the East and in due course visited Jerusalem for the third time in 1829. To his surprise, he found an estranged Jewish public, since the rabbis, with whom he had formed a courageous friendship during his former visits, had passed away in the meantime. Because of this, Wolff began working among the Greek Orthodox community and even declared that he would found two schools for them, one for boys and one for girls. This aroused the hatred of the community's leaders, who forbade any contact with him. The hostility reached a climax during a sermon which Wolff was giving in a café in the city. There, according to his testimony, a member of the community put some poison into his drink. Wolff became sick for several weeks and in July 1829 barely managed to escape from Palestine.[27]

The statement made by Wolff during his first stay in Palestine in the spring of 1822, that the doors of Jerusalem were wide open, planted a hope in the minds of the London Society leaders that conditions were ripe for the establishment of a first mission station. They therefore sent out a delegation headed by Lewis Way, a society member and philanthropist, together with another missionary, William Bucknor Lewis, who was nominated to set up a permanent basis in Jerusalem. In May 1823, after a stay in the south of France and in Malta, they sailed for the port of Tyre in order to spend the summer in the mountains of Lebanon. During their stay there, Way decided to carry out the idea conceived by Wolff a year earlier of establishing a seminary in the village of Antoura. This was intended for the training of missionaries on their way eastward, and to accustom them to the heat and to 'living on an Asiatic diet (which consists in a transition from potatoes to cucumbers, from roast beef to rice, &c.). Without these qualifications, our young men had better go to Poland and Germany, than be sent to Syria, to languish and die … .'[28] Lewis Way never managed to reach Jerusalem as his poor health forced him to return to England at the end of the summer of 1823.

His fellow delegate, William Lewis, who remained in Lebanon, had to complete the task alone, and set out on his journey, spending long periods of time among the Jewish communities of Safed and Tiberias. On 13 December 1823 he entered Jerusalem and found a Jewish community completely impoverished and in need of protection. Lewis remained in the city for five weeks, and before returning to Beirut he also visited Hebron to complete a meticulous examination of the conditions for the establishment of London Society institutions among the Jews of Palestine.[29] In May 1824 Lewis sent an exhaustive report on the situation of the Jews in Jerusalem in which he recommended the ways in which future emissaries could increase their chances of success. He suggested that the Jews in the city should not be treated as a single, homogenous group, but that the two main communities should be distinguished as separate groups. In his view, missionaries of German origin should work among the Ashkenazi community of Yiddish speakers, and British missionaries should be trained to work with the Arabic- and Ladino-speaking Sephardi community. For the placement of permanent mission stations, Lewis reported that the Jews lived in four cities – Jerusalem, Hebron, Safed and Tiberias – and in his opinion two stations should be set up at this stage: one in Jerusalem, which would include activities in Hebron, and the other in Safed, which would include the Jewish community in Tiberias. He therefore wrote to the London Society requesting them to spare him the need to study Yiddish and send a German missionary to Jerusalem for the Ashkenazi community, leaving him free to work among the Sephardim.[30]

The summary report of William Lewis in Palestine and his conception regarding the establishment of a permanent basis induced the London Society to dispatch another missionary to Jerusalem. The task was given to Dr George Edward Dalton (d.1826), a doctor by profession and a native of Wexford in Ireland. He was sent to enhance the work of the mission by making the London Society a pioneer in the field of medical missions in Palestine. In the summer of 1824 Dalton went to Malta, where he stayed for a few months because of the birth of his son, and at the beginning of 1825 he arrived with his family in Beirut.[31]

In April, Dalton continued on his own to Jerusalem, where he met his colleague, Lewis. A few days after his arrival, they were both caught up in the riots against the Pasha of Damascus and his attempts to crush it.[32] During the disturbances the Jewish community and the group of foreigners in the city suffered casualties. The two missionaries took part in calming the situation. Lewis intervened with the authorities and even succeeded in freeing one of the rabbis from prison, while Dalton occupied himself with treating the wounded. By mid-May, the gloomy atmosphere that these events cast over them raised their fears regarding the difficulties that might be expected when a permanent mission station would be set up in the city. Dalton reported that, 'Missionaries must come to this field prepared to wait, and now and then do "here a little and there a little".'[33] But he also found a glimmer of hope in his contacts with the rabbis of Jerusalem, who, in his judgement, highly esteemed those of British nationality. The reason for this and for the sympathetic attitude towards him apparently resulted from the medical assistance he had rendered to members of the Jewish community.

Dalton, who had left his wife and son in Beirut, spent some of his time examining whether the conditions in Jerusalem made it possible for missionaries to reside there with their families. He discovered that the practical problems and the tyrannical system of government made it difficult for the missionaries to remain. But there were also weighty reasons in favour of the missionaries settling in Jerusalem, especially those with families. In his view, if a realistic solution could be found by the acquisition of a residence with a garden attached, 'as it would not be prudent at all times for females to go out of doors', a permanent settlement in the city would be a possibility.[34] However, the unquiet increased in Jerusalem and only at the beginning of May 1825 were the missionaries able to take advantage of a temporary lull in the hostilities to escape to Beirut.

In the second half of that year, because of the doctor's ill health, Dalton and his family remained on the shores of Lebanon waiting for news that the riots in Jerusalem had died down. Only in mid-December was it possible to go there again, and he reached the city on Christmas Day. But Dalton did not live very much longer. On 3 January 1826 he expressed great satisfaction at being joined by 'the new Englishman' – a London Society missionary, John Nicolayson (1803–56), who had to spend the three weeks of their acquaintance at Dalton's sick bed. On 25 January 1826 Dalton died and was buried at his request in the cemetery of his Greek Orthodox friends on Mount Zion in Jerusalem.[35] On his deathbed he still had the strength to say that 'the friends of the cause in England have too high an opinion of what has been done here, for as to the establishing of a mission in Jerusalem, or any other place in the country, nothing has been done as yet'.[36]

STRIKING ROOT

A new era dawned in the history of the London Society in Palestine with the arrival of John Nicolayson (his original name was Hans Nicolajsen). There was no longer any need for exploratory expeditions to learn about the country and its inhabitants, nor failed attempts to set up a permanent mission station, but it was finally possible for the society to strike root in Jerusalem and to open the way for building a mission house. Nicolayson was born on 1 June 1803 in the town of Lügumkloster in Schleswig, Denmark, and was educated in the spiritual faith of the Danish Lutheran Church. While still a youth, he was seized with the desire to devote his life to missionary work, and in March 1821, before reaching the age of 18, he left his family and moved to Berlin in order to study at the seminary for missionaries – the above-mentioned Berliner Missionsschule of Johannes Jänicke.

In April 1823 Nicolayson was sent to London and spent two years in the society's training centre in Stansted. After completing his studies he was entrusted with the task of joining George Dalton in Jerusalem and filling the post of William Lewis who wished to return to England. On 21 December 1825, Nicolayson landed in Beirut and was received by Dalton's wife, who informed him, to his surprise, that the doctor had gone to Jerusalem in spite of his failing health. Nicolayson hurriedly left for Jerusalem on 27 December to join Dalton and keep him company in order to take advantage of the experience Dalton had acquired during his previous stay in the city. On reaching his destination and meeting Dalton, he soon found himself attending him at his deathbed. The loss of his colleague was a heavy blow to Nicolayson, who expressed his emotions in a letter to London in which he noted Dalton's exceptional qualities, stressed the great loss to the society, and asked for their compassion towards the grieving widow and orphans. He also solicited sympathy for himself, lamenting his bitter fate: 'young and inexperienced as I am in the work of the Lord, I am left the only Missionary of the Society in this country'.[37] During this visit, Nicolayson made no advance at all in setting up a permanent mission station. The events that had occurred and the distress they caused induced him to return the way he had come, to Beirut, on 17 February 1826. Two days before this he wrote in his diary that the events in Jerusalem had left him 'absolutely a solitary stranger in that then strange country … The two months I have spent in Jerusalem were a time of intense trial and testing to myself rather than of actual labour among the Jews.'[38]

He remained in Beirut until November 1826, and then rented an apartment in Safed, in the Galilee, where he resided until the middle of May 1827. During his stay there, Nicolayson made a thorough examination of the possibilities of establishing a mission in the Galilean city, and noted the stubborn objections of its residents. One of his conclusions was that activities of a medical nature would be of great assistance in capturing the hearts of the Jews. When he returned to Beirut there were increasing rumours of an impending war. Nicolayson was caught up in the midst of the tension created by the continuing struggle of the Greeks to free themselves from Turkish rule. Britain's pro-Greek intervention affected the attitude towards the Christians in general and to the foreigners who were British subjects in Palestine and Syria in particular.[39] A few of the Christian residents found refuge in the Lebanese mountains while the missionaries under British protection had to leave altogether. In mid-January 1828 Nicolayson returned to Beirut with Dalton's widow, and they were married there. But in May 1828, because of the circumstances resulting from the outbreak of the 1828–29 war between Russian and Turkey, the couple were forced to sail for Malta.[40]

During the next two years Nicolayson attempted to make a close observation of the Jews living in the Mediterranean basin, and especially of the Jewish communities in North Africa. To accomplish this task, the society dispatched Samuel Farman (1808–78), a young and inexperienced missionary, to join Nicolayson in September 1829 in order to complete his education in missionary work and improve his command of Eastern languages. In July 1831 Farman left Nicolayson and set out on a comprehensive tour of Palestine, staying for about a month and a half in Safed. He used his time there to establish contacts with the Jewish community and tour the surrounding area. Among other places, he visited Acre, where he became aware of the winds of war that were beginning to blow throughout the country and of the views of the public regarding the situation. Farman recorded his thoughts in his diary:

> Mahomed Ali is preparing a great army, whose destination is against Acre and Damascus. How far this report is to be depended on, I cannot say. The Christians and Jews greatly rejoice in the expectation of the event. Wherever I go, I am constantly asked, 'When will Mahomed Ali's army come?' or 'When will the English come and rescue us from the cruel tyranny of the infidel Moslems?'[41]

It seems that the local Jews and Christians under Turkish rule saw the European foreigners, nationals of foreign powers in

Palestine, as one group without making any distinction between the different nationalities.

At the end of August 1831 Farman was taken by surprise by the appearance of Nicolayson, who had returned to Palestine to purchase a building which could serve as a future mission house. The fresh breezes blowing across the country as a result of the expected conquest by Mohammed Ali encouraged Nicolayson. As an American journal put it:

> The inhabitants of Syria no longer look to Constantinople for their laws, but to the banks of the Nile where a man once a poor orphan boy in Macedonia has raised himself by the force of his character to an independent and powerful sovereignty; and as a patron of the liberal arts and sciences, emulates the renowned among the Caliphs of Bagdad.[42]

Such a state of mind led Nicolayson to write a report concerning the possibility of putting his work in Palestine into an organised framework. In his view, the influence of the foreign consuls in neighbouring countries had become stronger than ever before, and this improved the atmosphere in which the missionaries worked. He claimed that it was now possible to realise the plans for setting up a permanent mission station in Safed if a suitable building could be found. In Jerusalem, he noted, it was necessary to add at least one other missionary family in order to succeed in maintaining continual missionary activity. But the hopes of Nicolayson and Farman to obtain a foothold in Safed were disappointed and they both returned to Malta in September 1831.

In April 1832 Nicolayson and his family went back to Beirut and in mid-August Farman joined them once more. At the beginning of January 1833 Nicolayson welcomed another missionary, Erasmus Scott Calman (1796–1890), a converted Jew and a native of Bauska in Courland (now in Latvia), situated on the shores of the Baltic Sea. Calman made his way from England as an emissary of the London Society to his assigned station in Baghdad, but in Beirut it became evident to him that he would not be able to continue on to his destination through to Damascus in the near future, and so he changed his plans and chose to go instead to Jerusalem. Nicolayson, who had already been wanting for some time to return there, decided to accompany his new colleague.[43]

On 22 January 1833 Nicolayson and Calman reached Jerusalem and presented themselves, as a routine procedure, before the governor of the city in order to inform him of their arrival. The new order in Palestine after the Egyptian conquest had an effect even on the manner in which the missionaries were received. For the first time after the many earlier visits to Jerusalem, Nicolayson was given to understand that the governor would make every effort to be of service to him.[44] The sense of optimism continued to surround them throughout their visit to the city, and the contacts made by Calman, who spoke Hebrew, with the members of the Jewish community were conducted with great success. Nicolayson began searching for a suitable building and discovered that he would have no difficulty finding one. He was assisted by Joseph Amzalak (1778–1845), a wealthy Jew born in Gibraltar and holding British citizenship, whom he had met earlier. Amzalak had just then been on the verge of buying a new residence and offered to put his present house at the disposal of the mission. Both its size and location suited their needs perfectly, as Nicolayson noted in his diary, though he hastened to add that he did not know to what extent it was possible to rely on such a proposal.[45]

In the meantime, Calman was obliged to leave Jerusalem and complete the journey to his original destination in Baghdad. Nicolayson reluctantly accompanied him part of the way in Palestine in order to give him the benefit of his experience and to serve as his interpreter in his contacts with the Sephardi community. Although Nicolayson was unhappy to leave Jerusalem, he retained some measure of hope that their short stay in the city would lead to permanent residence. The two men visited Tiberias and Safed and then parted company, Calman going on to Damascus and Nicolayson returning to his family and his colleague Samuel Farman in Beirut. After a few weeks, Nicolayson took advantage of the fact that two American missionaries, William Jones Hardy and William McClure Thomson (1806–94), wished to settle in Jerusalem, and quickly joined them with the intention of renting a house in the city where his family could live together with Thomson's family, thereby confirming his view that two missionary families were necessary for the establishment of a permanent mission station. When the missionaries reached their destination they found that Amzalak had not yet bought a new residence; however he undertook to help in purchasing a building near his home. After difficult negotiations he managed to lease a building for Nicolayson for the period of one year beginning on 20 May 1833.[46]

Nicolayson preferred to spend the summer of that year in Beirut for organisational purposes, and on 22 October 1833 settled down with his family in their first permanent home. This is the mission house belonging to the London Society for Promoting

Christianity Amongst the Jews, which stands opposite David's Tower near Jaffa Gate in Jerusalem. It seems that it needed a man of determined character – one who had arrived in Jerusalem as a young, inexperienced missionary only 22 years old, going straight to the deathbed of a colleague – to take advantage of political changes in the region and to succeed in giving the society a firm base in the initial stages of its existence in the Holy Land. Nicolayson himself wrote in his memoirs:

> Only when the Egyptian army under the command of Ibrahim Pasha had entered Palestine was I able to return with my family from Malta to Beirut, and after the conquest of Acre and complete [Egyptian] control over the country [I managed] to settle for the first time in Jerusalem ... Therefore it should be noted that the first permanent settlement of the [Protestant] Mission in Jerusalem itself began only in 1833.[47]

About half a year had gone by since John Nicolayson had begun enjoying the comforts of living in the permanent residence of the London Society before he was faced with new troubles. At the end of May 1834 the city was swept up into a state of emergency when thousands of armed farm workers massed outside the walls. Revolts broke out in the regions of Nablus and Hebron in response to many of the new measures introduced by Mohammed Ali, but mainly because of the decree that every fifth Muslim in Palestine would be recruited into the army.[48] Although Nicolayson and his family as well as other Christians in the city, were not hurt, that the large military force encamped near their home close to Jaffa Gate did not augur well. On 26 May, when the rebels attempted to break into the city, the Egyptian soldiers defended themselves with canon shots from the top of the citadel and from the walls. At one o'clock in the afternoon another disaster occurred in the form of an earthquake, the first of a series of strong earthquakes that shook the city for several days.[49] Nicolayson recorded his feelings in his journal:

> To fill up the bitter cup now wrung out to the inhabitants of this city, the report of plague within the walls seems now fully established. ... Thus the number of God's four great and sore judgements is filled up – earthquake, war, scarcity, and plague, all within the narrow space of less than a month.[50]

The plague broke out in full force, and affected the Protestant families, every member of whom fell ill.

At the end of October 1834 Nicolayson found relief for the first time in months in the return of Erasmus Scott Calman sooner than expected. He could now, once again, devote himself with added energy to the work of the mission, reinforced by the valuable assistance of Calman, who was much liked by the Jewish community in Jerusalem. In November 1834 and in April 1835 Nicolayson took part in the tours conducted by his American missionary colleagues in Bethlehem and Hebron, during which he visited the local Jewish community. During that same winter Calman's health began to deteriorate and on 30 April, as a result of his frequent bouts of fever, Nicolayson had to send him back to Beirut. In the summer months Nicolayson's own health was undermined and at the end of October he also returned to Beirut.[51]

In the five-month period he spent away from Jerusalem, Nicolayson visited the mission station in Izmir and made the acquaintance of Simeon Rosenthal (d.1882), a native of the Danubian principate of Wallachia. Rosenthal, who was then in the process of becoming a Christian, was baptised on 14 April 1839 as Wildon Charles Simeon. Nicolayson performed the baptismal ceremony for the Rosenthal family in Jerusalem, the first to receive baptism in Palestine and to adopt the Protestant faith. The ceremony included the baptism of Rosenthal, his wife, his eldest daughter of 14 years, and his four-year-old son. Nicolayson was very moved as this was the first time he had conducted a ceremony for the conversion of a Jew. Rosenthal served the London Society as a talented missionary and was well liked by the Jewish community.[52]

Meanwhile, on 27 March 1839, a British political element was added to the religious one in the form of Vice-Consul William Tanner Young. Fourteen years prior to Young's arrival to man the new position in Jerusalem, the suggestion for such an appointment had already been made. In May 1825, after Dr George Dalton had completed his maiden tour of Jerusalem, he had sent his observations, which included the proposal for the appointment of a British consul in the Holy City, to London.[53] Of course, Dalton recognised the fact that this was a matter for His Majesty's government to decide and that Jerusalem did not have the status of a port city or trade interests that would obligate such an appointment. But, in his opinion, the number of foreign residents and the subjects of the great powers among the Jewish community, as well as the European travellers who occasionally passed through the city, justified a serious examination of this proposal. His point of view was naturally that of a missionary, and therefore Dalton went as far as to claim that, 'Could this be effected, it would afford a very interesting position for a pious man to hold. Few, perhaps, would have more opportunities of forwarding the objects of mission, and particularly among the European Jews resident in Jerusalem.'[54] However, Dalton's suggestion in 1825 for the appointment of a British consul in Palestine evidently did not go further than the limited audience of the journal in which it was published.

In October 1834 John William Perry Farren, the British consul in Damascus, visited Jerusalem. At the end of the visit and being impressed with that city's importance, he nominated Serapion Murad, an Armenian of Jaffa, who at this time was acting as the trade representative of Sardinia, to be the consular agent of Britain in Jerusalem, and he applied to the British Foreign Office to confirm the appointment. The mass of correspondence exchanged between London and its representatives in Damascus, Beirut and Alexandria with regard to the necessity of establishing such a position in Jerusalem strangled the initiative in its cradle. Only in 1836, when asked about the matter in connection with anxieties regarding the close political rapprochement of Russia and France to Mohammed Ali, did the Foreign Minister, Henry John Temple Palmerston (1784–1869), decide in favour of the idea and asked Patrick Campbell (1779–1857), the British consul in Egypt, to select someone suitable for the job. Campbell applied to his colleagues in Damascus and Beirut to help him choose a candidate. Niven Moore (1795–1889), the British representative in Beirut, quickly put forward the name of his business partner, William Young, and in September 1837, after lengthy negotiations with the Sublime Porte, the appointment of Young as the first vice-consul of Britain in Jerusalem was ratified.[55]

A year later, Anthony Ashley-Cooper, later the 7th Earl of Shaftesbury (1801–85) – the most enthusiastic public figure with no political affiliations, who was in favour of the idea of the restoration of the Jews and who became President of the London Society from 1848 until his death – recorded in his diary on 29 September 1838:

> Took leave this morning of Young, who has just been appointed Her Majesty's Vice-Consul at Jerusalem! He will sail in a day or two for the Holy Land. If this is duly considered, what a wonderful event is this! The ancient city of the people of God is about to resume a place among the nations, and England is the first of Gentile Kingdoms that ceases 'to tread her down'. If I had not an aversion to writing … I would record here, for the benefit of my very weak and treacherous memory, all the steps whereby this good deed has been done

... I shall always, at any rate, remember that God put it into my heart to conceive the plan for His honour, gave me influence to prevail with Palmerston, and provided a man for the situation who 'can remember Jerusalem in his mirth'.[56]

Two days before the prospective vice-consul arrived in Palestine, official confirmation was given of the decision to combine the political appointment with the concern for the welfare of the Jews, which also implied their return to the land of their forefathers. Palmerston sent a letter to Young in which he instructed him that, 'It will be a part of your duty as British Vice Consul at Jerusalem to afford protection to the Jews generally.'[57]

In the summer of 1840 there were increasing indications, even in Palestine, that another round of hostilities was to be expected in the struggle between Turkey and the Egyptian ruler. The young Sultan, Abdul Majid, having learnt the lesson of his father's defeat of June 1839, joined up with the European alliance of Britain, Russia, Prussia and Austria, which set out to drive Mohammed Ali, who was supported by France, out of the lands he had conquered. The war reached its climax with the surrender of Acre at the beginning of November 1840, heralding the end of Egyptian rule in Palestine. On 22 August, Nicolayson had already reported to London on the hostile activities that were about to occur in the region and concerning the position taken by the mission in this matter. The British consul in Alexandria sent out warnings and advice to British residents and merchants in Egypt, recommending that they organise themselves and keep up their guard because of the serious situation. At the same time, the governor of Jaffa published an edict that European ships, besides those flying the flag of France, which was an ally, would not be permitted to anchor along the shores of the city. In his report, Nicolayson added that, although one should express the hope that matters would calm down, from a realistic point of view the chances were in favour of war. He left it to the members of the mission to act as they pleased and to decide whether to remain in Jerusalem or to leave Palestine. He himself was determined not to leave Jerusalem and to put his faith in God. In any event, he was planning to write to his friend, the American consul in Beirut, to furnish him with a letter of protection, since it seemed preferable to him to be protected by a representative of a neutral power that was not party to the expected quarrel.

Each day, rumours continued to fly about imminent warfare, and Young, the British vice-consul in Jerusalem, who was then spending a vacation on Mount Carmel, decided to leave Palestine immediately. British missionaries took a similar course of action, and at their request, were given written permission by Nicolayson and the money needed for the journey. Nicolayson thought that he should also send away his family, who had been staying all this time in Bethlehem, but then decided to let them remain in Jerusalem for the time being since the dangers of travelling at that time constituted a greater threat than remaining. On 8 September 1840 all foreigners, except for a few Americans, left Jerusalem, and the London Mission House became still and silent with only the Danish missionary standing guard.[58]

The war came to an end. The first weeks after it were marked by a considerable amount of uncertainty and doubt concerning the return of Turkish rule in Palestine. On this subject Nicolayson remarked:

> Still it remains to be seen what will be the actual consequence of this return to the old Government – not I trust to the *old system* of that Government as existing before in that city. For if this were the case it would be greatly to be regretted in its bearing upon the whole country, but more especially upon native Christians and Jews, and upon *all* foreigners, who will, indeed, in either case, have much reason to regret the loss of many advantages by the change, unless adequately protected by the interposition of the European Powers on their behalf [emphasis in original].[59]

## EFFLORESCENCE OF A CHURCH

> It is well known that for ages various branches of the Christian Church have had their convents and their places of worship in Jerusalem. The Greek, the Roman Catholic, the Armenian, can each find brethren to receive him, and a house of prayer in which to worship. In Jerusalem also the Turk has his Mosque and the Jew his Synagogue. The pure Christianity of the Reformation alone appears as a stranger.[60]

The political conditions that were created by the establishment of Egyptian rule in the 1830s, which, on the one hand, enabled Jews to immigrate into Palestine, and, on the other, eased conditions for missionary work to be done, made it mandatory for the leaders of the London Society in 1834 to set up a church in the Holy City. Additional motives for realising this idea lay in the balance of power within the various Christian communities in Jerusalem. All these communities, except for the Protestants, had their own churches. John Nicolayson himself reached the same conclusion in 1835 after his stay in the company of the American missionaries and his joint tours with them. In March, he reported that his colleagues were not sparing any efforts in trying to set up a church of their own in Jerusalem, and wondered why the London Society refrained from doing so as well.[61] His words fell on attentive ears and in November 1836 Nicolayson came to London in order to give concrete shape to the idea of building a church. His discussions with the society leaders ended with their adoption of some of his proposals. In his view a Protestant church should be founded in which prayers would be conducted according to Anglican rites, so as to present the Jews of Jerusalem with a different kind of Christian establishment from others to be found in the city. They had been exposed to what he saw as the corruption of the Catholic, Orthodox and Armenian, churches which had been aggressive towards them and had strengthened their deep-seated prejudices against Christianity. Nicolayson tried to purchase a plot of land within the city walls near Jaffa Gate in the northwestern corner of Mount Zion close to the Jewish Quarter, and to erect a new building for the church. He assumed that he could obtain the necessary permits for the church from the Egyptian government, which then ruled over Palestine, and suggested that the best way to ensure this would be for the Foreign Office in London to send instructions to the British consul at the Egyptian court and submit through him a formal application in the name of the society.[62]

Having adopted Nicolayson's proposals, the president of the London Society requested the help of the Foreign Minister, Lord Palmerston. The latter ordered the British consul in Alexandria to request the permit from the Pasha of Egypt for the construction of a Protestant church and additional buildings for the missionaries in Jerusalem. At the same time, Palmerston instructed the British ambassador in Constantinople to make it clear to the Sublime Porte that Her Majesty's government would consider it of grave concern if there were any Turkish complicity with the other Christian communities in Palestine in trying to oppose the London Society.[63]

The London Society, after reaching its decision subject to obtaining the permits from Cairo and Constantinople, authorised Nicolayson to buy a plot of land suitable for the church and the additional buildings. Nicolayson returned to Jerusalem in October 1837, and a few weeks later the London Society sent him a letter reporting that the request for a *firman* (the term for 'permit' in the

2. Christ Church in Jerusalem, 1849

3.  Christ Church today

Turkish language) for the erection of the church had been rejected in the Turkish capital. The society leaders instructed him to act in any way possible to buy the land with or without buildings, and to continue his attempts to set up the missionary institutions in the spirit of the instructions he had received.[64] Their intention was to prepare immediately any of the existing buildings to serve as temporary prayer halls and residential quarters for the missionaries until the desired permit for the church was obtained.

On 22 July 1838, Nicolayson completed the redesigning of the temporary building as a chapel and conducted the first prayer meeting there in Hebrew. In September 1838 he managed to bypass the current prohibition in Palestine forbidding any foreigner to acquire land and to register it in his own name. After months of negotiating, Nicolayson engaged the services of an Armenian 'man of straw', who carried out the transaction and pledged to transfer the property at a later stage as an endowment to Nicolayson's ownership. On 16 August he acquired the first plot of land at the cost of £530,[65] and on 19 September he acquired an additional plot. The London Society now had two adjoining plots of land at its disposal with buildings adjacent to each other and with a garden and courtyard attached. A year later, the transfer of ownership was carried out in the name of Nicolayson as trustee of the London Society. On 24 October 1839, in the office of the Cadi (Civil Judge) of Jerusalem, a formal signing took place in which the Armenian 'straw man' transferred to Nicolayson all the documents of ownership that he had received, some of them being 150 years old.[66] The site acquired at the total price of £800 is used by the society to this very day and is situated '… on Mount Zion exactly opposite the castle of David, near the gate of Jaffa, and on the very confines of the Jewish quarter'.[67]

In mid-1839 a difficulty arose from an unexpected quarter. Young, the British vice-consul, who had recently arrived in Jerusalem, made a series of claims demanding greater involvement in the project. Among other things, he demanded that Nicolayson register the property in his name as well, as bearer of the title of British vice-consul. After several weeks, the leaders of the London Society rejected Young's demand. Regarding the claim that Her Majesty's representative should be registered as one of the owners of the property, the society observed that his appointment would one day be terminated and no one could guarantee that his replacement would support their cause to the same degree.[68] At the end of the year Young received explicit instructions from the Foreign Office directing him to extend his protection to the members of the society who were building a church in Jerusalem. In response, the vice-consul sent a letter of goodwill to London in which he expressed his views regarding the prospects of obtaining a *firman* for constructing a church. In his opinion, the application of the Foreign Office to the ruler of Egypt, who was in control over Palestine at the time, was fundamentally a mistake. Mohammed Ali had no authority to sanction the building of a Christian house of prayer in the Holy City, and he therefore suggested applying to Constantinople to demand a place of prayer for the Protestants whose residence in Jerusalem was already approved.[69]

In spite of the apparent goodwill shown by Young, the differences of opinion persisted between him and Nicolayson into 1840. At the beginning of the year the vice-consul insisted on examining the decisions of the London Society as found in the documents in Jerusalem. In response to Nicolayson's astonishment at this, the secretary of the society wrote that the London committee was surprised at Young's expressions and shocked that he could think of making any demands, and that he might have been granted his wishes if he had only made a polite and friendly request. The committee left it to Nicolayson to decide how he should act without fear of reprisals, since the primary duty of the vice-consul was to protect the interests of British citizens, and he would surely not be allowed to put any obstacles in their way.[70]

In the summer of 1840 the dispute in Jerusalem took on a personal aspect when Young expressed doubts about his ability to grant Nicolayson consular protection since he was still a Danish citizen. The secretary of the society reported to Nicolayson that echoes of the dispute between the mission and the consulate in Jerusalem had reached London by way of travellers returning from Palestine. Documents referring to this conflict continued to pile up in the diplomatic pouches in Jerusalem, Constantinople and London for several years. At the beginning of 1843 Young declared in a letter to Her Majesty's ambassador in Constantinople that he had not hidden his views of Nicolayson from the very start, and criticised the policy followed by the members of the society in Jerusalem who did not take the feelings of the Muslim population into account.[71]

It seems probable that in the dispute that arose between Nicolayson, who took the position held by the Anglican Church, and Young, who represented British foreign policy, there was a fundamental clash between political and religious interests in Palestine. To the same extent, it seems unlikely that the bureaucratic impediments that Young devised to hinder the erection of the church were planned at the actual initiative of the Foreign Office in London headed by Lord Palmerston, who was a supporter of the society and the idea for a church.[72] It is almost certain that it was the relationship between a veteran and experienced missionary who had spent several years investing all his energy and enthusiasm in this project, and a consul inexperienced in diplomacy who was not involved in this work, that caused Young to act in this way on his own initiative.

In any case, the pattern of relations between the London Society and the British consulate in Jerusalem was such that, while the missionaries enjoyed the protection of a British political entity simply by being British subjects, they were not, however, bound to act within the framework of conventional limitations imposed upon such an entity since they were members of a private society. At the same time, the British Foreign Office could quietly encourage the activities of the London Society, which generally conformed to its policies. In cases of diplomatic dispute, it could be claimed that those implementing the policy represented an autonomous society which was not subject to the British consulate in Jerusalem. This relationship between the London Society and the representatives of the British Crown in Jerusalem remained in the same format for many years.

In June 1839 Nicolayson had managed to overcome several difficulties, among which were a plague that had struck the city and a shortage of building materials and beasts of burden, and he began erecting a wall to separate the area purchased from a neighbouring mosque. The fact that until then the London Society had not dispatched an experienced architect who could take charge of the planning and oversee the construction process forced Nicolayson to draw up the plans for the church and the residential quarters himself. As a result of his engagement in this work and his familiarity with all its details, he requested and received permission from the London committee to purchase another plot of land with a building on it to the west of the area that had already been bought, in order to satisfy the needs of the growing missionary community in Jerusalem.[73]

At the end of December 1839 excavation work began on the foundations for the buildings, which were, without doubt, urgently needed and already officially authorised. On the 27th the builders exposed a magnificent ancient wall, which was sometimes 3 metres in width and 10 metres high. Nicolayson felt that the discovery of the wall, which fitted in almost exactly with the plans drawn up for the mission buildings, was a sign from heaven, and he naturally used it as a ready-made foundation. At the beginning of February 1840 the excavation work and exposure of the wall was completed and on the 10th of the month the cornerstone was laid. Under the stone Nicolayson buried 'a silver penny of Queen Victoria's coinage, & a five Piaster piece of the present Sultan [Abdul Majid], the former having date 1838, & the latter 1255, being the current year of the Hagira [the Muslim calendar]'.[74]

At the end of March 1840 the general assembly of the London Society sent its blessings on the completion of the first floor of the mission's building complex in Jerusalem and instructed Nicolayson to cancel his original plan to assign the second floor as a prayer hall, and instead to prepare immediate plans for the construction of a separate church building. For this purpose, in that very month, the society appointed a young architect William Curry Hillier (d.1840), who had evinced a strong desire to devote his time and talents to working among the Jews. He was ordered to set out at once for Jerusalem to guide the project to a successful conclusion and thereby release Nicolayson for missionary work. In April work began on the foundations of the church building, but after a few days it was stopped because of technical difficulties connected with the nature of the soil. It became clear to the excavators that on Mount Zion, as in most areas of Jerusalem inside the walls, one must penetrate down several layers of the ruins of earlier buildings in order to get to rock bottom, and this exhausting work involved repeated cases of collapse into the excavations being made.[75]

On 8 June 1840 building work on the southern wing of the first residential floor was finished, and at the end of the month two German carpenters arrived to begin work immediately on making the windows and doors for the completed rooms. On 7 July, Nicolayson reported with satisfaction on the arrival of the architect Hillier in Jerusalem, who spent the following three weeks making a thorough survey of the entire project, examined the structures already built and the plans for continued work. Hillier had just managed to send a letter to London on his findings about the quality of the work and the need to economise on building materials, before he fell ill with typhus fever. On 9 August 1840 he died and was buried the next day in the American cemetery on Mount Zion.[76]

The war of 1840 passed as recounted earlier, with Nicolayson remaining alone and unharmed in Jerusalem. In a letter dated 11 November, four days after the surrender of Jerusalem, in which he described in detail what had taken place in Palestine from his vantage point, he noted that he wished to make use of the intervening time before a new administration took control in Jerusalem. He asked for the advice and guidance of the society, as he was greatly tempted to create a *fait accompli* and complete the building of the church. He therefore urged his colleagues in London to take immediate steps to obtain the *firman*. In reply, the president of the society, Thomas Baring, applied to Palmerston and in a detailed letter asked him to take advantage of the favourable political situation now existing after the war and to exercise his influence on the Sultan to permit the establishment of the church.[77] Palmerston hastened to send suitable instructions to Her Majesty's ambassador in Constantinople, John Ponsonby (1770–1855). In his letter Palmerston repeated the request of the London Society for obtaining the *firman*, and noted that the British public would be greatly pleased if the Sublime Porte acceded to the request. In his view:

> A compliance by the Porte with this request would afford very great pleasure to the public in this country, for there is a strong and general feeling here, which is becoming daily more and more prevalent, that considering the deep obligations conferred upon the Porte by Christian Powers during the last twelve months, the Porte ought to permit the Christian worship to be openly performed in the city of Jerusalem.

Further on in the letter, the Foreign Minister leaves his ambassador in Constantinople to act in the matter to attain the objective according to his best judgement, but at the same time stresses the fact that, 'Her Majesty's Government takes a deep interest [in this matter] in which they are extremely anxious to succeed.'[78]

Before these letters were exchanged between London and Constantinople, Nicolayson had already sailed for England, in December 1840, because he thought that his presence there was vital for obtaining the desired *firman* for the church construction: 'Now or never.'[79] When he arrived in London he participated in the special gathering of the London committee, which discussed the matters concerning the mission in Jerusalem. One of its decisions was that definite steps should be taken to promote the establishment of the new church, which it termed 'The Apostolic Anglican Church at Jerusalem'. In addition to the decision on principles, the society also enacted a few practical measures, among which was the appointment of James Wood Johns as responsible for the project in place of the deceased Hillier, and young Edward James

Jonas as his assistant so that he could be trained to act as his replacement in case of need. This decision apparently resulted from the experience of Hillier's sudden death.[80]

When the discussions were over, the London Society instructed Nicolayson to stop over in Constantinople on his way to Jerusalem and provided him with letters from Lord Ashley and Foreign Minister Palmerston, ordering Ambassador Ponsonby to pave the way for Nicolayson's access to the Sultan's court. The intention of the politicians in London was to expedite the granting of an official *firman* that would protect the missionaries and at the same time give them a legal stamp of approval for establishing a church in Jerusalem.[81]

In Constantinople, Nicolayson immediately applied to the British ambassador to promote the cause for which he had come, but found himself dealing with an extremely cautious diplomat for whom the church in Jerusalem was not of primary importance. Nicolayson writes, 'Lord Ponsonby, the ambassador at that time, treated the matter with so much reservation that instead of removing the difficulties involved in obtaining the necessary *firman* for the establishment of a church in Jerusalem, he raised all the obstacles that he could possibly conceive.'[82] Nicolayson therefore reported back to London about his intention to leave Constantinople, but the society saw considerable value in his presence there, and ordered him to remain. The orders from London were also to put pressure on Ponsonby at every opportunity and in all possible ways in order to get the *firman*, and they even encouraged him to use bribery (*bakshish*, as it was commonly known) if need be, even if the sum seemed more than was reasonable.[83]

Until August 1841 a constant exchange of letters went on between Ponsonby and Nicolayson, which were characterised by the problems raised by the ambassador and the solutions proposed by Nicolayson. The latter even occasionally ended his letters with a veiled threat that failure in this matter would be a source of grief and disappointment for the Christian public throughout Great Britain, and no effort or means would be spared to prevent a refusal.[84] In August, the ambassador in Constantinople notified Nicolayson that the Sublime Porte had absolutely refused to grant the firman.[85] At the same time, Ponsonby wrote to Palmerston that he was sorry the question of building the church was ever raised since he believed that a direct appeal to the Ottoman government for a permit to establish a church would meet with immediate refusal, and therefore he did not act in this manner himself. However, his letter also contained a practical aspect. In his view, if a small chapel were to be built without much attention being drawn to it, it might be given official approval in the course of time, and later be expanded into a church. Ponsonby added that in his opinion no other way would succeed, and that he did not believe that a British demand, however strong, would cause the Sublime Porte to relent.[86] Palmerston's reply did not take long to come, and at the end of August he sent an urgent letter to Constantinople to say:

> I have accordingly to instruct your Excellency to apply earnestly for such a Firman. It cannot be supposed that at a moment when the whole of Syria has so lately been restored to the Sultan by the powerful intervention of Great Britain, so small a favour as this [permission to build a church] could be refused to the British Government upon grounds of a pedantic adherence to Mohammedan doctrine.[87]

In mid-September 1841, Count Karl Hans Königsmark, the Prussian envoy in Constantinople, allied himself with the British effort and met with the Turkish Foreign Minister. In spite of the fact that during the meeting the latter repeated the Muslim ruling that prohibited the establishment of new churches, an understanding was reached that the Protestants would be allowed, as in other places in the Empire, to build chapels next to their embassies or consular residences. Ponsonby summed up the results of the meeting and wrote to the Foreign Office in London in a softer tone:

> I have learned from others whom I employed to further the measure, that nothing more will be obtained than an unavowed permission from the Ottoman Minister for us to build an English Church in Jerusalem, and a promise that they (the Ministers) will order the Turkish authorities (including the Cadi) at Jerusalem not to oppose our erecting it, but on condition that the fabric be modest and unostentatious in appearance and dimensions, and not calculated to attract attention. I hope to have this promise in writing. The Porte will not, I fear, grant any Firman.[88]

This report apparently drew another urgent demand from London, since Ponsonby held a stern meeting in Constantinople a month later in which he employed harsh language towards the Turkish Foreign Minister, drawing his attention to the dangers that the Sublime Porte would cause himself by the insult offered to Her

Majesty's government because of his present refusal. The conversation ended with a quotation from the capitulation agreement between the two countries according to which Britain had the same rights accorded to 'the French, Venetian, and other Princes'.[89]

Nicolayson did not wait for the results of the interchanges between London and Constantinople and returned to Jerusalem. During July 1841 he was followed there by Jones, the new architect, appointed to complete the work with the assistance of professional builders from Malta. On his arrival, Jones sent to London his plans for the church which was meant, as he said, to be built in the Gothic or Norman style and to seat 300 worshippers.[90]

MEDICAL MISSION

During the year 1838 there were increasing signs that the mission station in Jerusalem was about to realise the hopes that had been hung upon it. In June Nicolayson consecrated the temporary chapel and conducted the first prayer service in Hebrew, and in September he completed the purchase of the land on which the church was to be built. For this reason the need arose to reinforce the mission station with additional missionaries, and, in accordance with its decision, the London Society sent the converted Jews, George Wildon Pieritz and Alexander Levi who arrived in Jerusalem in July 1838. These two men did not succeed in their work, and worse still, their attempts to approach the members of the Jewish community in the city called down the wrath of the rabbis upon their heads to the extent that they imposed a ban.

In December 1838 the society chose to try another course of action and dispatched two missionaries to Palestine, again converted Jews but this time also trained in medical work. The first was Albert Wilhelm Gerstmann (1815–41), a doctor by profession, and to serve as his assistant, the chemist, Melville Peter Bergheim (1815–90). The arrival of Gerstmann with his 'medicine chest' brought about the desired effect and infused new energy into the work of the mission. Before he could settle down in Jerusalem, he found a long list of instructions awaiting him from the London Society. The most important of these clearly defined his task:

> You are further directed to attend as a Medical Capacity first of all *gratis* to all who are connected to the Mission, & also to the poor Jews who may apply for advice or medicines. [From] Jews or others

who can afford to pay you are allowed to take a reasonable fee [emphasis in the original].[91]

Gerstmann arrived at the height of the plague that struck Jerusalem, beginning in the spring of 1838 and lasting for a whole year. At the end of a month – in which he offered medical treatment free of charge to the Jews of the city who fell ill, and especially to the poor and destitute among them who could not afford any medical care at all – the rabbis' ban was lifted.[92]

The gratitude of members of the Jewish community, and even some of their rabbis among them, was shown by the numbers who took an interest in the possibility of conversion. Nicolayson, who was surprised at the extent of this interest, wrote an emotional letter to Alexander McCaul (1799–1863), the Irish missionary who had long been a prominent activist in the London Society.[93] In his letter, Nicolayson expressed for the first time his sense of the immense importance that should be given to medical activity as the main component in missionary work. As though he had discovered a treasure trove, Nicolayson seized on the possibility of changing the nature of the mission in Jerusalem and went on in his letter to request that funds be raised for this purpose, using clear and unequivocal words:

> Our plan is to form something that may grow into a hospital. For this purpose we need one who will become the advocate of Jewish misery in happy England, present the claims of Abraham's descendants in Jerusalem. ... Such (as said) *You* either must become yourself, or find an equally suitable substitute. We can take no refusal, and offer you no other alternative. Yet be not alarmed at the name 'Hospital'. We are not going to erect a place like the hospitals in London [emphasis in the original].[94]

In October 1839, the scale of the epidemic reached its height, and the small medical unit in the mission functioned in full force. Gerstmann exerted himself night and day for the health of all the residents of the city and during that month treated scores of sick people daily, reaching sometimes even a hundred in one day. Bergheim also shouldered the heavy task and, besides working as a chemist, he performed purely medical procedures and simple operations. The dramatic rise in medical activity, added to the missionary considerations that accompanied it, demanded a reassessment of the situation. Nicolayson applied to the London Society and suggested setting up a hospital in Jerusalem. The society approved his request and set up a special fund with the aim of finding the resources for this purpose, and they even instructed him to draw an initial amount of £100.⁹⁵ Nicolayson took advantage of the preparatory work being done at the time to lay the foundations of new buildings, and requested that the roofs of the old buildings be renovated in order to install there the Mission Hospital in Jerusalem.

In January 1840 this hope was dashed. Although Gerstmann had recovered from the long illness he too had contracted, which until then had delayed the setting up of the hospital, his weak condition obliged him to return to England. The plans were thus postponed until a replacement could be found, and meanwhile the chemist, Bergheim, who was put in charge of the medical wing in the mission, was assisted by an American doctor, Cornelius Van Dyck (1818–95) then staying in Jerusalem. From August 1840 onward, the London Society published in its *Bulletin* a series of advertisements calling for candidates who thought themselves capable of founding a hospital in Jerusalem and managing the medical department. In March 1841 Nicolayson wrote with satisfaction that he was happy to hear that a suitable candidate had already been found.⁹⁶

AN ADDITIONAL PERSPECTIVE

An additional perspective is suggested here in the examination of this period, which is characterised by successive attempts of exploration and settlement. The London Society, which was in fact established by a German national, dispatched over a period of two decades a dozen missionaries to Palestine, mostly of German origin, and including only two British nationals, who remained in Jerusalem for only a few weeks. Many obstacles stood in the path of these emissaries, preventing them from settling in Jerusalem in the 1820s. The generally accepted view has rightly attributed the reasons for these obstacles mainly to the Ottoman regime, which did not allow for any kind of Protestant activity. However, even after the change in rule and throughout the 1830s when Cairo conducted a different policy and allowed the missionaries to gain a foothold in Jerusalem, the expected flourishing of missionary activity remained in abeyance.

It therefore seems undeniable that the London Society itself – as shown by its dispatching of a mixed variety of foreign emissaries and failure to send qualified British personnel available at that time – did not feel confident enough in its ability to take the necessary measures in establishing a significant presence in Palestine. Although the Danish missionary, John Nicolayson, managed to settle in Jerusalem and lay firm foundations for the future, talented as he was, he had to be satisfied with this achievement and to wait for some external factor to alter the status of the London Society in Palestine radically. Only at the beginning of the 1840s and only for a very short while, was the society able to spread its wings and play a highly significant part in Palestine. Ironically enough, even this breakthrough was engineered and led by another German national. It was then, and only then, that British missionaries began to arrive and to take up positions in Jerusalem.

## NOTES

1. Gidney, W.T. *At Home and Abroad*, p. 1
2. Jänicke founded the institution in 1800 with the help of, among others, British organisations, and remained in contact with the London Missionary Society for many years, during which time he trained additional missionaries for it. See Norris, H.H. *The Origin, Progress and Existing Circumstances of the London Society for Promoting Christianity Amongst the Jews: An Historical Inquiry* (London: 1825), p. 199. After his death the Berliner Missionsschule went into decline until its closure in 1849. See also Stock, E. *The History of the Church Missionary Society: Its Environment, its Men and its Work* (London: 1899), I, pp. 82–3; Gidney, *The History*, p. 76; Douglas, J.D. (ed.), *The New International Dictionary of the Christian Church* (Grand Rapids: 1974), p. 524.
3. Frey, J.S.C.F. *Judah and Israel; or the Restoration and Conversion of the Jews and the Ten Tribes*, 2nd edn (London: 1838), pp. 1–21; ibid., pp. 50–5 for his letter dated 24 November 1801; ibid., pp. 57–62 for the period spent in Gosport; Norris, *The Origin*, Appendix, pp. I-IV.
4. See Norris, *The Origin*, p. 20. According to a later version, after Frey completed his training and returned to London, he came into sharp conflict with top-ranking members of the London Missionary Society regarding his educational convictions and the attitude of the society towards its missionaries. The confrontations led to a mass of vicious rumours, personal recriminations and venomous letters that drove him out of that missionary organisation. See Bodleian, Dep. Cmj. d.54, for an article in the *Westminster Review* (January 1886), pp. 147–8.
5. Ibid.
6. *Jewish Repository and Monthly Communication Respecting the Jews, and the Proceedings of the London Society*, 1 (1813), pp. 27–8; Way, L. *Reviewers Reviewed; or, Observations on Article II of the British Critic* (London: 1819), pp. 24–5; Norris, *The Origin*, p. 23. The numerous dates that abound raise the question as to the exact date of the establishment of the London Society. We have selected May 1809 as this was when the society – set up to alleviate the plight of the

distressed, *mainly* those of the Jewish race – was transformed into a missionary society, the aim of which was the promotion of Christianity among the Jews *alone*, and it retained that title throughout the period being researched. Compare, for example, Way, *Reviewers Reviewed*, p. 25; Gidney, *At Home and Abroad*, p. 23; Gidney, *The History*, p. 34.

7.  The origin of the two ideological trends in the London Society date back to the disputes within the Anglican Church at the end of the seventeenth century between the 'High Churchmen' and the 'Dissenters'. The root causes of this split are outside the confines of this study, and on this matter see, for example, Perry, G.G. *A History of the Church of England* (New York: 1879), pp. 286–383, 495–575; and a brief account in Maurois, A. *History of England* (London: 1937), pp. 410–15.

8.  *Jewish Repository*, 1 (1813), pp. 105, 146–7, 164–5. The compound, which was in the Bethnal Green district, served as the Society's centre until it was sold in 1898. A tour of the area in 1997 revealed that during World War Two the site was completely destroyed and was rebuilt as a residential quarter. For the London Society institutions in the compound see mainly Ayerst, W. *The Jews of the Nineteenth Century: A Collection of Essays, Reviews and Historical Notices* (London: 1848), pp. 421–6.

9.  Simeon, C. *Memoirs of the Life of the Rev. Charles Simeon*, ed. W. Carus, 2nd edn (London: 1847), pp. 401–2; Way, *Reviewers Reviewed*, pp. 18–22; Abeken, H. *The Protestant Bishopric in Jerusalem: Its Origin and Progress. From the Official Documents Published by Command of His Majesty the King of Prussia and from other Authentic Sources* (London: 1847), pp. 136–7, App. E. Way inherited his wealth in 1794, having met by chance with a person also named Lewis Way, who willed that his property be devoted to religious causes. There are other versions stating that the name of the philanthropist was John Way. See, for example, Hopkins, H.E. *Sublime Vagabond: The Life of Joseph Wolff Missionary Extraordinary* (Worthing: 1984), p. 29.

10.  Nicolayson, J. 'Mittheilungen für eine Skizze der Geschichte der englischen Mission und des evangelischen Bisthums zu Jerusalem', *Zions-Bote*, 1 (1852), p. 6; Wolff, J. *Travels and Adventures*, 2nd edn (London: 1860), I, pp. 127–30. It has even been claimed that Lewis Way founded the society: cf. Gidney, *The History*, p. 58; see Way's obituary in *Jewish Intelligence, Monthly Account of the Proceedings of the London Society for Promoting Christianity Amongst the Jews* (March 1840), pp. 74–7. The Stansted estate is situated between Portsmouth and Chichester. Way maintained the seminary on his estate until 1826, the year it was transferred to the society centre in London: see St Albans for the collection of documents entitled 'Tracts Suitable for Imparting Information Relating to the Objects of the London Society for Promoting Christianity Amongst the Jews – Historical Notices', pp. 6–7; De le Roi, J.F.A. *Die evangelische Christenheit und die Juden* Vol. 3 (Berlin: 1892), p. 24.

11.  *The Jewish Era: A Christian Quarterly in Behalf of Israel*, IX (January 1900), pp. 14–19; De le Roi, *Die evangelische*, p. 18; Gidney, *The History*, p. 57; Friedman, M.L. *The American Society for Meliorating the Condition of the Jews, and Joseph S.C.F. Frey its Missionary: A Study in American Jewish History* (Boston: 1925), pp. 2–6. According to one version, Frey was forced to leave for the United States after being accused of adultery with Emma Josephson, the wife of the London Society treasurer: see Norris, *The Origin*, pp. 146–7. See Kochav, S. 'Beginning at Jerusalem: The Mission to the Jews and English Evangelical Eschatology', in Ben-Arieh, *A City Reflected*, p. 95, where Emma Josephson is

said to have been engaged in prostitution. For the activities of Joseph Frey in the United States, see mainly Frey, *Judah and Israel*, pp. 144–73. As a result of the resignation of the dissenters the real estate remained the property of the society. In 1823, in the offices of a New York notary, Frey signed the documents transferring ownership of the remaining land acquisitions to the London Society. See Bodleian, Dep. Cmj. c.120, for agreements dated 8 June 1823, 6 August 1823 and an additional document dated 26 August 1823 verifying the above.

12. Regarding the election of Baring, who refused to take office until the debts of the society were paid, see Abeken, *The Protestant Bishopric*, p. 137, for the letter sent by Baring to the secretary of the society in February 1840. A similar version is also given in Gidney, *The History*, p. 47.

13. Way, L. *A Letter Addressed to the Right Reverend the Lord Bishop of St. David's*, 2nd edn (Dublin: 1820), pp. 1–42. See there for the extensive description of the journey in a letter which Lewis Way sent from Moscow on 18 February 1818; the Earl of Bessborough, *A Place in the Forest: Being the Story of Stansted in Sussex* (London 1958), pp. 70–5; *Jewish Expositor and the Friends of Israel, Containing Monthly Communication Respecting the Jews, and the Proceedings of the London Society*, 2 (1817), p. 358.

14. Grajewski, P.B-Z. *The Struggle*, n.p.: 'The Mission in Jerusalem' [Hebrew].

15. Norris, *The Origin*, p. 295. On Tschudy, see Archive of the Gottlieb Schumacher Institute at the Keller House, Haifa, PTM.11: Letter from Tschudy to Blumhard in Basle dated 12 December 1826. The original is in the Archive of the Baslermission, Basle; ibid., Death notices, No. 230.

16. *Report*, 13 (1821), pp. 104–5. On Naudi, see Wolff, *Travels*, pp. 162–5; *Jewish Repository*, 2 (1814), p. 119. On Jowett, who remained in Malta until 1830, see Stock, *The History of the Church*, I, pp. 222–5. Most of the Protestant missionaries stayed over in Malta to acclimatise themselves and to receive up-to-date information about Middle Eastern affairs. In May 1823, the society even founded 'the Malta Jews' Society' intended as an information centre for all the missionary societies sending missionaries to convert the Jews to Christianity. See Protocol for the founding of that society in the diary of William Lewis in *Jewish Expositor*, 8 (1823), pp. 307–8.

17. *Jewish Expositor*, 6 (1821), pp. 16–23: a series of letters from Jowett and Naudi to London during the months of July–September 1820. Tschudy himself did not bother to report anything to London, and during 1821 the London committee dealt with this problem on several occasions. Tschudy was repeatedly commanded to send in his reports to the society. See, for example, Bodleian, Dep. Cmj, c.9: Protocols 1819–1821, No. 780 (27 March 1821); ibid., c.10: Protocols 1821–1823, No. 39 (22 May 1821), No. 209 (25 September 1821).

18. Wolff, *Travels*, I, pp. 173–4.

19. Bodleian, Dep. Cmj, c.10: Protocols 1821–1823, No. 262 (4 September 1821); ibid., No. 428 (26 March 1822). In the margin of the document it was later noted that its contents were transmitted to Tschudy on 9 April 1822 through the British consul in Aleppo. According to the Swiss missionary, the riots in Palestine forced him to leave for Malta in 1822, where a deputy of the society (most probably Naudi or Jowett) notified him of his dismissal. Tschudy continued to travel through Switzerland and Italy, and in December 1826, after becoming totally destitute, he applied for assistance from the Basle Mission. See *Keller*, PTM.11: Tschudy to Blumhard in Basle, 16.12.1826.

20. Wolff, *Travels*, I, pp. 2–8; see also Palmer, H.P., *Joseph Wolff: His Romantic Life*

*and Travels* (London: 1935); Hopkins, *Sublime Vagabond.*

21. *Jewish Expositor*, 9 (1824), p. 50: travel diary of Lewis Way; Wolff *Travels*, Vol. 1, p. 288.
22. Ibid., pp. 139–41; Hopkins, *Sublime Vagabond*, p. 75; Report, 13 (1821), p. 105.
23. Wolff, *Travels*, I, pp. 243–67; Gidney, *The History*, p. 105.
24. The source for the riots was the Damascus district governor who, in 1822, imposed heavy taxes that roused the anger of the inhabitants of Palestine. Until 1826, a rebellion was conducted against him, with its centre in Nablus and Jerusalem. For more extensive coverage see Manna, A. *The Sancak of Jerusalem Between Two Invasions (1798–1831): Administration and Society* (Jerusalem: 1986), pp. 32–3, which gives further references; *Jewish Expositor*, 7 (1822), p. 513: Wolff, from Aleppo to London, 1 August 1822; ibid., 8 (1823), pp. 108–15: Wolff, from Alexandria to London, 21 October 1822.
25. *The Missionary Herald, American Board of Foreign Missions*, 19 (December 1823), p. 378; *Jewish Expositor*, 8 (1823), p. 52; Gidney, *The Travels*, p. 104. The Americans later broadened their field of activity in the East with the assistance of the British consul, and chose Beirut as a permanent place of residence. See *Missionary Herald*, 20 (February 1824), pp.37–8. On the entire range of American activity in Palestine see Tibawi, A.L. *American Interests in Syria 1800–1901: A Study of Educational, Literary and Religious Work* (Oxford: 1966).
26. Wolf [sic], J. *Missionary Journal and Memoir of the Rev. Joseph Wolf, Missionary to the Jews* (London: 1824), pp. 346–7; *Missionary Herald*, p. 20 (Feb. 1824), pp. 33–40; *Jewish Expositor*, 9 (1824), p. 64: Wolff, from Jerusalem, 21 June 1823.
27. Wolff, *Travels*, I, pp. 419–29; *Jewish Expositor*, 14 (1829), pp. 438–40: Wolff, from Jerusalem, 4 May 1829; Hopkins, *Sublime Vagabond*, pp. 135–7.
28. *Jewish Expositor*, 9 (1824), pp. 49–50: travel diary of Lewis Way.
29. *Missionary Herald*, 21 (February 1825), p. 33; *Jewish Expositor*, 9 (1824), p. 20; Jowett to Wolff, 5 January 1824; ibid., 10 (1825), p. 341.
30. Ibid., pp. 13–17: Lewis from Antoura to Charles Sleech Hawtrey (1780–1831) in London, 28 May 1824.
31. Dalton obtained some glass in Malta for the windows of the Antoura College. He writes in this connection, 'I presume I shall have to turn glazier as well as doctor … .' See *Jewish Expositor*, 9 (1824), p. 390; ibid., 10 (1825), p. 309: Dalton, from Beirut, 17 January 1825; Gidney, *The History*, p. 119.
32. During the rebellion against the governor of Damascus, he himself went out to the region in 1825 and the missionaries in Jerusalem were caught up in the throes of the insurgency. The rebellion was quelled within days through the assistance of the governor of Acre. For this, see Spyridon, S.N. 'Annals of Palestine 1821–1841', *Journal of the Palestine Oriental Society*, 18 (1938), 63–152. Published in *Extracts from Annals of Palestine 1821–1841, Ms. – Monk Neophitos of Cyprus* (Jerusalem 1979), pp. 18–28.
33. *Missionary Herald*, 23 (February 1827), pp. 35–6; *Jewish Expositor*, 11 (1826), pp. 135–8; ibid., pp. 74–6: Dalton, from Beirut, 23 May 1825.
34. Ibid., p. 178: Dalton's Palestine diary, 18 April 1825; ibid., pp. 74–6: Dalton, from Beirut, 23 May 1825.
35. Ibid., p. 73; Archive of the LJS at the Israeli Trust of the Anglican Church, Jerusalem: Nicolayson's Journal, I, 25 January 1826; *Jewish Expositor*, 12 (1827), pp. 140–4. His gravestone was later transferred to the Protestant cemetery on Mount Zion, where it remains till today. For Nicolayson, see below.
36. Ibid., p. 143.
37. *Jewish Expositor*, 12 (1827), p. 25: Nicolayson, from Beirut, 13 March 1826.

38. *Jewish Intelligence* (January 1857), p. 7.
39. This involvement reached its height on 20 October 1827 in the defeat of the Turkish–Egyptian fleet in Navarino by the European alliance under British command. With regard to the involvement of the Great Powers in the Greek rebellion, see, for example, Marriott, *The Eastern Question*, pp. 212–21.
40. Nicolayson 'Mittheilungen', p. 8; *Report*, 21 (1829), pp. 64, 67. On the war over the Greeks that broke out with the announcement of Czar Nicholas I on 26 April 1828, see, for example, Marriott, *The Eastern Question*, pp. 221–5.
41. *Monthly Intelligence of the Proceedings of the London Society for Promoting Christianity Amongst the Jews*, 3 (July 1832), p. 99: Farman's diaries, 20 July 1831. The sense of expectation of the invasion of Mohammed Ali was already felt in the air during the years 1827–28, following his involvement in the suppression of the Greek revolt. On this, see Manna, *The Sancak*, p. 43.
42. *Missionary Herald*, 29 (December 1833), p. 440.
43. *Monthly Intelligence*, 3 (October 1832), p. 146; ibid. (October 1833), pp. 180–1. On Calman see his obituary in *Jewish Intelligence* (April 1890), p. 49.
44. ITAC: Nicolayson's Journal, I, 24 January 1833; *Monthly Intelligence*, 4 (December 1833), p. 185. The inclination to showing tolerance evinced by the Egyptian authorities towards the Christian minorities in Palestine during the period of Egyptian rule was already expressed in 1831, a few months before the invasion, by the message that Mohammed Ali sent to the foreign consuls in Egypt regarding his intention to grant equality and fair treatment to the minorities subject to his sovereignty. Other expressions to this effect can be found in documents throughout the decade of Egyptian rule in Palestine. For example, a research delegation sent by the Scottish mission in 1839 went as far as to say that the Christian missionaries enjoyed freedom of activity in Palestine to a greater extent than, for example, under British rule in India or Malta. See Bonar, A.A. and M'Cheyne, R.M. *Narrative of a Mission of Inquiry to the Jews from the Church of Scotland in 1839*, 3rd edn (Philadelphia: 1845), p. 173.
45. *Monthly Intelligence*, 5 (January 1834), p. 13. On Joseph Amzalak and his family see detailed account in Glass, J.B., and Kark, R. *Sephardi Entrepreneurs in Eretz Israel: The Amzalak Family, 1816–1918* (Jerusalem 1991), pp. 46–85. Later on, Joseph's son, Haim Amzalak (1828–1916), served as British vice-consul in Jaffa. See ibid., pp. 121–33.
46. ITAC: Nicolayson's Journal, I, 30 March 1833 to 7 April 1833; ibid., 8 April 1833 to 22 April 1833.
47. Nicolayson, 'Mittheilungen', p. 8.
48. On this matter see, for example, Spyridon, 'Annals', pp. 33–73. The suppression of Muslim fanaticism by Ibrahim Pasha and the free hand given to foreign minorities in religious affairs revived the yearnings for the Ottoman Sultan and led to insurrection. The decree concerning the recruitment of soldiers was only one among a series of other decrees concerning such things as the disarmament of citizens and the imposition of taxes. The rebellion was quelled by the expedition of Mohammed Ali to Palestine at the head of a large army and the beheading of the rebellious leaders. The heavy hand that Ibrahim Pasha laid upon the Muslims of Palestine gained him many nicknames. For example, the British traveller Alexander Keith (1791–1880) compared his rule to an 'iron rod'. See Keith, A. *The Land of Israel According to the Covenant with Abraham, with Isaac and with Jacob* (Edinburgh 1843), p. 475.
49. ITAC: Nicolayson's Journal, II, 19 May 1834 to 26 May 1834; Macalister, S. 'Gleanings from the Minute-Book of the Jerusalem Literary Society', *Palestine*

*Exploration Fund Quarterly Statement* (1911), pp. 83–9, where there is a summary of the events contained in the lecture given by Mrs Nicolayson at the conference of the Jerusalem Literary Society in March 1851.

50. ITAC: Nicolayson's Journal, II, 17 June 1834.

51. *Missionary Herald*, 32 (July 1836), pp. 251–4. After recovering, Calman continued to deal with matters concerning the Jews in Baghdad, Damascus and Beirut. In 1839 he joined the Church of Scotland delegation to Palestine and travelled in its company to visit Jewish communities in Eastern Europe and Prussia. In November 1839 his travels ended in London, and it was only after the war of 1840 that Calman returned to Jerusalem. See Bonar and M'Cheyne, *Narrative of a Mission*, p. 240 ff. As a result of his travels with the Scottish delegation, Calman sent a letter at the beginning of August 1840 to Lord Ashley (see below), in which he states his belief in the need and possibilities of settling the Jews of Europe in Palestine. See Calman to Ashley, 3 August 1840, as addendum to the letter from Ashley to Palmerston of 25 September 1840 in Hyamson, A.M. *The British Consulate in Jerusalem in Relation to the Jews of Palestine 1838–1914* (London 1939–1941), II, pp. LXVIII-LXXIII.

52. Bodleian, Dep. Cmj, d.59: register of baptisms of Christ Church Jerusalem. Rosenthal was registered as the first person to be baptised; for a full report on this including a 'programme' and an invitation to the baptismal ceremony in Jerusalem, see Archive of the LJS at Christ-Church, Jerusalem: Nicolayson's Journal, III, 13 April 1839, 14 April 1839; *Report*, 31 (1839), pp. 75–6. On Rosenthal, see also Bodleian, Dep. Cmj, d.100, for a pamphlet entitled 'The History of Simeon Rosenthal'.

53. Although a year earlier, in May 1824, William Lewis had made a similar suggestion to the London Society, this was phrased along very general lines. In his opinion, in order to protect the Jews who were not Ottoman citizens in Jerusalem, a consular agent should be appointed without regard to nationality. See *Jewish Expositor*, 10 (1825), pp. 16–17: Lewis, from Antoura, 28 May 1824.

54. Ibid., 11 (1826), p. 76: Dalton, from Beirut, 23 May 1825.

55. Vereté, M. 'Why was a British Consulate', pp. 319–40.

56. Hodder, E. *The Life and Work of the Seventh Earl of Shaftesbury* (London: 1886), I, p. 233. From the conclusion of the quotation it is hinted that the British Foreign Minister appointed the vice-consul in Jerusalem under Ashley's influence in order to advance the idea of the restoration of the Jews, and that Young himself was supportive of this idea. Most of those who have dealt with this question think likewise. M. Vereté, in his aptly turned remarks, refuted this claim and proved in his article that Ashley's words were written retrospectively, and that he had no hand in the appointment, which was clearly made for political reasons. Vereté bases his refutation on the fact that no earlier mention of this matter is made by Ashley, or in any of the society's journals. See Vereté, M. 'Why was a British Consulate', pp. 316–45. In Nicolayson's journal, discovered long after Vereté had researched the subject, we found that in November 1838, a few months before the vice-consul came to Jerusalem, it was written that 'we shall at length have the advantage of a Consul ... especially such a man as Mr. Young'. See Christ Church: Nicolayson's Journal, III, 8 November 1838. This study assumes that the truth lies somewhere in between.

57. Archive of the British Foreign Office at the Public Record Office, London, 78/368, p. 130: draft of letter to Young by John Bidwell, secretary to the British

Foreign Minister, 31 January 1839.
58. The British, who were a party to the conflict, chose to leave Jerusalem, while the group of Americans from Beirut, being subjects of a neutral country, thought it was safer to be in Jerusalem and moved there until the storm died down in January 1841. Christ Church: Nicolayson's Journal, III, 8 September 1840; *Jewish Intelligence* (November 1840), p. 361: Pieritz (a converted Jew, who will be discussed later) on board a British warship in Beirut harbour to London, 19 September 1840; ibid. (December 1840), pp. 393–4: Nicolayson to London, 13 September 1840.
59. Report, 33 (1841), p. 58; *Jewish Intelligence* (June 1841), p. 209: Nicolayson in London, 31 March 1841.
60. Bodleian, Dep. Cmj, d.59: pamphlet entitled 'Hebrew Church at Jerusalem', Feb. 1834; *ITAC*, Correspondence from London, I: Letter by James B. Cartwright (1798–1861), secretary of the London Society, 12 December 1834.
61. *Jewish Intelligence* (January 1836), p. 17.
62. ITAC, London Committee Resolutions, No. L166 (16 December 1836).
63. Ibid., No. L283 (14 March 1837): Foreign Office to the president of the London Society, 10 March 1837.
64. Bodleian, Dep. Cmj, d.59: 'Hebrew Church at Jerusalem' (February 1834), p. 4; ITAC, unclassified documents, power of attorney to Nicolayson from the secretary of the London Society dated 19 June 1837; ibid., London Committee Resolutions, No. L294 (18 March 1837); ibid., Nicolayson's Journal, II, 23 October 1837; ibid., correspondence from London, I: Cartwright letter, 30 November 1837; ibid., London Committee Resolutions, No. L580 (23 January 1838).
65. Christ Church, Nicolayson's Journal, III, 17 August 1838, 19 September 1838; ITAC, Nicolayson's Journal, II, 20 April 1838; ibid., 13 May 1838.
66. Bodleian, Dep. Cmj, c.135: lists of ownership documents copied on 14 March 1877. Details of the purchase in October 1838 in document No. A.a.1; transfer of land on Nicolayson's name in October 1839 in document A.a.5; Christ Church, Nicolayson's Journal, III, 24 October 1839. See there for detailed report on the signing ceremony in the *Mahkamah* (court building) of Jerusalem together with all the oriental trappings; ibid., 28 October 1839; ITAC, London Committee Resolution, No. L1753 (24 December 1839).
67. Johns, J.W. *The Anglican Cathedral Church of Saint James Mount Zion Jerusalem* (London: 1844), p. 3.
68. ITAC, London Committee Resolution, No. L1521 (23 July 1839).
69. FO, 78/368, p. 144, No. 9: draft of the Foreign Office in London to Young in Jerusalem, 20 December 1839; ibid., 78/413, p. 213, No. 1: Young to Palmerston, 30 January 1840.
70. ITAC, correspondence from London, I, 15 February 1840.
71. FO, 195/210, p. 52, No. 3: Young in Jerusalem to Stratford Canning, 1st Viscount Stratford de Redcliffe (1786–1880) in Constantinople, 26 January 1843.
72. The altercations found expression in the correspondence between Young in Jerusalem and the directors of the society in London. It is safe to assume that any initiative of the Foreign Office would not have had recourse to the mailing services of the vice-consul in Jerusalem but would have found its way directly to the offices of the society, which were also situated in London.
73. Nicolayson completed the sketch of the plan on 3 September 1839. See Christ Church, Nicolayson's Journal, III, 3 September 1839; Bodleian, Dep. Cmj,

c.125: List of purchases carried out in the church compound.

74. Christ Church, Nicolayson's Journal, III, 10 February 1840.

75.  Egerton, F. *Journal of a Tour in the Holy Land, in May and June 1840* (London: 1841), p. 23; Olin, S. *Travels in Egypt, Arabia Petraea, and the Holy Land* (New York: 1843), I, p. 130.

76. Bodleian, Dep. Cmj, b.51: Johns, *The Anglican Cathedral*, p. 4; Christ Church, Nicolayson's Journal, III, 9–10 August 1840; *Jewish Intelligence* (November 1840), p. 359: Nicolayson to London, 31 August 1840.

77. ITAC, London Committee Resolutions, No. M1024 (12 January 1841): Nicolayson, from Jerusalem, 11 November 1840; ibid., No. M1096 (9 February 1841): Baring to Palmerston, 1 February 1841.

78. *Correspondence Respecting the Condition of Protestants in Turkey, 1841–1851, Presented to the House of Commons in Pursuance of their Address of March 27, 1851* (London: 1851), p. 1: Palmerston to Ponsonby, 8 February 1841.

79. Christ Church, Nicolayson's Journal, III, 28 December 1840; *Report*, 33 (1841), p. 58; *Jewish Intelligence* (June 1841), p. 209: Nicolayson in London, 31 March 1841.

80. ITAC, London Committee Resolutions, Nos M1303, M1314, M1315 (26 March 1841); ibid., No. M1244 (16 March 1841); ibid., Nos M1352a to M1352e (13 April 1841); Johns, *The Anglican Cathedral*, p. 4.

81. ITAC, London Committee Resolutions, No. M1320 (26 March 1841), No. M1354 (13 April 1841).

82. Nicolayson, 'Mittheilungen', pp. 11–12. Cf. Tibawi, *British Interests*, p. 38, where the author creates the impression that Ponsonby was actually glad to help and even took initiatives of his own.

83. ITAC, London Committee Resolutions, No. M1814 (13 July 1841) with reference to Nicolayson's letter from Constantinople, 16–17 June 1841.

84. Ibid., Collection of unclassified letters, 29 May 1841–18 August 1841; ibid., Nicolayson in Constantinople to Ponsonby, August 1841.

85. Christ Church, Nicolayson's Journal, III, 29 July 1841; ITAC, London Committee Resolutions, No. M2072.

86. Ibid., Collection of unclassified letters: Ponsonby to Palmerston as Appendix 7 to Ponsonby's letter to Nicolayson, 17 August 1841; ibid., London Committee Resolutions, No. M1946 (17 August 1841).

87. FO, 78/429: Palmerston to Ponsonby, 28 August 1841.

88. *Correspondence Respecting*, pp. 6–7, App. 6: Königsmark to Ponsonby, 12 September 1841; ibid., pp. 5–6: Ponsonby to Palmerston, 15 September 1841. After the erection of Christ-Church and until November 1854 the British consul resided in a building belonging to the London Society in the church compound.

89. Ibid., p. 7: Ponsonby to Lord Aberdeen, 7 October 1841; Ibid., p. 8: Ponsonby to Rif'at Pasha, 11 October 1841.

90. Johns, *The Anglican Cathedral*, p. 4. For detailed reports on the building process in its initial stages, including technical details, sketches, cost of building materials and the employment of workmen, see ibid., throughout the album; ITAC, London Committee Resolutions, No. M1352 (13 April 1841); ibid., No. M2359 (23 November 1841). See Williams, G. *The Holy City: Historical, Topographical and Antiquarian Notices of Jerusalem* (London: 1849), II, p. 587, where the author does not spare his criticism of the London Society. In this connection he writes, 'At Jerusalem ... a church capable of accommodating four or five hundred persons was commenced, while as yet there were

but eight or ten individuals for whom it would be available, and even they were there simply with a view to its construction.'

91 ITAC, Correspondence from London, I: Cartwright, from London, 2 August 1838.

92. Christ Church, Nicolayson's Journal, III, 28 December 1838; ibid., 8 January 1839. From January to April 1839 Gerstmann treated 355 patients of the three faiths. See table in *Report*, 31 (1839), p. 76.

93. McCaul was born and educated in Dublin. His encounter with the philanthropist, Lewis Way, led him to join the ranks of the London Society, where he served as missionary in Poland and Germany for ten years. His daughter, Elizabeth Anne (1825–1921), later the wife of James Finn (1806–72), the second British consul in Jerusalem, was educated in Poland. In 1830 McCaul returned to England where, besides his position as Professor of Theology in Kings College, London, he was the head of the educational establishments of the society and served as its vice-president from 1854 until his death. See the obituary in *Jewish Intelligence* (January 1854), pp. 2–10, where the words of his eldest son, Joseph B. McCaul, are quoted from the preface to his publication: *A Memorial Sketch of the Rev. Alexander McCaul*. Regarding Alexander McCaul's book, *The Old Paths*, in which he wrote his commentaries on the Talmud, it has been said, 'The year [1840] was one of triple curses and tribulations: a blood libel in Damascus, an increase in the Sodomic trials and evil decrees against the Jews in Russia, and above all: in that year a lampoon was published called "The Old Paths".' See A. Fürst, *New Jerusalem*, Jerusalem 1944, I, pp. 5–10 [Hebrew].

94. This plan was first recorded by Nicolayson in his diary. See Christ Church, Nicolayson's Journal, III, 28 December 1838, 11 February 1839.

95. ITAC, correspondence from London, I: Cartwright letter, 25 July 1839, containing a quotation from the decision of the London committee.

96. Ibid., 4 August 1840; *Jewish Intelligence* (August 1840), p. 272; ibid. (September 1840), p. 296; *Report*, 33 (1841), p. 53: Nicolayson in London 31 March 1841.

# 2

# 1842–1845

## THE ANGLO-PRUSSIAN BISHOPRIC

We see that, during the political gyrations that occurred in the years 1839–42, many took an interest in saving the souls of the Jews in Jerusalem. The Prussian Minister ... said among other things that: 'The situation in which Palestine remains under Turkish rule, and especially the fate of the Jews, has drawn the attention of the King of Prussia because of his deep religious sentiments, and it is necessary to use all possible means to wrest Bethlehem, Nazareth and Jerusalem from Turkish hands.'[1]

Christian Karl Josias von Bunsen (1791–1860), the friend and confidant of the King of Prussia, Friedrich Wilhelm IV (1795–1861), was the originator of the idea to establish a Protestant bishopric in Palestine.[2] Bunsen was born in the county of Waldeck in the Kingdom of Hessen, and studied theology, philosophy and history at the University of Jena, where he received his doctoral degree. In 1816 he went to Rome, married an Englishwoman, Frances Waddington, and served as the Prussian envoy to the Vatican until 1838. The friendship between Bunsen and the Prussian king arose from their common fields of interest and shared character traits. The two were of the same generation and were moulded by the same intellectual, cultural and political forces that were then current in Prussia. Above all, they shared a similar interest in the history of the early church and in its literature, art and architecture. As a believing Christian, Friedrich Wilhelm was aware of the evolution of the Evangelical Church and of the link between church and state. One of the main features in his mental outlook was, in his own words, a deep commitment to the establishment of a Christian entity that would be able to withstand the forces of corruption in the modern era. He saw the system of correlation between the government and the church in England as a model to be followed, and therefore responded with enthusiasm to Bunsen's proposals to institutionalise formally the cooperation between the Anglican

Protestants and their German brothers in faith.

The idea of establishing an Anglo-Prussian Protestant bishopric in Jerusalem had occupied Bunsen's mind for a very long while. In 1838, while serving as the Prussian envoy at the Papal Court, he was compelled to leave his position by order of the Papal See as a consequence of his involvement in the dispute between Protestant Prussia and the Vatican.[3] The humiliation he suffered in Rome goaded him into an attempt to weaken the power of the Catholic Church, which he deemed responsible for his disgrace, through the strengthening of the Protestant Church. Thus there is an undeniable link between Bunsen's personal frustrations and his plans to set up a Protestant bishopric in Jerusalem.[4] On 10 December 1838, exactly one year after the Pope's allocution on his banishment from Rome, Bunsen met privately with Lord Ashley, a London Society man, and they put their heads together to draft the 'Jerusalem Plan.' Another clue to Bunsen's motives can be found in the letter he sent in that month to Friedrich Wilhelm in which he proposes launching a 'campaign against the Pope and his liars – with Britannia as my ally!'.[5]

Bunsen opened his attack on two fronts – religious and political. He had already dealt with the religious aspect in 1838 and 1839 while on an extended vacation in England, after leaving Rome and before his appointment as Prussian Ambassador in Berne, Switzerland. During his stay in London, Bunsen developed his ideas concerning Anglo-Prussian cooperation together with certain prominent British personalities, among whom, as mentioned earlier, were leading members of the London Society, Lord Ashley and Alexander McCaul. In 1840 Bunsen returned to England for another long visit and began working on the 'Jerusalem Plan' in greater detail. A central factor in his discussions with his English friends on their common project was the land in Jerusalem recently acquired by the London Society and the establishment of their mission station there. It was now possible to build upon solid realities, and so Bunsen and his English friends thought it best 'to transform this private foundation into a national and generally Christian-Evangelical one. This could only have happened if the Anglican Church established a Bishopric there.'[6]

The political front was broached in August 1840 when Bunsen wrote to Gladstone, then only a Member of Parliament in the general ranks, but later the Prime Minister of England:

The fact that an English church has been founded on the Holy Mount in Jerusalem is certainly a sign from God. Would you not

wish to take an active advantage of the favourable political circumstances which could be attributed to Divine Providence?[7]

In his reference to favourable political circumstances Bunsen
almost certainly meant the London Agreement, which had been
formulated three weeks earlier, whereby four European powers
undertook to assist the Ottomans in their struggle with Egypt.
Bunsen thought that the debt owed by Constantinople in return
for this agreement would make it possible to gain concessions in
Palestine.

These ideas and the steps taken to promote them were in
harmony with the general outlook of Friedrich Wilhelm, who
supported the plan in its entirety. 'The King had from his early
youth cherished the idea of amending the condition of Christians
in the Holy Land; where, as throughout the Turkish empire, the
position of all Christians was altogether ignominious, and that of
Protestants doubly so.'[8] Friedrich Wilhelm's imagination was fired,
and by July 1840 he had come to agree with the view that the time
had come to utilise the London Agreement in order to push
matters forward in Palestine and to promote Protestant
Christianity. In that same month he approached his European
colleagues and tried to obtain their commitment to work for the
sake of Palestine and for the status of Christians in the East
through an understanding reached with the Sublime Porte, so long
as it was still possible to make demands upon the Sultan *before* war
broke out. But his European allies showed a lack of interest, war
broke out and the propitious moment passed. At the end of 1841
the King once more raised his suggestion in the European capitals,
but again to no effect. The victory of the allies, the defeat of Egypt,
and the return of the Turks to Palestine before any agreements had
been made with the Sublime Porte had undermined the timely
opportunity to 'twist the arm' of Turkey and obtain its consent to
establish a bishopric in Palestine. All that could be gained from the
Sultan or his representatives was the general promise to protect
the European subjects living within the borders of the Empire.[9]

According to the accepted theory regarding the establishment
of the Protestant bishopric, Prussia proposed that Britain, as the
dominant power in Europe, should set up a joint bishopric with
her at the end of the war, since the British fleet had played a central
role in the battle to oust Egypt from Palestine and since the British
ambassador in Constantinople had a strong influence in the
Sultan's court. Such a theory implied that the way to establish the
bishopric entailed a British demand on the one hand, and an

Ottoman permit on the other. However, no request was actually submitted to receive a *firman*, either from London or from Berlin, and in any case no decision to grant a *firman* for a Protestant bishopric was endorsed in Constantinople.[10] In fact, the Sublime Porte even expressed surprise at the steps taken without notification or formal application, and complained about the agreement signed between Britain and Prussia under the assumption that the Sublime Porte would serve merely as a 'rubber stamp'. Constantinople announced that it did not recognise the Protestant bishop and also lodged a formal protest. Ottoman permission for the installation of the Jerusalem bishop was received retroactively, 11 years after his entry into the city.[11]

At this time intensive contacts were made between London and Constantinople to obtain a *firman* for the Protestant church on Mount Zion. These contacts are reflected in the stacks of documents found in several archives. It is very probable that this created the impression of similar contacts for establishing the bishopric.[12] The problem of getting a permit for the unprecedented step of installing a Protestant bishop in Jerusalem was resolved by Palmerston, the British Foreign Minister, in a letter to Lord Ponsonby, the British Ambassador in Constantinople:

> Her Majesty's Government conceives that no special permission for this purpose will be required from the Porte. This bishop will like any other British or Prussian subject have a right to reside in any part of the Turkish dominions, and the spiritual functions which he will exercise will in no way whatever interfere with the Mahometan subjects of the Sultan … you will make no communication on the subject to the Turkish Government till you receive instructions from the Secretary of State to do so.[13]

Conceivably, Friedrich Wilhelm, who wished to improve the living conditions of Protestants in the East, and especially those of the tiny German community, understood that the political situation and new-old Turkish administration would not be conducive to the creation of a totally new bishopric. He had come to realise that strong opposition could be expected from France and Russia for any Protestant initiative that might undermine the traditional status of seniority for their own churches in Palestine. For this reason, the King preferred to forgo the formal permit of the Sublime Porte for the Protestant bishopric and to bypass the need for such a permit altogether. He adopted Bunsen's plan in its entirety and decided to rely on those institutions that had already been given authorisation to exist in Palestine, i.e. to collaborate with the London Society, which had a foothold in Jerusalem, to convert the buildings in its possession into an independent church under the patronage of the two leading powers in the Protestant Church, and to set up the bishopric on the basis of the existing realities.[14] He therefore suggested that the British, who wished mainly to found a 'Jewish Church', establish a joint bishopric for the two countries on the basis of the society's mission station in Jerusalem.[15]

In order to carry out his plan, the King of Prussia recalled Bunsen from Berne in April 1841 and sent him to London to find out:

> In how far the English National Church, already in possession of a parsonage on the Mount Zion, and having commenced there the building of a church, would be inclined to accord to the Evangelical National Church of Prussia a sisterly position in the Holy Land.[16]

Bunsen laid out the proposal in London in June 1841, and the British government, with the prodding of Lord Ashley, who was a close friend of Bunsen's, did not hesitate in readily accepting the Berlin proposal, declaring itself prepared to offer its full support for the benefit of the Protestants in the East. In September, as an indication of the seriousness of his intentions, and in order to speed up the process, the King of Prussia offered to finance half of the joint venture on Mount Zion out of his own private funds, and transferred £15,000 into a fund with the annual interest going to the bishopric.

In the meantime, the two sides tried to reach an agreement over the formal divisions of responsibility in the future bishopric while preserving the unique character of each church within the partnership. In the framework of understandings it was agreed that the bishop in Jerusalem would be nominated by each partner in turn and that the Archbishop of Canterbury would hold power of veto over the candidate proposed by the Prussian Crown. In order to enable the bishop chosen by the Prussians to extend his protective authority over the Anglican members of the Jerusalem congregation, the British Parliament passed a special law – the Jerusalem Bishopric Act – which allowed for the nomination of a non-British subject as an Anglican bishop outside the borders of Britain. The law was then ratified by Queen Victoria. At the suggestion of the Prussian King, the British chose the first candidate and proposed the election of a leading member of the London Society, Alexander McCaul. But McCaul immediately refused the offer, and thought it would be more appropriate if the first appointee of the Protestant bishopric in Jerusalem were a descendant of Abraham. On his recommendation they chose a prominent personality in England who met such requirements – a converted Jew and veteran missionary of the London Society, Michael Solomon Alexander (1799–1845).

## THE ALEXANDER PERIOD

Alexander was born on 1 May 1799 in the town of Schönlanke in the duchy of Posen as the son of a Jewish rabbi. His father died in 1817 and three years later Alexander went to London where he was exposed for the first time to the Christian Holy Scriptures. In order to avoid succumbing to his inner prompting and accepting the new faith, Alexander began wandering through the cities of England, serving as rabbi and tutor. In 1824 he married Deborah Levy (1804–72) and a year later finally made up his mind to convert to Christianity and to join the London Society. At first Alexander served as a society missionary in Europe, mainly in Posen, his native district, and then returned to serve in London.[17]

On 11 November 1841, with great pomp and splendour, Alexander was consecrated in London as the first Protestant bishop in Jerusalem. The election of a London Society missionary to such a high position placed it in the limelight. It was now clear that the establishment of the first Protestant bishopric in Jerusalem was made possible by the society's foothold in the city, and this gave great satisfaction to the leaders of the society in London. Applications from clergymen regarding possible participation in the plans taking shape were received with much gratification.

The society announced its readiness to put all its institutions at the immediate disposal of the bishopric, to nominate the bishop as the head of its mission station in Jerusalem, to establish a church and build a residence for him, and to provide all the personnel needed for the bishopric from among the Society's ranks.[18] Besides the special fund set up for the immediate support of the bishopric, the general feeling of satisfaction was expressed in the society's journal of November 1841: 'The Committee of the London Society [are] deeply sensible of the honour put upon them in the selection of a beloved and respected member of their own body to fill the Episcopate.'[19] Two weeks before Alexander's departure from London, he was granted the position of head of the mission in Jerusalem. In December 1841 the first Protestant bishop in

Jerusalem sailed from the shores of England on board the
*Devastation* – a warship that Her Majesty had placed at his
disposal.[20] He carried with him clear instructions to direct his
efforts 'to the conversion of the Jews, to their protection, and to
their useful employment'.[21]

On 2 January 1842, with an escort of 100 horsemen, Bishop
Alexander entered Jaffa Gate to fulfil his mission in Jerusalem. His
entry into the city stirred great excitement among the large
entourage accompanying him:

> just as the new comers turned their heads to admire the Titan-like
> masonry of the tower of Hippicus ... the guns thundered forth the
> salute for the eve of the *Courban Bairam*. Thus, by an odd chance, the
> Protestant Bishop made his public entry into one of the four holy
> cities of Islam ... on the occasion of one of the greatest festivals of
> the Mahometan [*sic*] religion.[22]

Even the local population stood wonderstruck. What
impressed them more than anything else, in view of their familiarity with the lifestyle of the Catholic high clergy, was the fact that
the new bishop was married to a 'bishopess', as they put it. Their
amazement increased at the sight of the bishop's children riding
on donkeys at the tail end of the procession, drawing loud excla-
mations from the onlookers: 'Vescovini, Santa Maria!' (little
bishops, holy Mary!)[23]

The bishop and his large family spent their first days in
Jerusalem with the veteran missionary John Nicolayson. But they
were soon taken ill and until the end of summer had to stay in the
Monastery of the Cross, outside the city walls, while another
building was made ready for their use. After a time they moved
away to join the medical staff, Edward Macgowan (1795–1860) and
Melville Bergheim, who also had to leave the city because of poor
health. The whole group settled down temporarily in a building
on a plot of land leased by the society in the village of Jifna (biblical
Gophna) north of Ramallah. In October 1842 Alexander returned
to Jerusalem to his new residence, a fine house which until then
had been used by the American missionary George Backus
Whiting (1801–55) who had just moved to Beirut. It was leased
from a friend of the Mission, Joseph Amzalak, and stood opposite
the Citadel next to the building complex of the London Society.[24]

Since Alexander had come to Palestine without a permit from
the Turkish authorities, he presented himself immediately after his
arrival before the Pasha of Jerusalem. At the end of the meeting an
explicit directive was issued that proclamations should be made

4. John Nicolayson, founder of the Mission in Jerusalem

from the minarets that, 'He who touches the Anglican Bishop touches the apple of the Pasha's eye.' But this formal visit and its outcome did not prevent the governor of Jerusalem later on from putting obstacles in the path of the society and the bishops. As one of Alexander's biographers puts it, the Pasha 'seems to have forgotten all about the apple of his eye'.[25]

The arrival of the new bishop, one of the London Society's very own, filled the hearts of the missionaries with great hopes for the development of the small mission station in Jerusalem. These aspirations were constantly expressed in the society's journal:

5. Michael Solomon Alexander: first Protestant bishop in Jerusalem

The consecration of the Right Rev. Michael Solomon Alexander as Bishop for Jerusalem commences a new period in its history ... The past has been the seed-time. The feast of in-gathering has now begun. What the friends of Israel longed, and prayed, and laboured for, was not simply the conversion of a few individuals, but the resuscitation of the Jewish people, the resurrection of the Jewish Church.[26]

Lord Ashley also gave voice to his expectations unequivocally in his letter to Alexander before his departure for Palestine:

We [the members of the committee] confidently trust that the Faith, and zeal for the conversion of Israel which marked your course in a humbler station and a foreign land, will, by God's grace, burn with tenfold brightness in the land of your Fathers.[27]

6. Dr Edward Macgowan: founder of the first hospital in Jerusalem

During his brief term of office Alexander did indeed fulfil these expectations and turned the mission station of the London Society and the Protestant bishopric in Jerusalem into a unified body. His first act as bishop was to ordain as priests two German mission-aries who had actually been serving in Egypt in another missionary society and were sent to Jerusalem for their ordination rites. When Alexander reported this to the London Society, as he diligently continued to do throughout his term of office, he added a marginal comment: 'I confess I should have been glad if Jewish missionaries of *our Society* had been the first to receive ordination from the first Hebrew Bishop of the Anglican Church in Jerusalem [emphasis in original].'[28] On numerous occasions the bishop acknowledged this identity between the two synonymous roles he had assumed – that of the Protestant bishop and that of the head of the London mission station in Jerusalem. Sometimes, when he delivered a sermon before the small community in the Society's prayer house, which he called 'our chapel', he even solicited donations for the various funds of the London Society.

In mid-June 1845, the priest Heinrich Johann Abeken (1809–72), a close confidant of the Prussian king who had been involved in setting up the bishopric and recorded its history, visited Jerusalem and was impressed by what had so far been achieved. He wrote to his friend, Christian von Bunsen, 'I have now become far more convinced than I was in London of the importance and necessity of basing the efficiency of the Bishopric upon the Mission to the Jews, and preserving it in the most intimate connexion with it.'[29]

The growing activity of the mission station in Jerusalem during Alexander's term of office blossomed into full florescence. Besides the two outstanding institutions of the society – the hospital and the church, which will be discussed in full at a later stage – new institutions were established with his enthusiastic support. These included a college for converts, a school for vocational training, a book depository that also served as a salesroom for sacred texts, and even a small school for boys and for girls. In this period as well the society wisely managed to acquire a plot of land for a cemetery which symbolised, perhaps more than anything else, the firm hold that the London Society had taken in the Holy Land.

### The College

In May 1843, after a suitable building had been prepared in the Christian Quarter near Damascus Gate, the bishop consecrated the new Hebrew College in Jerusalem. This institution was intended to provide a framework for training new converts and those still in the process of conversion as potential missionaries. Besides religious studies they were taught the English language and introduced to the rules of Hebrew grammar. Administration of the college was entrusted to a converted Jew, Ferdinand Christian Ewald (1802–74) who was born in Maroldweisach near Bamberg, Bavaria. Ewald joined the ranks of the London Society in 1832 and served as its emissary to North Africa until he was selected to accompany Bishop Alexander to Palestine and to work as a society missionary in Jerusalem. His assistant at the college was Erasmus Scott Calman. In its first stage, the College had four students – three rabbis who had begun the process of conversion and Edward Jonas, assistant to the church architect James Johns. In December 1843 William Douglas Veitch (1801–44) arrived to serve as a priest

of the bishopric, and after Ewald left Jerusalem, Veitch administered the college in his place. In spite of the success that this institution proved to be professionally, the directors had to close its
doors in 1846 after the death of Alexander because of the lack of
funds for its upkeep. Veitch left his post, and Calman went over to
work at the Mission Hospital.[30]

## School of Industry

There was a basic assumption that whoever showed an interest in
conversion would immediately lose the fixed allotment he
received for his upkeep provided by the charity funds doled out by
the heads of the Jewish communities in the four sacred cities of the
Holy Land – Jerusalem, Hebron, Safed and Tiberias. This impelled
the society to find a solution, and since their declared policy was to
avoid any kind of direct cash handouts to the converts, the natural
solution was to train them in some productive work in order to
enable them to earn their own living. In 1843 the society set up a
School of Industry headed by Christian Hauser in order to train
converts in carpentry work for building construction and in wood
carving, and at the same time to teach them acceptable working
habits.[31] The fact that the institution was attended by young Jews
who had never before engaged in this kind of occupation in a
similar framework made it necessary to enforce strict rules of
behaviour.

The following list gives a few of these regulations formulated
by the directors of the institution:

1.  Work to begin at 7 a.m. and close at 6 p.m. Dinner hour from 12
    a.m. to 1 p.m.
2.  Any workman who wants to leave work for a few hours, must
    give notice to the foreman, or whoever is in charge.
3.  Any one who does not attend to his work and is found playing
    or disturbing another workman, taking up his time with any
    other work, will be liable to a fine, not less than five Piasters.
4.  Immorality, use of profane language, lack of obedience to the
    master's orders will for the first time be punished by a fine of
    not less than five Piasters, the second time 10 Piasters and the
    third time with instant dismissal.
5.  No workman must take the tools of another without the
    master's consent.

6.  Meals may only be taken at the dinner hour: under no circumstances may they be had during working hours.
7.  Any one taking tools from the workshop will the first time be fined, and on repeating the offence will be dismissed.
8.  Smoking is strictly forbidden during work hours, and on the premises.[32]

This vocational institution had originally been set up to produce furniture for the church under construction, for the hospital and for the other mission buildings. The delays in the construction of the church diverted most of their efforts into serving the needs of the small Protestant community and foreign travellers passing through. After a few years the institution began to decline and only at the end of 1848 was it opened again in an expanded framework with a new name – 'House of Industry' – to be discussed later.

### The Book Depôt

Another institution founded at the initiative of Bishop Alexander was the Book Depôt, which was opened during the first half of 1844 at the edge of the Jewish Quarter. Its purpose was to sell the Jewish sacred scriptures in many languages and to distribute freely the Christian scriptures and the society's journals. The Book Depôt was run by converted Jews who were engaged in reading passages from the Bible and the New Testament to unlettered Jews. This reading was a means for holding discussions with the Jews coming in and out, and creating initial contact with them. The opening of the Book Depôt naturally aroused a storm in Jerusalem and from the beginning a ban was imposed (but later removed) on the Jews who frequented it.[33]

### The Cemetery

Early attempts were already made in 1839 by John Nicolayson to acquire some land for a London Society cemetery site in Jerusalem. In June of that year he reported that, with the collaboration of Vice-Consul Young, he had located a suitable plot of land on Mount Zion that would meet this need, but that he had postponed closing the deal until matters were clarified about land acquired earlier for residential construction.[34] During the course of the year, the acquisition of the cemetery plot on Mount Zion was no longer on the agenda, and in November the society records show that Nicolayson had requested approval for an additional plot site. In March 1840, after various misunderstandings developed between the vice-consul and the society regarding the church building, the London committee instructed Nicolayson to reach some kind of arrangement with Young about the cemetery plot. However, since the mission leaders anticipated a conflict of opinions over the burial of society members who were not British citizens, i.e. converted Jews, they ordered Nicolayson to put the interests of the London Society first, and to purchase, at the same time, another plot of land to be set aside for this purpose.[35]

Young then managed to acquire a good cemetery site:

> It is a Parallelogram of 156 feet long and 60 feet broad – It is 335 paces West of the Jaffa Gate and 182 paces East of that Turkish Burial-Ground which is in the vicinity of the Upper Pool of Gihon, North West of the City.[36]

He later requested and received approval from the Foreign Office in London to build walls around the site. Among those buried in this cemetery were Ewald's wife in January 1844 and Bishop Alexander in December 1845. However, because of its proximity to the Muslim cemetery and all the problems this entailed, the small British community in the city was forced to find a new site. In January 1844, during negotiations with Constantinople about the *firman* for building the church, Nicolayson also asked the Sublime Porte for a permit to buy a plot of land for a cemetery on Mount Zion outside the city walls, where other Christian burial grounds were situated.[37]

Only in the spring of 1848 did the British consul general in Constantinople and his colleague in Jerusalem receive a *firman* to purchase a cemetery plot for the Protestant community. The Second Bishop in Jerusalem, Alexander's successor, bought the site 'on the southern declivity of Mount Zion' and surrounded it with a sturdy wall. The purchase price for this plot, meant jointly for British and German burials, came to £350, which was partly covered by London Society funds. The bishop quoted in his diary the appeal he made to his German associates to effectuate their joint ownership even if only symbolically, by making a contribution towards the land purchase.[38] When the new cemetery was consecrated, the small number of headstones from the American and British graves were transferred there from the previous cemetery near Mamilla Pool and from the Catholic and Greek Orthodox cemeteries on Mount Zion.[39]

THE CHURCH IN JERUSALEM

And when Nicolayson had come in the year 1840 to build the church there, he naturally found impediments and troublemakers on the part of the Ishmaelites [Arabs] who were hostile to the Protestants. – But since it was difficult for the Consul Finn to walk the distance daily on foot to the Church of the Holy Sepulchre, an official permit was sent from Constantinople, by the hand of the Ambassador there, to build a small church near the home of the Consul, a special church for him, and in this way the construction of the church was commenced.[40]

On 28 February 1842 Bishop Alexander laid the first row of stones upon the concrete foundations that had just been completed at the site of the church to be built, and on 1 November in that same year the ceremony for laying the cornerstone was held.[41] On this festive occasion Alexander's wife Deborah inserted in the cornerstone a parchment scroll on which it was written:

The foundation stone of this church erected on Mount Zion Jerusalem by the London Society for Promoting Christianity Amongst the Jews was laid this first day of November (All Saints Day) in the year of our Lord MDCCCXLII [1842] and the seventh year of Her Majesty Queen Victoria by Mistress Alexander the lady of the Right Reverend the Anglican Lord Bishop of the United Church of England and Ireland in Jerusalem.[42]

Once the ceremonies were over and the construction work once more became a mere matter of routine, disputes broke out with the architect, James Johns, who was entrusted with the construction of the church, and the London Society decided to forgo his services.[43] After both sides had gone their separate ways, Johns published in 1844 a de luxe edition of an album called *The Anglican Cathedral Church of Saint James, Mount Zion, Jerusalem*, which included drafts of the architectural designs and sketches for the church. The Society appealed against its publication claiming that the sketches were its own property. In response to these claims, Johns sent a well-reasoned letter declaring that the sketches were made after his departure from Jerusalem on the basis of the drawings that he had made there and which were not those he had undertaken to transmit to the society. His letter went on to express surprise at the complaints being made since, in his view, the society should not object to anything that might eventually serve its own ends.[44] Johns was replaced in January 1843 by

Matthew Habershon (1789–1852), and in conjunction with him the society appointed R. Bates Critchlow to be construction supervisor.

At the same time, the King of Prussia, Friedrich Wilhelm IV, who viewed Johns's plans as being too oriental, put forward a plan of his own, which, in his opinion, had the mark of evangelical modesty and was based on drawings made by the Prussian architect August Stüler (1800–65). In February 1843 the Prussian consul in Beirut was asked to help persuade the British to adopt the King's plans, but the construction work had by then reached a stage that did not allow for changes to be made. The church was eventually built according to Matthew Habershon's plans, which had to be drawn up on the basis of what Johns had left unfinished at the construction site.[45]

In the meantime, the stream of visitors to Palestine grew stronger and the small Anglican community increased proportionately until it became necessary to enlarge the temporary chapel of the London Society in Jerusalem. The winter rains at the end of 1842 were not very beneficial to the building and rendered the temporary chapel on the second floor of the mission house completely unusable. Nicolayson decided to make some minor alterations and by dispensing with a few functional features managed to extend the interior space. After a year had passed and with the Christmas of 1843 approaching, construction was completed of another building that could accommodate 150 of the Protestant faithful. On Christmas Eve, 32 members of the Jerusalem community attended the prayer service in the new chapel, which was named the 'St James Chapel'.[46]

The construction work on the church was progressing slowly with the tacit consent of the Turks, when it was suddenly interrupted by a decree of the governor of Jerusalem in January 1843.[47] Bishop Alexander and John Nicolayson went to Constantinople to lay their case there, and on the way they stopped over in Beirut to consult with the British consul, Colonel Hugh Henry Rose (1801–85). The consul dissuaded the bishop from making a sudden appearance in Constantinople because he thought this would cause consternation among the representatives of the European Powers in the capital of the Ottoman Empire, and embarrass Her Majesty's ambassador. Nicolayson continued on alone to Constantinople, but his efforts were in vain and he did not succeed in revoking the decree.[48] The complaints of the British consuls in the region induced London to renew the diplomatic struggle in Constantinople to obtain the *firman* for the church. The fact that the Turks had violated the understandings that they would not object to the construction work, so long as the church was built within the British consular compound and in an unobtrusive style, caused great disappointment in Britain. The Foreign Office in London instructed the ambassador in Constantinople to renew contact with the Sublime Porte in order to redress matters the best he could, either by obtaining the *firman* or by renewing the understandings reached in September 1841. Throughout 1843 negotiations continued, characterised mainly by the attempts of the Turks to question the very right of the London Society to own land. For example, a conjecture was raised that the land on which the church was being built was Muslim holy ground (*Wakf*). All these claims were rejected by the Foreign Office, but the efforts to straighten out the matter continued to come up against a solid wall of resistance.[49]

In January 1844 the negotiation process went into high gear. The construction of the church in Jerusalem once again appeared on the diplomatic agenda as a result of the sharply worded petition sent from Jerusalem to Constantinople by persons hostile to the society. The petition put forward two main allegations: the first questioned the very legality of purchasing land in order to build a church; the second claimed that there was no precedent for a permit of this kind that allowed for the building of a church in a place where no earlier church had stood in the past. Bunsen, who was then the Prussian ambassador in London, joined the struggle to oppose the petition. In a long and well-reasoned memorandum to Palmerston, he noted that in his view the involvement of Nicolayson with Stratford Canning, the British ambassador in Constantinople, was of vital importance to his efforts to change the decision of the Sublime Porte. As to the matter itself, Bunsen added that the Protestants in Jerusalem did not need any precedent of this kind since on the Mount Zion site where the church was being erected there once stood a Jacobite church, which was only later turned into mosque.

In the second part of his memorandum, Bunsen raised a few essential points upon which he had previously agreed with the Foreign Minister – George Hamilton Gordon, Earl of Aberdeen (1784–1860). He noted, 'Sir Stratford Canning *should be apprized* of the object of Mr Nicolayson coming to Constantinople. At the same time he, the Ambassador, has been instructed to do what is possible to carry the *Firman now* [emphasis in original].' He then added that Karl Hans Königsmark, the Prussian ambassador to Constantinople and his replacement, Karl Emil Gustav von M. Le Coq (1799–1880), had received orders to assist Canning. In his view, the joint demand of London and Berlin for a *firman* from the Sublime Porte was justified because it was intended for building a church for the consuls of Great Britain and Prussia. Therefore the proposal to be submitted to the Sultan should declare:

> ... that the Church is no ostentatious building and will not form a prominent object but be contained within a square formed of dwelling- and school-houses, including the Church from all sides.

At the end of his memorandum, Bunsen suggested preparing for other issues that might arise in the course of further negotiations with Constantinople, and went into detail regarding the placement of the buildings within the church compound and regarding construction costs.[50]

It appears that Palmerston studied Bunsen's memorandum with utmost seriousness, since only a few weeks after he received it the British ambassador placed a letter on the desk of the Turkish Foreign Minister, Rif'at Pasha, that was meant to solve the crisis over the church in Jerusalem and to resolve the differences between the two countries. In his opening statement, Canning declared once more that the church was meant to serve the consulates of Great Britain and Prussia and was to be erected within their building compound. He went on to stress that his country saw it as part of its policy not to interfere in matters concerning the religious communities in Jerusalem and expressed the wish that these words would satisfy the Sultan. In order to remove any doubts, he concluded by quoting the words of Lord Aberdeen: 'Bearing this character, Her Majesty's Government are unwilling to suppose that the Turkish Government will offer any further opposition [to the erection of the church].'[51] Although Constantinople offered no further opposition, it chose to employ the usual delaying tactics and shifted the whole matter over to the governor of the Saida (Sidon) district. The latter was requested to advise the authorities in the capital city of his opinion on the issue and postponed his reply for nearly a year.

In March 1845 a petition was presented to the British Foreign Office on behalf of the London Society signed by fifteen thousand supporters led by the Archbishop of Canterbury. The petition reviewed the entire history of the society since its establishment and concluded with a demand in no uncertain terms that the Foreign Minister immediately and resolutely, through the Crown's ambassador in Constantinople, remove the obstacles standing in the path of the church builders in Jerusalem. The main motive behind this demand was the ban imposed on the Protestant Church throughout the Ottoman Empire while other religious communities enjoyed a freedom of activity. The society's supporters were very sharp in their demands, especially since Constantinople was in debt to London for the military assistance it had recently received in reclaiming control over Palestine and Syria.[52]

Concurrently with the publication of the petition, Ashley also applied directly to Lord Aberdeen concerning the same issue. It may be assumed that these measures bore fruit because at the beginning of September the Sublime Porte transmitted a memorandum to Canning in Constantinople in advance of publishing the *firman* for the church building. According to this, the main reason for the Turkish compliance was:

> the strong relations of friendship between Great Britain and the Sublime Porte, and more particularly in conformity with the constant desire of his Imperial Majesty to confirm the special relations and amity and good understanding between him and Her Majesty the Queen.[53]

On 10 September 1845 an order was published that was addressed to the Turkish governor in the region permitting the construction of the Protestant church in Jerusalem:

> It has been represented both now and before, on the part of the British Embassy residing at my Court, that the British and Prussian Protestant subjects visiting Jerusalem meet with difficulties and obstructions owing to their not possessing a place of worship for the observance of Protestant rites, and it has been requested that permission should be given to erect, for the first time, a special Protestant place of worship within the British Consular residence at Jerusalem. Whereas it is in accordance with the perfect amity and cordial relations existing between the Government of Great Britain and my Sublime Porte, that the requests of that Government should be complied with as far as possible ... When, therefore, it becomes known unto you, Walee [governor] of Saida, Governor of Jerusalem, and others as aforesaid, that our royal permission has been granted for the erection, in the manner above stated, of the aforesaid place of worship, you will be careful that no person do in any manner whatever oppose the erection of the aforesaid place of worship in the manner stated, and you will not act in contravention hereof.[54]

On 16 October 1845 the *firman* was presented through the consuls of Britain and Prussia in Jerusalem to the governor of the city. Two days later, at the head of a large delegation, he visited the site of the proposed building and declared that in contradiction to what was stated in the *firman* the church was not situated in the consular area, and he delayed the start of construction until this matter could be clarified. During the ensuing weeks, with the energetic and adamant assistance of the British ambassador in Constantinople, the obstacles were removed. His intervention led to a new and more firmly worded permit than the previous one for the erection of the church and this was issued on 9 December 1845.[55]

## THE HOSPITAL IN JERUSALEM

The first and foremost of the Amalekites [biblical enemies of the Israelites] was the English hospital. It was the spearhead which unfortunately succeeded in carrying off Jews who were innocent or of weak character, and brought in its wake the terrible ban against the mission hospitals. It was the only Christian hospital which treated Jews alone! And what kind of treatment – root treatment! Till this very day the old building of the English hospital in the Old City carries the symbol of detestation and abomination: at the doorway to the courtyard there is a large crucifix depicted on the exterior of the house side by side with a mezuza.[56]

The medical enterprise of the London Society in Palestine was abandoned when most of the missionaries left Jerusalem during the second Mohammed Ali crisis in 1840. Seeing that the work done by the missionary doctors had left an impression on the Jews of Jerusalem, and realising how essential it was to continue this enterprise in order to achieve the goals of the society during the 1830s, the society leaders were encouraged to give substance to their decision of March 1841 to renew their activities after the enforced interruption of the war. It was resolved to carry out the plans for founding a hospital for the Jews and that next to it 'a School be established in Jerusalem under the immediate direction and management of the Head of the Medical department, and in which Surgery and Pharmacology is to be taught'. Also that Dr Edward Macgowan should be informed that his offer to go out and serve as a doctor at the Jerusalem Mission was accepted, and that, 'His professional character stands too high to make it necessary for him to transmit his Testimonials.'[57]

Bergheim, the first of those who left England to rehabilitate the medical department, arrived in Jerusalem in the summer of 1841, while Macgowan joined the entourage of Bishop Alexander and arrived in January 1842. At the end of his first month of work, Macgowan sent a detailed report describing the poor state of health of the Jerusalem Jews, his activities among them and his recommendations for the construction of a hospital and dispensary by the London Society. He urged the London committee to arrive at some practical decision on this matter and hinted that it would be possible to economise on the expenses of the medical department by growing medicinal herbs. Macgowan even exhorted the society to let him lease some land for this purpose and to employ a local worker. While still awaiting permission from London, he began to renovate a small building for use as a clinic to render first aid to Jewish patients and as a centre for the sale of medicines. Assisted by Bergheim, Macgowan even conducted a few simple operations with the aid of equipment he had bought in England.[58]

In mid-1842 permission was received from London to set up a modest hospital, and Macgowan immediately set to work. At the same time the society missionaries in Palestine requested that the construction of the mission buildings and hospital be completed, as these would form, as they put it, a centre in Jerusalem comparable to the one in London called 'Palestine Place'. In September, Macgowan managed to lease a building for a period of 11 years at the cost of £25 per annum. The building was in the vicinity of the society's dispensary on the eastern slopes of Mount Zion facing the city and near the Jewish Quarter, only a few minutes' walk from the site where the new church was being built. The hospital was planned to hold 12 beds on two separate floors, the lower one for men and the upper for women. At the same time, Macgowan proposed to set aside a separate wing for pilgrims and British tourists needing medical attention, and to charge fees for this so as to cover expenses independently and even to generate income.[59] With the arrival of Matthew Habershon, the architect appointed for constructing the church, they both began with the renovations of the hospital and the additional wing to the existing structure. In February 1843 work was intensified because, as mentioned above, the construction of the church was halted at that time and many of the workers were diverted to the hospital project.

In December 1844 the Jews' Hospital in Jerusalem was opened and within days was filled to capacity.[60] The new institution filled the hearts of the missionaries with pride which found expression in the frequent reports to London. The society journal published many of Macgowan's letters, one of which described a typical day at the hospital:

> It has frequently been my wish during the last month, that our friends in England could get a peep at the hospital on one of my days for the admission of patients. The scene that would meet their eyes would be one of uncommon gratification and interest. They would see the waiting room full of patients, besides a crowd of others thronging the doors of the hospital, who had been too late for admission, but who are patiently waiting, in the hope of being attended to when the first applicants shall be dismissed. Every three or four minutes the door of the consultation-room opens, and out comes a patient with his prescription in his hand, which he takes to the dispensary, which is situated on the other side of the street. This lasts for about two hours, during which the crowd of patients in the street are waiting – some standing, others seated, or lying on the ground or on the steps of the door. Some of them, naturally enough, lose patience, and, on the opening of the door, endeavour to force their way into the consulting-room, and are with difficulty prevented from doing so. Their turn, however, comes at last, when it becomes necessary to discriminate between those who really require advice, and those who are suffering from want. To the most necessitous of the latter a ticket is given for the matron of the hospital, who is in attendance in an adjoining room, and who, on receiving the ticket, gives out of her stores which have been provided by the kind friends in England, some articles of clothing, flour, or relief in a little money, according to the wants of the applicant.[61]

Even before the dedication ceremony of the hospital, the missionaries in Jerusalem had already anticipated opposition by the heads of the Jewish community to the hospitalisation of Jewish patients in a Christian establishment, in spite of the three years' experience in operating the dispensary, which succeeded in serving a wide public. They tried to make things easier for the patients and those accompanying them as far as possible and even set up a kosher kitchen. But, in spite of the foreseen difficulties, the missionaries never expected such a violent reaction from the Jews.

Because of the segregated character of the Jewish community in Palestine, it used a variety of methods to draw back into its folds anyone who even appeared to be on the verge of converting to Christianity. Heavy social pressure was brought to bear on the candidate for conversion, going as far as to impose divorce, the removal of children from the parent's care, and finally a total ban of excommunication, which implied the denial of the right to be buried in a Jewish cemetery and no hope of eternal bliss. But, above all, the community took advantage of the basis for its economic survival – the charitable donations and their distribution – to deprive the convert of his source of subsistence.

Six weeks after the opening of the medical establishment, one of the patients died there. The two chief rabbis in Jerusalem made his Jewish burial conditional on having all the patients in the hospital, including the Jewish attendants, leave it immediately, and that no Jew would be allowed to enter its gates in the future. Several letters went back and forth for an entire week between the rabbis and the director of the hospital, and between the latter and the British consul in Jerusalem and the Foreign Minister in London. Since all these letters were futile, the missionaries were forced to bury the deceased patient in the British cemetery.[62]

The seriousness of this event from the viewpoint of the Jerusalem rabbis induced them to take the gravest measure in their power without delay, and they issued a ban saying:

All Israel shall hear and fear. As the horribleness in Israel upon Mount Zion, was clearly seen, from the affairs of the Freemasons' [*sic*] hospital, whose sole object wish & desire, by it, is to bring the souls of our brothers, of the house of Israel into their uncleanness (may the merciful one deliver us!) therefore the chief, great, wise & learned man of the holy congregation of the Sephardim, met together with the chiefs & leaders of the holy congregation of the Ashchenazim Perushim & Khasidim, who reside here in Jerusalem our holy & glorious city (may she be built & established!) & at the head of the meeting was also the highly honourable & wonderful Rabbi, who is full of the glory of the Lord, famous in piety, the crown of our heads the First in Zion (may the Lord keep & preserve him!), & all agreed to proclaim in the camp of the holy congregations above mentioned, as follows, – By the power of our holy law & the might of the holiness of Jerusalem our holy city with as a heavy anathema as that of Joshua the son of Nun, & as that of Rabbi Gershon [*sic*]; we give notice that no man shall dare to enter the hospital above mentioned, whether a patient for his recovery, or a healthy person to serve there. Let both man & woman take warning by this our edict. We also inform all our brethren of the house of Israel that whosoever shall enter the said hospital; their meat & drink shall become, through a heavy excommunication as unlawful food – their bread and wine shall become as the bread & wine of idolaters, all their children will not be circumcised (amongst the holy assembly, neither will he be called up to the reading of the law) nor shall he have any part in the God of Israel, he will also not be purified, after his decease, by Jews, nor buried in their burial ground. We

caution also the Shokhatim [ritual slaughterers] of all the congregations, not to kill a fowl for those, of the house of Israel, who shall
enter the hospital. Likewise we charge our vendors of meat, by the
same powers, not to sell meat to any man or woman, who shall enter
the hospital; should they, however by any device, get meat from our
vendors, then the dishes will be unlawful, the man or servant,
through whom they got it, incurs the above mentioned curse. All the
above mentioned curses shall be likewise upon every one, who will
advise or induce any of the children of Israel, to enter the said
hospital; but ye brethren, of the house of Israel, who cleave to the
Lord, hear & your soul shall live. Whosoever shall transgress this
our edict, renders himself liable to all the penalties above
mentioned; but good blessings & prosperity will come upon those
that hear our words. May the merits of our brethren of the house of
Israel, & of Jerusalem our holy & glorious city defend us that none
of us shall be led astray. Amen & so be the will of God![63]

The implication of such a ban in those days meant the expul-
sion of the excommunicated person from the Jewish community or
death by utter deprivation. The publication of this ban resulted in
the complete desertion of the hospital by everyone within 24
hours.

During the weeks that followed, force of circumstance made
the Jews of Jerusalem slowly trickle back to receive the hospital
services. However, the community providers remained adamant,
and for every instance of a Jewish patient dying in the medical
establishment they raised difficulties about burial. For example, at
the end of the summer of 1845, when a Jewish mother and her
baby died, the father of the family pleaded for help from the rabbis
but was totally rejected. They claimed that the very hospitalisation
in the Mission Hospital stripped them of the right to Jewish burial.
After lengthy discussions in which the London Society missionaries and the British consul in Jerusalem were involved, the rabbis
agreed to permit the burial at ten times the normal cost.[64]

The distress of the patients' families, which had become a
common phenomenon, created the need for a special burial place
for those Jews who died at the hospital. At that time there was a
plot of land for sale near the Jewish cemetery, and the society
wished to allocate this for the immediate burial of the Jewish
mother and child. When the rabbis heard of the expected sale they
hurriedly agreed to bury the bodies in Jewish graves, but the sale
was nevertheless carried out and the plot of land was bought for
£12. This plot was called, and is still called today, 'Ras el-Amud'
and is situated on the side road leading from Jerusalem to the

Dead Sea on the southern slopes of the Mount of Olives and above the village of Siloam (Shiloah).[65]

In January 1846 another Jewess died in the hospital, and, after the rabbis of Jerusalem again refused to allow her Jewish burial, the body was interred in the cemetery bought by the mission for this purpose. The burial, which was the first since the plot was purchased half a year earlier, aroused great anger among the Jewish population, and they enlisted the support of the Jerusalem governor, who threw the Arab owner and the Jewish dealer into prison and ordered the sale cancelled. Attempts to change this ruling through the British embassy in Constantinople were fruitless and the London Society lost the cemetery plot.[66]

The missionaries, of course, laid the blame on the community leaders and not on the Jewish population, which generally appreciated the medical services. Careful distinction was made between the rabbis of the Ashkenazi community and those of the Sephardi community. The latter, which represented the larger community in Jerusalem and were less dependent upon the charity allocations coming from abroad, showed greater tolerance towards the mission. The society missionaries assumed that the Sephardi rabbis would not have taken such drastic measures as preventing a Jewish burial and that the action of the Ashkenazi rabbis was caused by an internal split between the Hasidim and the Perushim, which necessitated a strong hand in order to maintain the distinction of each sect. The missionaries realised that the eagerness of the Jerusalem Jews to receive medical and welfare services provided by the London Society, and the influence this gave to the Christian church, undermined the authority and position of the Ashkenazi rabbis, who, in the society's view, were mainly concerned with 'the preservation of its own narrow and exclusive dominion, over the minds and bodies of its victims' and therefore did all they could to oppose the mission.[67]

The person who led the campaign of criticism against the Jewish community leaders of those days was naturally the director of the hospital, Edward Macgowan. His choice of words went beyond the mere need to repel the antagonism towards the institute that he headed, and his criticism was broad and sweeping:

> In fact Rabbinism is a system far more refined, complicated, and exacting than Popery itself. It embraces not only the religious observances, but rules with despotic control every act of civil life. Claiming the exclusive superintendence of meats and drinks, and determining the lawfulness or unlawfulness of the same, it sepa-

rates by a broad demarcation the Jewish community from all the rest of mankind.[68]

The opposition of the Jerusalem rabbis to the hospital and to the entire medical enterprise of the London Society had a positive outcome in that it generated independent Jewish initiatives, led by Moses Montefiore (1784–1885), who took action more than once during the course of that century:

> When Montefiore heard in the year 5603 [1843] that the British Mission Society had set down its stake in Jerusalem as well, and had installed a special doctor to cure the body and even more so, the 'soul', he hastened to send here Dr. Simon Fränkel [1806–80] together with medicines to heal those who were poor and sick free of charge in order to cut off the arm of the Mission … [69]

Fränkel arrived in Jerusalem in mid-1843. The further the renovations of the Mission Hospital advanced, the more he realised how vital it was to set up a rival Jewish hospital. He recorded his thoughts in a Jewish journal:

> It is well-known to you that the Missionary Society strains every nerve to make proselytes; they leave nothing undone. Thus they have erected a hospital in which none but Jews are to be admitted. No Jew, it is true, will enter it, if he can help it; but what shall the poor, unfortunate, sick and houseless do? Who, after all, can blame him for it? and what is the consequence? … At any time a hospital would have administered relief to the sick and suffering; now, it will like-wise counteract the efforts of the Mission – an object which, in my opinion, every one of our brethren should, and will keep in view.[70]

Fränkel was welcomed gladly by the London Society doctor, and the missionaries were pleased at the establishment of a Jewish hospital, knowing that it was their activities that had induced the philanthropic patrons of the Jewish community to act themselves. Dr Macgowan, director of the Mission Hospital, wrote that, 'every friend of Israel would rejoice that Christian benevolence had provoked such a charitable jealousy among them'.[71] After the dedication ceremony of the London Society hospital in December 1844, the Jewish hospital also opened in one of the finest buildings in the Jewish Quarter, which had once served as a military medical facility during the Egyptian occupation a few years earlier. The two-storey spacious building was well equipped and the patient occupancy was as high as that of the English Mission Hospital.

SAFED

> The situation of Safed is very picturesque, on a high hill nearly 3000
> feet above the Mediterranean. ... The scenery is very bold, like the
> fine mountain scenery of Italy or Switzerland. Here grow the olive,
> the vine, pomegranate, walnut, almond, and a variety of other kind
> of trees; but we could not see the myrtle groves which other trav-
> ellers imagine to have seen, nor the large sycamore tree under
> whose shade thirty travellers, with their camels and horses, are said
> to have rested.[72]

Safed, being one of the four sacred cities of the Jewish people in
the land of Israel and having a large Jewish population, was an
obvious attraction for the London Society from the very first.
Attempts to settle in the city were already made during the
exploratory expeditions of the British missionaries in the 1820s and
1830s, but it was only in the period of Bishop Alexander and with
his encouragement that the society came to a decision to actually
secure a foothold there. At the end of May 1843 two new missionaries – the converted Jews, Paul Heiman Sternschuss and
Alexander Isaac Behrens (1820–82) – left Jerusalem to open a
mission station in Safed. John Nicolayson, who had lived in the
city 16 years earlier and knew it well, joined the expedition in
order to pave the way for his colleagues. On 2 June 1843 the group
reached Safed together with Tanoos Kerm, a native Muslim, who
had already bought a building for them. He joined them to facilitate the bureaucratic procedures and to serve as their interpreter
and also to be a teacher in the school to be established. As soon as
they arrived they were disappointed to find that the previous
owner had not yet vacated the building. It was only with the energetic measures taken by their Muslim merchant friend that it was
finally possible, on 17 June 1843, to open the mission house which
became the first in a series of institutions set up by the Safed
mission.[73]

The situation that faced Sternschuss and Behrens was different
from that which they had encountered in Jerusalem. Safed still
bore the scars of a devastating earthquake, which had occurred on
1 January 1837 with a death toll of thousands. Sternschuss wrote in
his diary that the city was steeped in misery and looked like a
mound of ruins. Because of the constant looting and other tribulations that the city suffered as a result of the earthquake, no well-to-
do Jews wishing to settle in Palestine dared risk coming to Safed.
According to his impressions, all the Jews of Safed, with a few

exceptions, were miserably poor. The wretched physical conditions to which they were exposed were merely a prelude to the difficulties facing the missionaries in their contacts with the city population. Safed, because of its isolated location and its being nearly inaccessible under nineteenth-century conditions, prevented the Jews from being exposed to outside influences. The segregation this imposed on the inhabitants created a community that obeyed to the letter whatever the rabbis said, and one that was far less open to the overtures of the Protestant missionaries. As soon as they arrived, the two missionaries were met with the violent opposition of the Jewish community leaders, who at first tried to expel them from the city. When they did not succeed, they began to persecute any Jew who associated with the missionaries. And, as in similar cases, they denied them a share in the charity funds sent from Jewish communities abroad. Sternschuss himself had harsh words for this state of affairs in the letter he sent from Safed to London: 'The Jews here are complete slaves of the persons who have the management of the rent for distribution; but if any one displeases them in the least, he is immediately threatened with the loss of the weekly and monthly charity money.'[74] The vehement antagonism met by the missionaries in their contacts with the community leaders in Safed was expressed by the local Jews who said that if a missionary converts a Jew 'he must dig a grave for him' at the same time, since it would be impossible to protect his life in that city.[75]

The harsh winter of 1843 in Palestine did not spare the Society's missionaries and badly affected the mission house. Sternschuss and Behrens expressed the hope that they would endure the rest of the season without trouble and drew much encouragement from the single ray of light that had managed to steal through the darkness – that the opposition to their very presence had lessened a little. In order to take advantage of this opportune moment, the society decided to use the tried and trusted formula and to add a medical wing to the mission station in Safed. Sternschuss was transferred to Baghdad, and his place was taken by a medical missionary, the converted Jew, Dr Anton Abraham Kiel, a native of Courland who had previously served at the mission station in Jaffa. His medical work prompted the rabbis to take action, and they rented a building to be used as a Jewish hospital, but, when they realised that the members of their congregation preferred the London Society doctor, they gave up the idea.

At the beginning of 1844 a new calamity descended upon the young mission station. Local Muslims began to mistreat the British

missionaries, apparently because of the tensions between warring
Arab factions in the area, and perhaps not without the encouragement of the Jewish community leaders. At the end of January the
attempts to attack Alexander Behrens reached a climax with the
connivance of one of the armed guards of the governor, who did
not bother to intervene. When real danger threatened their lives,
Behrens and Dr Kiel were forced to leave the city with the sense
that there was little chance left to establish a British missionary
presence in Safed.[76]

In order to make a closer examination of the new situation in
the city, the society sent a fact-finding delegation headed by the
English missionary J.O. Lord, under the assumption that his
British origins would facilitate matters. He was accompanied by
the converted Hungarian rabbi, Abraham Tymmim, who was originally to have gone with him to Hebron to set up a mission station
there. They arrived in Safed at the end of February 1844, and this
fact-finding delegation became a permanent one there since Lord
and Tymmim found that the city had quietened down. They were
accorded a friendly welcome by the Jewish population and
continued their work there without interruption throughout 1845.
During the course of 1846 there was no continuous missionary
presence in the city owing to the illness of Lord, who had to go to
Malta for a period of convalescence. But, in spite of this, the society
bought another building in Safed.[77] Only in the heyday of the first
wave of Jewish immigration to Palestine during the 1880s did the
society renew its activities in full scale in this Galilean city.


JAFFA


Jaffa is situated 37 miles north-west of Jerusalem, on a sandy
promontory, washed on three sides by the waves of the
Mediterranean. From the sea Jaffa presents, with its houses rising
tier upon tier, a very imposing appearance, like that of a fortress
town, such as Toledo, which it resembles. With its luxuriant gardens
and the mountains in the background it offers a most picturesque
scene ... The harbour is wretched in the extreme, ships having to
anchor a considerable distance out at sea. Passengers are landed,
often with much difficulty and danger, in small boats ... The town
has been greatly enlarged and improved in recent years, and the
wall, which formerly surrounded it, has been removed, but its old
streets are still narrow and dirty.[78]

The modest port of Jaffa, which served as the main point of entry into Palestine and was called the 'port of Jerusalem', acquired a major role when it changed from being a small city at the beginning of the nineteenth century into one that was second only to Jerusalem in importance by the end of that century. Its significance as the gateway through which thousands of travellers came and went every year, many of them tourists and pilgrims – some of them Jews – did not escape the eyes of the society missionaries, nor those of Bishop Alexander. He had stayed in Jaffa for a short while because of the illness of one of his daughters and had noted the hidden potential for the establishment of a mission station to work among those arriving from the moment they set foot on the soil of the Holy Land. In November 1842 he recommended that if the society could find a suitable person it should send a representative to Jaffa, since the city served as the port of Jerusalem and many Jews landed there on their way to the Holy City.[79]

The recommendations of the bishop were realised only in 1846, after he had passed away. The society rented a building and installed a Book Depôt like the one in Jerusalem. They appointed a Jewish convert, Christian Wilhelm Hanauer (1810–73), a native of Fellheim near Memmingen in southwest Bavaria, to take charge of this institution and the reading of chapters from the scriptures to the Jews visiting it. Dr Anton Kiel was also stationed in Jaffa after he left Safed because of the antagonism shown towards him there. Kiel engaged himself in medicine on a limited scale among the small Jewish community and gave medical assistance to those passing through the city.[80]

HEBRON

There is no part of Palestine which I have visited, so well cultivated as the country around Hebron. On the evening of our approach to the city, we passed for miles through scenes of ravishing loveliness, varied with hill and dale, of wood and corn fields, and vineyards, illuminated by the rays of the declining sun ... Nothing could be conceived more rich, brilliant, and smiling than this garden of Eden.[81]

Hebron, also one of the four sacred cities of the Jewish people in the land of Israel, had stirred the imagination of the London Society missionaries, not least because of the heart-warming descriptions of the emissaries who had visited it. In contrast with the enthusiastic depictions of the city, the Jews of Hebron were described in less flattering terms. In most of the accounts they were portrayed as the hard core of fidelity to Judaism, and according to other sources they were 'fanatical, and their spiritual bondage and thraldom complete'.[82] In January 1843 Bishop Alexander together with his family and a few missionaries went down for a comprehensive tour of Hebron. This was one more of the many tours that had been made by the society missionaries since the 1820s. The group stayed among the Jews of the city for a few days and received first-hand impressions of the character of the community and the possibility of setting up another mission station besides the one in Jerusalem. Christian Ewald, who was one of the members of the delegation, wrote that he and the bishop felt the importance of continuing the missionary work that they had just begun and that they planned to return to the city.[83]

In its annual report for 1843 the society announced, in response to the reverberations that reached London after this visit, that it intended to set up a permanent base in Hebron. It chose Dr Thomas Kerns for the task, and he set out in December 1844 to examine whether attitudes had changed during the two years since the last visit and to rent a suitable building for the mission house. Kerns arrived in Hebron and tried for several days to obtain a permit from the Bedouin governor to reside permanently in the city, and also requested to lease a suitable building through him. Kerns, who set down his impressions in detail, reported on the corrupt government, which imposed a rule of terror over the Jews of the city, and recommended that the attempts to settle in Hebron be postponed for a while. After a few days he returned to Jerusalem. Two months later, in February 1845, the missionaries Lord and Tymmim made another attempt to settle in Hebron, but they were unable even to rent a room, and were then transferred to the mission station in Safed, as mentioned earlier. The society felt these attempts were enough for the time being, and therefore decided that Hebron would be a substation of the main one in Jerusalem, and that missionary work would be carried out through regular visits to the city.[84]

## TIBERIAS

Another of the four sacred cities was Tiberias, which had a large Jewish population but was not considered a very important site for a missionstation. It appears that the reason for this was the oppressive heat that greets the visitor in summer and makes such a deep impression on the European traveller that it is given special mention in the written reports.[85] Consequently, it was its sister city, Safed, that was chosen as the London Society centre in the Galilee, while Tiberias remained a substation where missionary work was conducted through occasional visitations. During a visit in 1843 missionaries wrote that Tiberias had the potential for the establishment of a mission station but could not be tolerated as a place of residence except during the winter season. Contacts with the Jewish population in the city were also not very encouraging. The Jews of Tiberias did not arouse their admiration, and visitors who stopped by in Tiberias after the earthquake of 1837 portrayed them in painful detail, saying that the survivors were poor, emaciated and filthy, looking like the shadows of their brother Jews in Europe.[86]

In February 1844 Bishop Alexander visited the northern part of Palestine and during his stay in Tiberias gained the impression that the city deserved an independent mission station without any connection to the one in Safed. His report reached London, and it was noted at the committee meeting of that year that the London Society intended to appoint a missionary to set up a mission station in the city. This decision was not carried out in practice and the London Society never did establish a mission station in Tiberias. The missionaries were content with regular visitations, setting up an encampment on the outskirts of the city and reporting about the large crowds around the little camp 'eager to have their bodily ailments attended to, and willing to listen to the proclamation of the Gospel'.[87]

## CHRISTIAN VON BUNSEN

We chose to devote a fifth part of our research solely to a short period of four years because of their great importance. The Anglo-Prussian bishopric in Jerusalem was of prime importance to the Protestants in Palestine and transformed the London Society foothold, which contained a handful of missionaries, into a centre that gripped the imagination of millions of Protestants in the Western world and held them spellbound. The creation of the bishopric, as with any other major event in history, did not emerge out of careful international planning but simply from the personal motivations of one vigorous character.

Certain aspects in the life history of Christian von Bunsen, the Prussian ambassador in Berne, combined together with his ardent faith in the idea of the restoration of the Jews, weighed the scales in favour of the intricate set of circumstances that made it possible to establish the bishopric. The dominant incentive for the creation of a Protestant entity that would counterbalance the presence of the Catholic Church in Palestine was generated by the insult Bunsen suffered at the Vatican Court. He found fellow believers in England whom he came to know well through his marriage to an Englishwoman, and during the long periods of time that he spent in London he associated with top-ranking leaders of the London Society and became acquainted with its modest activities in Jerusalem. He found the instrument to propel his idea forward in the person of his good and faith-inspired friend the King of Prussia, who employed the full weight of his political power and provided half the cost of the enterprise from his private purse.

Bunsen was therefore the key figure in the establishment of the Anglo-Prussian bishopric by means of the London Society foothold in Jerusalem. In this way he unintentionally granted the society the legitimacy and international recognition necessary for its transformation from a modest holding into the very centre of an enterprise then seen as the most outstanding Protestant achievement in the nineteenth century. After the decision was made to establish the bishopric, it was headed by another German – also a member of the London Society. Immediately after his arrival, Bishop Alexander began to make the bishopric a concrete reality and paved the way for the society's advancement by establishing institutions and deepening the ties with the Jewish communities in Palestine.

The era of Bishop Michael Solomon Alexander in Palestine ended at the close of 1845. Since the area of his responsibility as the Protestant bishop in Jerusalem also extended southwards to Africa, Bishop Alexander went down in the winter of 1845 to visit the Jewish community in Egypt. On 23 November, in the village of Ras el-Wadi, before he could reach Cairo, the bishop expired. Those accompanying him brought his body back to Jerusalem and buried him on Saturday night, 20 December 1845, by the light of torch flames in the former London Society cemetery near Jaffa Gate. Except for in Jerusalem, the city in which he was buried, the bishop did not live to see much benefit from the activities of 'his' society in Palestine.[88]

NOTES

1.  Grajewski, P.B.-Z. *The Struggle of the Jews against the Mission from 1824 till Our Times* (Jerusalem: 1935) (Hebrew).
2.  William Ewart Gladstone (1809–98) writes in his memoirs about the bishopric: '… which I believe to have been the child of Bunsen's poetic and energetic brain', in Schmidt-Clausen, K. *Vorweggenommene Einheit: Die Gründung des Bistums Jerusalem im Jahre 1841* (Berlin and Hamburg: 1965), p. 88, n. 24. See also 'The Three Anglican Bishops in Jerusalem', in *The Church Quarterly Review*, XVIII (April–July 1884), p. 330, where it is mentioned that Bunsen was the bishopric's first originator. For a more detailed account of the establishment of the bishopric see mainly Abeken, *The Protestant Bishopric*; Hechler, W.H. *The Jerusalem Bishopric, 1841: Documents Chiefly Reprinted from a Copy of the Original German Account, 'Das Evangelische Bisthum in Jerusalem', Geschichtliche Darlegung mit Urkunden: Berlin, 1842* (London: 1883); Bunsen, F. *A Memoir of Baron Bunsen, Drawn Chiefly from Family Papers by his Widow Frances Bunsen*, 2nd edn, 2 vols (London: 1869); Schmidt-Clausen, *Vorweggenommene Einheit*; Smith, H. *The Protestant Bishopric in Jerusalem* (London: 1847); Horn, S.E. *The Jerusalem Bishopric 1841* (Minnesota: 1978); Greaves, R.W. 'The Jerusalem Bishopric, 1841', *English Historical Review*, 64 (July 1949), pp. 328–52; Welch, P.J. 'Anglican Churchmen and the Establishment of the Jerusalem Bishopric', *The Journal of Ecclesiastical History*, 8 (1957), pp. 193–204; Geldbach, E. *Der Gelehrte Diplomat* (Leiden: 1980); Lückhoff, M. 'Prussia and Jerusalem: Political and Religious Controversies Surrounding the Foundation of the Jerusalem Bishopric', in Ben-Arieh Y. and Davis M. (eds) *Jerusalem in the Mind*, pp. 173–81.
3.  The crux of the argument between Prussia and the Vatican was the question of mixed marriages between Catholics and non-Catholics. Since Bunsen was very aggressive in his representation of Prussia's position that favoured granting permission to marry, he was forced to leave Rome. Regarding this matter, which is not a subject for this research, see Schmidt-Clausen, *Vorweggenommene Einheit*, pp. 72–84 where further sources are given; Barclay, E.D. *Fredrick William IV and the Prussian Monarchy 1840–1861* (Oxford: 1995), pp. 77–81.
4.  Years later, in the summer of 1882, the German ambassador in London sent a letter to the British Foreign Minister regarding the intentions of the King of Prussia, who wished to cooperate with Britain in setting up the bishopric. Friedrich Wilhelm IV thought that the bishopric was meant, first and foremost, to demonstrate Protestant unity in the face of the older churches. See Bodleian, Cmj, d.53 for the collection of documents submitted to the British Parliament in July 1887 entitled *Correspondence Respecting the Protestant Bishopric at Jerusalem* (Germany No. 1. 1887): Georg Herbert Münster (1820–1902) German Ambassador in London, to George Leveson Gower, 2nd Earl of Granville (1815–91), British Foreign Minister, London, 17 July 1882. Bunsen's motives for thwarting the Catholic Church, which served him in establishing the bishopric, are echoed in the journal of the Church Missionary Society published in the spring of 1887, which states that Friedrich Wilhelm and Bunsen, who had shown such great interest in setting up the joint bishopric, proposed that the Anglican and Lutheran churches should unite in a common effort to enlighten the Eastern churches and assist them in opposing the encroachments of Rome.

5. Barclay, *Fredrick William IV*, p. 81.
6. Schmidt-Clausen, *Vorweggenommene Einheit*, pp. 88–100; Barclay, *Fredrick William IV*, p. 81. In the biography of Bunsen written by his wife, she states that he himself was the originator of the idea to harness the society to this enterprise. See Bunsen, *Memoir*, I, pp. 368–9.
7. Schmidt-Clausen, *Vorweggenommene Einheit*, p. 89, n. 26: Bunsen to Gladstone, 3 August 1840.
8. Bunsen, *Memoir*, I, p. 367: Bunsen in London to Friedrich Perthes, 12 October 1841; Hechler, *The Jerusalem Bishopric*, pp. 25–6.
9. Abeken, *The Protestant Bishopric*, pp. 37–9.
10. In July 1841, at the beginning of the discussions between Prussia and Britain, the idea was raised to send through the British ambassador in Constantinople an application for the recognition of the bishopric, but this was not carried out. See Bunsen, *Memoir*, I, p. 373: Bunsen to his wife, 13 July 1841.
11. Regarding the opposition of Constantinople to the establishment of the bishopric, see Lückhoff, 'Prussia and Jerusalem', pp. 178–9.
12. ITAC, collection of unclassified letters: extensive correspondence between Ponsonby and Nicolayson from 29 May 1841 to 18 August 1841.
13. FO, 78/429: Palmerston to Ponsonby, 27 September 1841.
14. In this regard, Nicolayson wrote:

> Without pretending to trace the origin of the plan of an Anglican Bishopric at Jerusalem … I may yet observe that the existence of the English Mission to the Jews there was known to and favourably regarded by all the high parties who have since concurred in that plan. It has become favourably known to … the King of Prussia through some of my assistants in the Mission who were Prussian subjects.

See ITAC, collection of unclassified letters: Nicolayson in Constantinople to Canning, 21 February 1844 – a memorandum on the subject of the Jerusalem bishopric and its connections with the London Society. For the conception of Friedrich Wilhelm see Bodleian: offprint from *The Christian's Monthly Magazine and Review* (February 1846), entitled 'The Jerusalem Bishopric', p. 7; this article can also be found in the collection of pamphlets in the Archive of the Anglican Church at Lambeth Palace Library, London, H6572.J4 (1.6).
15. Abeken, *The Protestant Bishopric*, pp. 137–40; Hechler, *The Jerusalem Bishopric*, App., p. 66: Memorandum of the Prussian Minister for Religious Affairs, 1 November 1841. For the general attitude towards the relationship between the location of the London Mission in Jerusalem and the establishment of the Protestant bishopric see Latourette, K.S. *A History of the Expansion of Christianity*, Vol. 4: *The Great Century* (New York and Evanston: 1941), p. 39. On the differences of shade between the Prussian conception in which the German Protestants in the East were of primary concern, and the British conception which was geared to the idea of the restoration of the Jews, with regard to the establishment of the bishopric, see Stock, *The History*, I, p. 422. On the opposition of Russia and France to the previous initiatives of Friedrich Wilhelm to conduct a joint Christian administration in Palestine, see Carmel, A. and Eisler, J.E. *Der Kaiser reist ins Heilige Land: Die Palästinareise Wilhelms II, 1898*, (Stuttgart: 1999), Ch. II.
16. St Albans, memorial booklet for Bishop Alexander: *Two Sermons, Preached … on Occasion of the Death of the Right Rev. Michael Solomon Alexander* (London: 1846), p. 63; Lambeth, H5672.J4 (2.8), pamphlet entitled *The Jerusalem Bishopric*

*and its Connection with the London Society for Promoting Christianity Amongst the Jews* (1887), p. 5; also found in Bodleian, Dep. Cmj, d.138; ibid., d.153.

17. For details regarding Alexander see *Jewish Records*, 23 (1825), pp. 2–3; Ayerst, *Jews of the Nineteenth Century*, pp. 297–301; Corey, M.W. *From Rabbi to Bishop: The Biography of the Right Reverend Michael Solomon Alexander, Bishop in Jerusalem* (London: [1956]), pp. 9–44; Gidney, *The History*, pp. 207–9.

18. ITAC, London Committee Resolutions, No. M2063 (15 September 1841). The society even outdid itself in setting up a special foundation to raise additional funds to finance the bishopric. See ibid., No. M2150 (12 October 1841); Hechler, *The Jerusalem Bishopric*, App. p. 79: British letter of guarantee for the financial support of the bishopric, 15 November 1841.

19. *Jewish Intelligence* (November 1841), p. 384.

20. At first the Admiralty offered the frigate *Infernal* but Alexander refused to travel in a ship bearing this name. He finally had no choice but to compromise with travelling on the *Devastation*. See Tibawi, *British Interests*, pp. 50–1.

21. Hechler, *The Jerusalem Bishopric*, App. p. 110: declaration of principles for the establishment of the bishopric, 9 December 1841. In the declaration of intentions that accompanied the establishment of the bishopric, a special section was devoted to the framework of relationships with other churches. It was stated there that:

> He [the elected Bishop] will establish and maintain, as far as in him lies, relation of Christian Charity with other Churches represented at Jerusalem, and in particular with the Orthodox Greek Church [to which most of the Christian Arabs in Palestine belonged]; taking special care to convince them, that the Church of England does not wish to disturb, or divide, or interfere with them; but that she is ready, in the spirit of Christian love, to render them such offices of friendship as they may be willing to receive.

22. *The Times*, 27 January 1842. On the colourful entry of the bishop into Jerusalem see several additional sources, e.g. *Jewish Intelligence* (April 1842), pp. 127–8: Alexander, from Jerusalem, 25 January 1842; ibid., p. 129: Nicolayson, from Jerusalem, 24 January 1842; Ewald, *Journal*, pp. 24–6.

23. Von Hase, K. *Kirchengeschichte auf der Grundlage akademischer Vorlesungen*, (Leipzig: 1892), III, p. 556. On the personal aspects of the life of Alexander and his family during his term of office in Jerusalem, see detailed account in Lambeth, MS.3394-5: incomplete autobiography of Deborah, wife of the bishop, written between the years 1857 and 1859; ibid., MS.3396: diary of Alexander's wife describing their journey to Mount Carmel in February 1845; ibid., MS.3397: biography of Alexander in typescript, compiled by E.W. Wilson and M. Ransom.

24. Williams, *The Holy City*, I, p. 20. Whiting moved to Beirut when a general decision was made by the American mission to transfer the centre of their activities there after the Anglican bishop began his period of service in Jerusalem. See Tibawi, *American Interests*, p. 101.

25. Corey, *From Rabbi to Bishop*, pp. 69, 81.

26. *Jewish Intelligence* (December 1841), p. 391.

27. Lambeth, MS.3397: Ashley to Alexander, 9 January 1841.

28. *Jewish Intelligence* (May 1842), p. 161: Alexander, from Jerusalem, 25 January 1842.

29. Ibid. (November 1845), p. 375: Abeken, from Jerusalem to Bunsen, 7 July 1845; Abeken, *The Protestant Bishopric*, p. 155.

30. Gidney, *The History*, p. 237.

31. ITAC, Jerusalem Local Committee Minutes Book, I, No. 120 (28 February 1843): Hauser's appointment; ibid., No. 135 (21 March 1843): establishment of this institution including the agreement with Hauser on the definition of his duties as head of the School of Industry.
32. Bodleian, Dep. Cmj, d.62: Regulations entitled 'Rules of the L.J.S. House of Industry, Carpentry & Turnery Department, Jerusalem'; ibid., see later document which includes many additional rules.
33. A vestige of that same book depot can be found today incorporated within its modern counterpart near the gate of the Christ-Church compound in Jerusalem.
34. Christ Church, Nicolayson's Journal, III, 3 June 1838.
35. ITAC, London Committee Resolutions, No. L1669 (14 November 1839), No. M147 (3 March 1840).
36. FO, 78/581, No. 13: Young in Jerusalem to Aberdeen, 30 May 1844.
37. ITAC, collection of unclassified letters: Nicolayson in Pera (a residential quarter for diplomats in the vicinity of Constantinople) to Canning, 6 January 1844. Regarding the American and British cemeteries on Mount Zion, see for example Ben-Arieh, Y. *A City Reflected in Its Times: New Jerusalem – the Beginning* (Jerusalem: 1979), pp. 63–6 (Hebrew).
38. Gobat S. and Thiersch, H.W.J. *Samuel Gobat, Bishop of Jerusalem: His Life and Work* (London: 1884), p. 256.
39. In the summer of 1904, when the cemetery was nearly filled up, a plot of land of a little more than one acre was purchased on its eastern side. The purchase was carried out in a complicated deal between the bishopric, the consuls of Britain and Germany, the three British missionary societies and representatives of the German community. The purchase was financed mainly by the Church Missionary Society in exchange for ownership of the nearby Gobat School. See Bodleian, Dep. Cmj, d.59: copy of the detailed agreement between the parties dated 4 June 1904. On the cemeteries, see mainly Mehnert, G. *Der englisch – deutsche Zionsfriedhof in Jerusalem* (Leiden 1975).
40. Grajewski, *The Struggle*, n.p.: 'The First Pastor: Johannes Nicolayson' (Hebrew).
41. ITAC, Jerusalem Local Committee Minutes Book, I, No. 72 (8 November 1842). As customary in those days, two ceremonies were performed, the first marking the beginning of the work, and the second, a more festive one, was the insertion of a written scroll and gold coins in the first stone to be placed on the foundations, which had by then reached ground level.
42. Johns, *The Anglican Cathedral*, p. 13. The text is quoted from a hand-drawn illustration (No. 6) of the scroll by the author.
43. ITAC, Jerusalem Local Committee Minutes Book, I, No. 84 (13 December 1842). It states there that Johns was fired for his inefficiency in the project for which he was sent to Jerusalem. Additional decisions regarding this matter were taken during discussions in the society forum. Most of these dealt with suspicions about the way he handled the budget for the church building. See various decisions taken on 13 December 1842 and others on 27 December 1842.
44. Bodleian, Dep. Cmj, d.59: copy of letter from Johns to the society, April 1844.
45. Schütz, C. *Preussen in Jerusalem (1800–1861): Karl Friedrich Schinkels Entwurf der Grabeskirche und die Jerusalempläne Friedrich Wilhelms IV* (Berlin: 1988), pp. 126–41. See ibid., p. 133: Stüler's sketches; ibid., p. 137: Habershon's sketches. For Habershon's proposal see ibid., p. 86.

46. Isaacs, A.A. *Biography of the Rev. Henry Aaron Stern, D.D., for more than Forty Years a Missionary Amongst the Jews* (London: 1886), p. 26.

47. ITAC, Jerusalem Local Committee Minutes Book, I, No. 104 (17 January 1843). The order to stop work was transmitted to the London Society through the British consul in Jerusalem. Apparently the missionaries, having noticed that Young refrained from protesting against the new decree, disclaimed responsibility, and informed the Pasha that he took no stand in the matter, assumed that their consul had collaborated in the work stoppage.

48. FO, 195/210, p. 52, No. 3: William Tanner Young in Jerusalem to Stratford Canning in Constantinople, 26 January 1843; ITAC, Jerusalem Local Committee Minutes Book, I, No. 110 (14 February 1843). Throughout that year Alexander continued to express in writing his anxiety about the suspension in the building process. For example, he wrote in September that:

> I was sorry to learn … that our Church affairs were not proceeding as we had hoped … . It would at all events be very desirable to have the matter settled if possible one way or the other, for if the Church is not to be built, we might then proceed with the building of the houses, which we greatly need.

See Lambeth, MS.3397: Alexander to Canning, 20 September 1843.

49. ITAC, collection of unclassified letters: reply of Nicolayson in Jerusalem to Ashley in London, in which he puts forward certain points that Ashley could make use of in the memorandum he was going to send to Ponsonby in Constantinople; *Protestants 1851*, pp. 10–11: Lord Aberdeen to Canning, 4 October 1843; ibid., Canning to Aberdeen, 1 December 1843.

50. The petition is not in our possession. Its existence can be derived from the memorandum written by Bunsen to Palmerston on 6 January 1844. See ITAC, Collection of unclassified letters.

51. *Correspondence Respecting*, p. 13: Memorandum Respecting Suspended Buildings at Jerusalem: Canning to Rif'at Pasha, 31 January 1844.

52. Bodleian, Dep. Cmj, d.53: petition presented to Lord Aberdeen on 18 March 1845.

53. *Correspondence Respecting*, p. 41: memorandum from the Sublime Porte to Canning, 2 September 1845.

54. Bodleian, Dep. Cmj, d.55: Translation of the royal decree given on 10 September 1845 to the governors of Saida, Jerusalem and others, handwritten document No. 72 among a collection of pamphlets.

55. ITAC, Jerusalem Local Committee Minutes Book, I, No. 299 (28 October 1845); ibid., No. 302 (18 October 1845): letter from the British consul in Jerusalem to Bishop Alexander; ibid., No. 423 (16 December 1845): Henry Newbolt, deputy consul in Jerusalem to Nicolayson, 12 December 1845.

56. *Yated Ne'eman* (29 June 1990), Suppl., pp. 10–11: article entitled 'War Against the Mission' (Hebrew).

57. ITAC, London Committee Resolutions, Nos M1329, M1330, M1337 (26 March 1841).

58. Bodleian, Dep. Cmj, c.125: lease agreements and the purchase of parts of the pharmacy building; *Jewish Intelligence* (October 1841), p. 353; ibid. (May 1842), pp. 162–5: Macgowan, from Jerusalem, 1 November 1842. See also additional reports throughout the year; ibid. (September 1842), p. 316: Macgowan, from Jerusalem, 1 July 1842.

59. Bodleian, Dep. Cmj, c.125: listings of leases from November 1843 till September 1857; ITAC, Jerusalem Local Committee Minutes Book, I, No. 57

(27 September 1842); *Jewish Intelligence* (July 1845), pp. 241–2; ibid. (January 1843), p. 21: Macgowan, from Jerusalem, 1 November 1842; ibid. (May 1843), p. 172: Macgowan, from Jerusalem, 28 February 1843. The building, today used as a hostel, can be found at the end of Bikur Holim Street in the Old City of Jerusalem.

60. For these details and many others about the work done in the hospital until the end of the nineteenth century, see ITAC, Medical Reports, from January 1845 onwards. During 1845 the number of beds available at the hospital was doubled to 24, and in that same year 1,000 Jews visited the pharmacy. In 1846 the number rose to 2,000 and it was reported that there were 215 patients and that 1,500 home visits were made. For further information about the hospital see Schwake, N. *Die Entwicklung des Krankenhauswesens der Stadt Jerusalem vom Ende des 18. Bis zum Beginn des 20. Jahrhunderts* (Herzogenrath: 1983), II, pp. 108–91.

61. *Jewish Intelligence* (January 1847), p. 21: Macgowan, from Jerusalem.

62. FO, 78/625: Young in Jerusalem to Aberdeen in London, 31 January 1845; ibid.: the chief rabbis to Macgowan, 21 January 1845; ibid.: Macgowan to Young, 21 January 1845; ibid.: Macgowan to Young, 22 January 1845, in Hyamson, *The British Consulate*, I, No. 43 and appendices, pp. 67–70; ITAC, Jerusalem Local Committee Minutes Book, I, No. 271 (28 January 1845).

63. Ibid., collection of unclassified documents: original letter of excommunication in Rashi script with a handwritten English translation alongside.

64. See several reports of Dr Macgowan in ITAC, Medical Reports, throughout 1845.

65. Bodleian, Dep. Cmj, c.125: purchase documents marked Hospital Cemetery at Siloam. I.

66. FO, 195/210: Newbolt to Canning in Constantinople, 17 February 1846, in Hyamson, *The British Consulate*, I, No. 48 and Appendices, pp. 82–6; ibid.: Newbolt to Canning, 25 March 1846, in Hyamson, *The British Consulate*, I, No. 50 and Appendices, pp. 87–94; ITAC, Jerusalem Local Committee Minutes Book, I, No. 333 (27 January 1846); ibid., No. 335 (24 February 1846).

67. *Jewish Intelligence* (April 1845), p. 110: Macgowan, from Jerusalem, 4 February 1845.

68. Ibid. (May 1846), p. 158: Macgowan, from Jerusalem.

69. Grajewski, P.B.-Z. Letter from Montefiore to the rabbis of the Jewish community', in *In Memory of the First Zionists* (Jerusalem: 1928), Ch. 11 (Hebrew). Regarding Simon Fränkel who was trained in medicine in Munich and before his arrival in Palestine served as ship's doctor in the Dutch Navy, see also Grajewski, *In Memory of the First Zionists*, 2nd edn (Jerusalem: 1929) Ch. 19; Ewald, *Journal*, p. 102.

70. *Allgemeine Zeitung des Judenthums* (4 March 1844): Fränkel, from Jerusalem.

71. *Jewish Intelligence* (April 1845), p. 110: Macgowan, from Jerusalem, 4 February 1845. For a similar formulation see *Allgemeine Zeitung des Judenthums* (13 May 1843).

72. *Jewish Intelligence* (November 1849), p. 369: from the diary of Christian Ewald; Gidney, *Sites and Scenes*, I, pp. 53–4.

73. Bodleian, Dep. Cmj, c.125: listing of ownership documents numbered: K.a.1, K.a.2, K.a. 4.

74. *Jewish Intelligence* (November 1843), pp. 388–9: Sternschuss, from Safed.

75. Gidney, *Sites and Scenes*, I, p. 55.

76. Lambeth, MS.3397: Alexander in Jerusalem to Baring, 28 October 1843. The

bishop reported on five attempts to assassinate Behrens in his home in Safed by the Turkish subject hired for the purpose.

77. Bodleian, Dep. Cmj, d.63: memorandum of the London Committee Resolution No. P.265 testifying to the purchase; *Report*, 39 (1847), p. 38; Gidney, *The History*, p. 251.
78. Gidney, *Sites and Scenes*, II, p. 119.
79. *Jewish Intelligence* (February 1843), p. 59: Alexander from Jerusalem, 30 November 1842.
80. ITAC, Unclassified documents: agreement in Arabic for the lease of a building in Jaffa belonging to the Armenian monastery for a period of one year from 27 May 1846. Hanauer, who was called Moshe Ben-Michael Halevi before his conversion to Christianity, was baptised in Jerusalem in September 1843. See Bodleian, Dep. Cmj, d.59: Jerusalem Register of Baptisms, 24 September 1843. Some time afterwards his son, James Edward Hanauer, was born. J.E. Hanauer, who was to become a London Society missionary even better known than his father, will be discussed later on.
81. *Jewish Intelligence* (September 1848), p. 285: Macgowan, from Jerusalem, 29 June 1848.
82. See, for example, Gidney, *Sites and Scenes*, II, p. 111; Gidney, *The History*, p. 247.
83. On this visit see Ewald, *The Journal*, pp. 157–75.
84. ITAC, Jerusalem Local Committee Minutes Book, I, No. 267 (24 December 1844).
85. See, for example, Gidney, *Sites and Scenes*, I, p. 50, where it states that: 'Tiberias is the hottest place in Palestine.'
86. Robinson, E. *Biblical Researches in Palestine and the Adjacent Region* (London: 1856), III, p. 255.
87. Gidney, *Sites and Scenes*, I, p. 50.
88. Regarding the circumstances of his death in Egypt see mainly *St Albans*, Memorial pamphlet for Bishop Alexander: *Two Sermons, Preached ... on Occasion of the Death of the Right Rev. Michael Solomon Alexander* (London: 1846): Veitch, from Cairo, 26 November 1845, pp. 83–5; ibid., pp. 88–94; ITAC, Jerusalem Local Committee Minutes Book, I, No. 319 (9 December 1845): Veitch, from Cairo, 27 November 1845; *The Times* (26 November 1845).

# 3

# 1846–1881

## THE GOBAT PERIOD

The lengthy intermediate period between the death of the first Protestant bishop in Jerusalem, Michael Solomon Alexander, and the inauguration of the new Jerusalem bishop was not beneficial to the London Society mission station. The total identification that existed between the modest mission station in Jerusalem and the prestigious institution of the bishopric during the Alexander period had raised the missionary enterprise to heights it had not earlier known. Now, after the death of the charismatic figure who had led this forward stride, a feeling of depression overcame those engaged in the missionary field in Palestine. The experienced missionary, Erasmus Scott Calman, gave voice to this feeling in his letter to Alexander's widow written a few months after her husband's death:

> The affairs of the Jerusalem mission ... is neither I fear prospering nor is it in a healthy state. The Jerusalem mission has lost much in my estimation and judgment of what is really true and valuable, by the removal of the Bishop your late beloved husband who acted as a connected link between Jews and Gentile. Since that event, I am sorry to say, everything here has assumed a form of isolation and separation.[1]

In Calman's opinion all the spiritual energies were being diverted to the interrelationships between missionary workers in Jerusalem rather than to propagating the gospel among the Jewish community. If this situation did not change quickly, he continued, the 'thaw in the sun will freeze again in the shade'.

According to the guiding principles laid down at the time when the bishopric was founded, it was up to the King of Prussia, after Alexander's death, to select his own candidate for the Protestant episcopate in Jerusalem. Friedrich Wilhelm IV, having accepted the proposal of Bunsen, his ambassador in London and his good friend (who had most probably consulted his English friends and especially Lord Ashley), offered the position to Samuel Gobat (1799–1879), then serving in the ranks of the Church Missionary Society. Gobat was a native of the village Cremines near the town of Moutier situated in the Jura mountains in the Canton of Berne, Switzerland, and had received his training at the Basle mission. At the time that he was offered the position he was acting as deputy director of the Protestant College in Malta and had spent many years of service as a missionary in Syria and Egypt, but more particularly in Ethiopia. Gobat willingly accepted the high position and entered the gates of Jerusalem at the end of December 1846.[2]

As soon as Gobat's expected appointment as Bishop of Jerusalem became known, the leaders of the London Society urged him to assume concurrently the title of vice-patron of their society. In a series of letters he sent to London during August 1846, Gobat thanked them for their kind suggestion, accepted the position, and at the same time laid down his policy regarding the Jews. In mid-August he wrote, 'I am one with your Committee in feelings, in hope, in prayer, and in activity; I shall, therefore, always feel it a high privilege to act with one accord, to pray in the same spirit, and to wait for the appointed time with all the faithful members of the Society.'[3]

However, an article in the London Society journal of September 1846 revealed the first indications of his conception (as a member of the Church Missionary Society) of his role as bishop and the place which the Jews occupied in his order of priority – a conception that later led to a change in his policy. This article quoted a correspondent for the *Augsburg Gazette* of Berlin as having reported that Gobat intended to direct his efforts more towards the Muslim population than to the Jewish one. In a note appended to that article the London Society leaders added hopefully, 'We are, however, assured, on the very best authority, that that eminent person has no project whatever of turning away from the Jews.'[4] Having installed himself in Jerusalem, Gobat was sometimes suspected of not liking the Jews very much, mainly because he placed difficulties in the path of those wishing to convert. It is recorded in his biography that, although his heart was full of love towards the Jews of Jerusalem, his experience of human nature inhibited him from expressing his feelings, and he avoided excessive emotion. In his own words, 'I tremble whenever the missionaries send me a convert [Jew], for either he is insincere from the beginning, or, if he commences by being honest and in earnest, he will soon be spoilt by the flattery of the friends of Israel in England.'[5]

Gobat was not fully in accord with the views of the friends of the Jewish people in Britain, who believed in the idea of the restoration of the Jews. These friends thought that the return of the Jewish people to Palestine should be fostered even before their conversion, and they were prepared to invest huge sums to that end. Gobat maintained that efforts should be fully invested in converting those individuals already living in Palestine. At the beginning of 1847 the bishop himself stated in his diary that to the best of his knowledge those who had appointed him did not intend him to work solely among the Jews. He felt, as Paul had done in his era, that his mission was to direct his efforts 'to the wise and to the ignorant, Greeks [Orthodox], Romanists [Catholics], Armenians, [Muslims], Turks, &c ...'.[6]

In its journal of January 1848, the society published Bishop Gobat's public appeal to its readers. In this article, the first in a series of the London Society New Year messages published during the 33 years of his episcopate, Gobat described the situation of the converted Jews and the enormous difficulties faced by the missionaries in Jerusalem. He referred once again to the now familiar occurrence of excommunication by the Jewish community of any member who showed an interest in Christianity, which put the onus of their economic support upon the mission station. The accepted solution of transferring the converted to other cities also created difficulties because of the high cost of travel to be paid for by the society. The missionaries, therefore, shared the cost out of their own pockets and at the expense of their own families' livelihood. Gobat went on to deplore the fact that so much was invested in assisting the Jewish population:

> The Jews here, seeing that the Hospital at Jerusalem, an excellent institution, but which is chiefly beneficial to the unconverted Jews, by reason of their overwhelming majority, is eminently prosperous; and hearing that an institution is to be put in foot at Jaffa, in favour of the Jews, *as* Jews, and to the *quasi* exclusion of proselytes, whilst the mission here is deprived almost of all the means of relieving the wants of believing Israelites, have come to the conclusion that the missionaries are acting contrary to the views of the 'Christian public in England'. The fact that assistance was granted indiscriminately even to those who would never convert, lowered the motivation of those who considered doing so [emphasis in original] .[7]

His words were taken as the opening shot of a demand for donations from the readers of the journal. He insisted that those possessing the means must come out and help, otherwise the work of the missionaries would cease. He envisaged the community in Jerusalem as coming to a standstill, and that the church being built would be left as testimony and monument to Protestant impotence. Gobat took advantage of the platform placed at his disposal to give renewed expression to his view as a missionary, which contained more than a hidden allusion to the anticipated policy change in the Protestant bishopric in Jerusalem. He announced the good news to the readers that he had received a written directive (*fatwa*) from the Mufti of Beirut that there was no legal hindrance for Arab Christians to transfer from one Christian community to another. The directive, which applied to all citizens of the Ottoman Empire, permitted also the Druse and Jews to adopt the Christian faith. Gobat was thus able to express overtly his policy of working with the Arab-Christian community as well, and to bring it into the ranks of the Protestant faith. At the end of his article he reported that he had just leased a building to serve as a new school, which, while being nominally for Jewish girls, would not turn away girls of other faiths. In November 1847 the gates of the Diocesan School were opened to about 20 girls and boys – Jews, Christians and a few children of Jewish converts. This educational institution did not easily succeed in retaining its pupils for very long, since the Jewish parents, under community pressure, took their children out after a few months. But Gobat was convinced that the experience of coming into contact with the Christian faith, which the pupils brought home with them, would one day prove that the attempt had not been in vain.[8]

During 1848 Gobat initiated the first missionary enterprise among the Arab-Christian community in Palestine. Besides appointing two missionaries to read the Scriptures to the Jews in Jerusalem and Jaffa, the bishop nominated three more to do the same work among the Arab population. In September of that year Gobat increased his activities among the Greek Orthodox Arabs by inaugurating a school in Shechem, far away from the supervising gaze of the heads of their community in Jerusalem. Although the latter soon placed a ban on the bishop, this did not prevent him from continuing his activity in Shechem and from setting up, a few years later, many more educational institutions in other Arab villages.

### *The Basler Pilgrims Mission*

Besides his direct efforts among the local Arab population, the bishop encouraged and even initiated the arrival of other

Protestant elements, which he directed to act among the various community groups in Palestine. The first institution, which hastened to take advantage of Gobat's appointment to his high office in Jerusalem, was the Basler Pilgermission of St Chrischona near Basle. The head of this mission, Christian Friedrich Spittler (1782–1867), had already made plans for activity in Palestine, and had consulted with Gobat for many years prior to the latter's appointment as bishop. In September 1846 Spittler sent his first two emissaries to Palestine – Ferdinand Palmer (1818–92) and Conrad Schick (1822–1901) – pioneers in a distinguished missionary enterprise. In days to come the mission established the 'Bruderhaus' in Jerusalem, which, among other things, served as a training centre for Protestant missionaries on their way to setting up mission posts in Africa. He also founded the Spittler & Co. trading house in Jerusalem, which was later to become the largest private bank in Palestine, owned by Johannes Frutiger (1836–99), and more especially the Syrian Orphanage founded by Johann Ludwig Schneller (1820–96), which turned into the largest Protestant missionary institution in the Middle East.[9]

*The Deaconess Sisterhood*

Another institution that began its activities in Palestine during the Gobat episcopate was the Deaconess Sisterhood of Kaiserswerth in Düsseldorf. The bishop urged the head of the institution, Theodor Fliedner (1800–64) to send two sisters to assist in medical work in Jerusalem. Fliedner wrote to the London Society and proposed to send two additional sisters to help them. In April 1851, Fliedner himself accompanied the four women to Jerusalem. Two of them, whose expenses were covered by the society, were employed as nurses in the society's hospital under the director, Dr Edward Macgowan. Soon afterwards the sisters set up their own small hospital under the professional guidance of the same Dr Macgowan, who served for a long while as the official doctor in this German institution and who praised the faithful work of the sisters with much enthusiasm. The other two Deaconess sisters devoted themselves to the education of Arab girls in a small school they established in the compound of their hospital.[10]

*The Church Missionary Society*

Above all else, Bishop Gobat should be given credit for the widespread activity of the Church Missionary Society in Palestine. This society was founded in 1799 as an integral part of the Anglican Church with the aim of setting up missions among the pagan idol worshippers in Africa and the East. The Church Missionary Society began its activities in the Mediterranean area in 1815 and chose Malta as its centre. Additional mission stations were opened in Greece, Turkey and Egypt, resulting in the decision to act also among the Eastern churches and the Muslims. However, in the course of time, it was forced to reduce its activities in the region to a minimum because of the lack of resources and local failures. The establishment of the Protestant bishopric in Jerusalem was received by members of the Church Missionary Society with great interest and the election of Bishop Gobat, a missionary of this society, to the position of second bishop in Jerusalem was an encouraging sign that Jerusalem and not Malta would be a suitable centre for missionary activity in the Levant.[11]

After Gobat proposed that the Church Missionary Society make Palestine the springboard for its activities, its leaders met together in June 1851 and instructed their Alsatian missionary, Frederick Augustus Klein (d. 1903), to leave for Jerusalem. Klein and his medical colleague, Dr Carl Sandreczky (1810–92), arrived in the Holy City and laid the groundwork for wide-ranging missionary work, which in time included the establishment of scores of educational institutions throughout the country. Thousands of Arab-Christian members of the Eastern churches, as well as Muslims and a few Jews, were educated in these institutions.

The entry of the Church Missionary Society into Palestine ended the exclusivity that had characterised the activity of the London Society until then, and eroded its status as the representative of British interests, which had been stated in the principles laid down for the institution of the bishopric in 1841. No longer was missionary work devoted to the Jewish community alone, but was extended to members of the Eastern churches as well. The London Society also found it obstructive that the Church Missionary Society – invited to work in Palestine by the Swiss missionary Samuel Gobat, who was of German orientation – employed missionaries mainly of German nationality. Since the Church Missionary Society was not very selective in its target population, it began working among the Jewish community as well and encroaching upon the very meagre successes of the London Society, which felt this to be an intrusion into its own sphere of activity. Tensions were created by the tendency of certain Jews to apply to educational institutions run by the Church Missionary

Society because they felt more at ease in the company of the German-speaking missionaries.

During 1873, towards the end of his term of office, Bishop Gobat gradually began to transfer the mission stations and the educational institutions that he had set up around the country into the hands of the Church Missionary Society. This eventually led, in 1875, to a gathering of its leaders at a conference called 'The Mohammedan Conference' which ended with the decision to give full weight to missionary work among the Muslims in Palestine. The Church Missionary Society, therefore, increased its support for Gobat's initiatives and took upon itself the entire responsibility for the bishop's enterprises. Later on, it set up many additional schools throughout the country, even though the Turkish government allowed for the establishment of educational institutions only in areas where there was a mixed Christian and Muslim population. Sometimes it even closed down schools that did not fulfil those conditions. However, in most cases, the local chiefs overlooked the regulations and allowed the Church Missionary Society to function in areas that were preponderantly Muslim, so that the village children could receive a suitable education.[12]

From this it can be seen that with the change in missionary policy of the Church Missionary Society, which was active mainly in Arab villages and no longer competed with the London Society for the souls of Jewish community members, relations improved between the two missionary societies in Palestine. In time, when the German–British partnership in the Protestant bishopric ended, the rivalry between the two societies was buried, and a new opponent arose to challenge both of them in the form of a third British missionary society.

## DECLINE

The first signs of enervation in the activities of the London Society in Palestine appeared during the course of 1851, a year in which missionary work produced no more than a single Jewish convert. In its annual report, the London committee expressed its dissatisfaction with the activity which was conducted on so limited a scale and did not meet expectations. The main reason for the decline in successful missionary activity, was probably the growing detachment of the London Society from the bishopric, which began after the appointment of the second bishop in Jerusalem. In his traditional New Year letter to the London Society journal, Gobat made his first extensive review of his energetic efforts in setting up a network throughout the country of educational institutions that were intended for the Arab population, especially that of the Greek Orthodox community. The fact that most of his efforts and attention were devoted to those who were not the target group of the London Society, and that he contributed nothing to the society's own efforts, marred its chances of success. The widening gap between the bishop and the London Society was evident in the very terms the bishop chose to employ in his New Year letter, where he referred to the leaders of the London Society as 'they' and no longer as 'our Society', which his predecessor Alexander had done.[13]

The arrival of Klein, the first missionary of the Church Missionary Society, and the appointment of the German pastor Friedrich Peter Valentiner (1817–94), who was sent to work side by side with Bishop Gobat, made it imperative for the London Society to examine the situation thoroughly. Although the society expressed its approbation in its report on the arrival of the missionaries in Jerusalem, the loss of its monopoly in missionary activity in Palestine led to changes in its projected plans for that country. Nicolayson was recalled to London in order to hold discussions with the society leaders and to find suitable solutions for the new state of affairs created in Jerusalem. At the end of the talks a decision was reached to reinforce the missionary garrison in Palestine. In October 1851, the London Society dispatched Edward Richmond Hodges (1826–81) to assist in missionary work, and a month later the pastor, John Christian Reichardt (1803–73), was summoned to Jerusalem to examine the situation at first hand and to submit his recommendations. For this purpose, at the beginning of December, he invited most of the London Society missionaries in the region, as well as emissaries of other missionary societies, to hold a conference for a few days. During this conference, the work of the missions was discussed in all its aspects, and at the end detailed and intensive reports were presented with a long list of resolutions mainly with regard to the reinforcement of the missionary enterprise in Palestine.[14] The first act to be carried out in the wake of the reports was the installation of a prominent emissary in Jerusalem. In February 1852 the London Society sent the experienced pastor Henry Crawford (1815–63).[15]

During the 1850s various events occurred that contributed to the decline of the London Society missionary enterprise in Palestine. The most significant event was the Crimean War, which led to, among other things, the disruption of the channels through which donations were sent from the Jews in the Diaspora – the main source of support for the Jewish community in Palestine. Some of the foreign residents in the country promoted local charity initiatives for the benefit of the Jewish population, the leading figure being the British consul, James Finn. He set up a small agricultural farmstead called 'Abraham's Vineyard' outside the city walls, where scores of Jewish families in Jerusalem were enabled to make a living.[16] The London Society missionaries also tried to relieve the distress the best they could. Yet, just in this very difficult period for the Jewish community in Palestine, when a real advantage could have been taken of this distress to increase missionary activity and harvest the gains, they did not do so. The initiatives for assistance taken by wealthy Jews in the Diaspora inspired great hopes in the Jewish community and distanced it from missionary enterprises.

Among the Jewish personalities who were active in the country, distributing funds, and setting up welfare institutions for the Jewish population, were three prominent figures. The first was Albert Cohn (1814–77), who came in 1854 as a representative of the Rothschild family to establish a hospital. The second was Moses Montefiore, who came in 1855 and bought, among other things, a plot of land outside the walls of Jerusalem intended as a site for a hospital, but later used to construct a windmill and residential neighbourhood called 'Mishkenot Sha'ananim'. The third was Ludwig August Frankel (1810–94), an emissary of Elise von Herz-Lämel, daughter of the aristocratic Austrian Jew, Simon Lämel (1766–1845), who arrived in 1856 and built a school within the city walls. These men reduced the need of the Jews for the society institutions and thereby lessened its influence among the Jewish population during that time. The final blow was given the society on 6 October 1856 by the death of John Nicolayson, pioneer among the missionaries.[17]

Nicolayson's place as head of the London Society Mission in Palestine was taken for a few years by Henry Crawford, mentioned above. At the end of 1860 he fell ill and, in January 1861, the missionary, Joseph Barclay (1831–81), was appointed to replace him. Barclay was born in August 1831 in Mourne Lodge in County Tyrone, Ireland. He was educated in Dublin, where he obtained an MA degree in theology in 1853. In 1858 he entered the services of the London Society and was stationed in Constantinople until his appointment brought him to Palestine in March 1861. In 1866, while he was in Jerusalem, this highly gifted man, who was conversant with several languages, including Greek, Latin and Hebrew, was granted an honorary doctorate by the University of Dublin.[18]

Barclay's days in Jerusalem were marked by the continual decline of the London Society in Palestine. The relations between the head of the mission and Bishop Gobat were correct but restrained. As a British national and a member of the Anglican Church, Barclay thought that anyone who was not trained as a pastor in that church was not suited to the office of bishop. He also claimed that the English community in Jerusalem was neglected because of the close connections between Gobat and Germany and his obligations to the Prussian Crown. In addition, Barclay even criticised the institution in which he served and the quality of its members. In his view, the administration of the London Society was conducted without talent, and the policy and allocation of resources to the mission stations in the world resulted in poor achievements in terms of the number of Jews converted. In October 1868, Barclay commented, 'While men [in the service of the London Society] at home could get better pay, those abroad who asked for some increase were treated as impudent, and flung aside like a sucked orange.'[19]

In May 1870 Barclay sent the directors of the London Society a letter of resignation from his position as head of the mission in Jerusalem. The meagre budget allocated to the mission station had also affected his own salary, and, since he had to finance his stay in Jerusalem from his private funds, he chose to leave the ranks of the society. Its directors in London hastily decided to forgo the services of the critical missionary in Jerusalem, and recorded in their journal that personal reasons had led Barclay to tender his resignation. Nevertheless, during the 1870s he sometimes agreed to go out on the society's fundraising missions. In August 1876 he was asked by the society leaders to return and fill the position of head of the mission in Jerusalem once more, since no candidate could be found for this vacant post. But the residual resentments he had accumulated towards the end of his previous term of service there caused him to formulate a response in the following manner: 'However anxious I might be to revisit the former scenes of my labours, I must now give up that pleasure.'[20]

The declining trend that had affected the society continued its descent after July 1870, when Barclay left Jerusalem, and is evident from the constant need for replacements of those appointed to head the mission there. During the first eight years of that decade, nine missionaries served in this capacity for brief periods of time.[21]

At the end of the 1870s, Arthur Hastings Kelk (1835–1908) was sent out as head of the mission in Jerusalem and remained at this post for 22 years, the longest period of service in this mission. Kelk was a native of Worthington, near Birmingham, UK, a descendant of an old clerical family and a Cambridge graduate. At the university he was carried away by the missionary spirit that swept across the country in the 1850s. After being rejected by the Church Missionary Society, he was ordained a pastor by the London Society and sent to serve as tutor at the Malta Missionary College and elsewhere. In 1878 Kelk was offered the position of head of the mission in Jerusalem and went there in November for a few months in order to examine the conditions in Palestine and his ability to fill the high position faithfully. He returned to London, and in November 1879, after accepting his official appointment, he went back to Jerusalem.[22]

Kelk was not at first considered to be a brilliant missionary, but he was exceptionally gifted as an administrator, a quality that enabled him to take the society out of its period of decline and lead it in a new direction. He himself noted as much at the end of his term of office:

> Those twenty years' experience were of great use to me as head of the mission like that at Jerusalem, but they did not help me to become an effective missionary … perhaps the management of men is of more importance in such a post than being individually a missionary.[23]

### Relations between the Society and the Bishopric

The apparent opposition of interests between the heads of the London Society mission and the Protestant bishopric in Jerusalem, which resulted from their different view of their target population and the differences in style and methods used to attain their objectives, were not revealed in the official publications of the society and the bishopric. Over the years, the society refrained from overt criticism of the particular preferences shown by Bishop Gobat and it would be difficult to discern even a hint of censure.

At the beginning of their period of partnership, about a year and a half after Bishop Gobat was installed in Jerusalem, he refused to hold a baptismal ceremony for two Jews because they both refused to acquire a useful trade for their livelihood. They were therefore forced to leave Jerusalem and the mission institutions that had so greatly desired their conversion. The editor of the society journal, who certainly must have disagreed with the bishop, added a note to his article on this matter, saying in a very hesitant and diplomatic tone, 'The Committee do not feel at liberty to offer any comment upon the bishop's rule. There may be circumstances which make this test of sincerity expedient at Jerusalem.'[24] A few years later, in his annual letter to this same journal, the bishop gave wide coverage to his activities among the members of the Eastern churches. The society, in its annual report, withheld publication of this reprise of the bishop's views and confined itself to commenting that it had no doubt of 'His rectitude of purpose and conduct in those points regarding the Eastern Churches ... so that its contents need not be recapitulated here.'[25]

Another aspect of the relationship between the bishop and the society in later years can be deduced from the longstanding argument that went on in the small Protestant community in Jerusalem, which was known as the 'Rosenthal Case'. This affair has already been thoroughly treated elsewhere, and the present study is interested only in examining its repercussions upon the above-mentioned relationship. The essential matter in this affair was the judicial claim made in 1849 by Dr Edward Macgowan, director of the London Society Hospital, against Simeon Rosenthal, who was appointed as the society's inspector of its construction projects in Jerusalem. Rosenthal was accused of embezzling the funds intended for the purchase of building materials and for the salaries of those working at the construction site of the mission station, and as a result he was relieved of his duties by the London Society.[26]

In 1857, the affair once more occupied public attention in Jerusalem when the British consul, James Finn, wished to appoint Rosenthal, then serving as an interpreter at the British consulate, to replace him during his absence from the city. In a written declaration sent to the Foreign Office in London, Bishop Gobat protested against the unsuitable appointment and his protest was seconded by three members of the London Society: Dr Edward Macgowan, his assistant, Edward Atkinson, and the pastor, William Bailey (1823–98). Rosenthal demanded satisfaction at the British consulate and the uproar reached a climax when Consul Finn prevented the four complainants from leaving Jerusalem. However, out of respect for the bishop, he limited the restriction to 'two hours at a time'.[27]

The sensitive situation in which the London Society found itself when three of its members joined up with the Protestant bishop against two other of its supporters, Consul Finn and Rosenthal – the first converted Jew in Jerusalem – obliged the society to offer some explanations. It chose to attribute the protests of Macgowan, Atkinson and Bailey to personal motives and by doing so clearly defined the type of relationship that existed between the society and the bishopric. Apparently, in order to soften the antagonism that was created between the London Society and the consulate, the former endeavoured to blur the unanimity of opinion in this case between itself and the bishopric. For this reason, the editor of the society journal emphasised that he was not taking any stand in the Jerusalem dispute:

> It seems necessary to mention ... that while the Bishop of Jerusalem and the Jews' Society have ever worked most cordially together, they are independent of each other in their action in the Holy Land. His Lordship is neither the agent nor the missionary of the Society; nor is the Society's work under the direction or controul [*sic*] of the Bishop; neither therefore can be considered responsible for the acts or proceedings of the other.[28]

At a later time, in 1867, when the affair continued to arouse interest in Jerusalem, Bishop Gobat reacted by stating that the fact that he was identified with the Society and its members filled him with joy.

## THE HOSPITAL IN JERUSALEM

In contrast with the general decline in the activities of the London Society mission in Jerusalem, its medical wing underwent an impressive development during the Bishop Gobat period, and the hospital in Jerusalem became the flagship of the entire missionary enterprise. The hospital expanded until, by the late 1840s, it contained 30 beds. The Turkish authorities in Jerusalem, who seem at first to have hindered the hospital's development at the demand of the rabbis, gradually removed their objections and changed their attitude completely after some of the governor's relatives needed medical attention and received it.

The reputation of the hospital spread throughout the region and Jewish patients often arrived from neighbouring cities, mainly Damascus, Aleppo and Beirut. The thriving institution and early intimations of its changing image for some of the Jewish population broke down the wall of prejudice against the hospital and

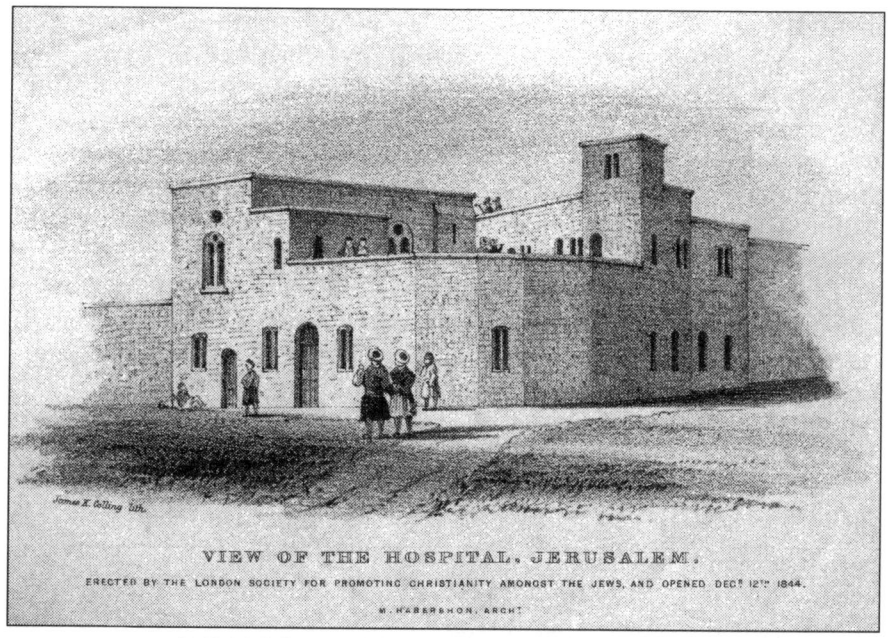

VIEW OF THE HOSPITAL, JERUSALEM.

ERECTED BY THE LONDON SOCIETY FOR PROMOTING CHRISTIANITY AMONGST THE JEWS, AND OPENED DEC! 12TH 1844.

H. HABERSHON, ARCH!

7. British hospital for the Jews in Jerusalem, 1844

8. Waiting room in the British hospital

brought into its waiting rooms even wealthy and well-respected members of the Jewish community. In 1850 the Chief Rabbi of Jerusalem chose to be hospitalised there, and at the same time allowed its doctors to operate on his daughter, whose eyes were infected. The hospital director felt so exuberant because of the change in attitude that he declared, 'Nothing could more forcibly prove to me how entirely the opposition to the hospital had died away amongst the Jews.'[29]

Yet it appears that this statement was inaccurate, since generally speaking the Jewish community in Jerusalem maintained their opposition to the activities of the hospital. The frequent application of the ban placed on those entering its gates did not stop some of them from preferring medical assistance to economic welfare. The dilemma faced by the Jews of Jerusalem – especially those without means – caused the society members in certain cases to offer the essential necessities of life to patients in the period following their release from hospital.

During the years under discussion, certain outstanding personalities were appointed as doctors in the Jerusalem hospital. The first was Edward Macgowan, and, after his death, Dr Thomas J. Chaplin (1830–1904) took his place in December 1860. Chaplin served as the hospital director for 25 years and acquired senior status in Jerusalem both as doctor and as medical researcher. He devoted his spare time to the study of leprosy, developing new methods of treatment, and his research was considered the most authoritative in this field. Besides his work he also took part in 1867 in setting up the Lepers Hospital in Jerusalem and served as the doctor of that institution for as long as he stayed in Palestine. In 1881 he even participated in the construction process of a new building for the Lepers Hospital until the day he left for England.[30] Towards the end of his stay, Chaplin was involved in the establishment of St John's Ophthalmic Hospital and with the finding of a suitable site for it. After his return to England he continued to take part in the discussions of the hospital's management committee in London.[31]

Chaplin was also engaged in other fields, and conducted independent scientific research. After the founding of the Palestine Exploration Fund (PEF) in 1865, he contacted the researchers in the country and the results of his studies began to appear in the PEF Quarterly Statement and in other publications. The main fields in which the Jerusalem physician gained a scientific reputation were meteorology, historical geography and archaeology. Chaplin remained in Jerusalem until 1 January 1886 and then returned to

London, where he served as the chief supervisor of all the London mission stations around the world.

The general trend that appeared at the start of the 1840s, in which the Jewish population was prompted into independent action by the establishment of missionary enterprises, continued throughout the 1850s. The Crimean War, which cut off the Jews of Palestine from numerous sources of income abroad, caused harsh deprivation in Jerusalem. Albert Cohn, the Rothschild delegate mentioned above, who was sent in 1854 to inaugurate the Jewish hospital, addressed his audience at the dedication ceremony and stressed the motive for its establishment:

> We, *your own brethren*, will do these things for you, that the sick may not be driven to seek these things from strangers, who speak another language, or to eat food which no Jew ought to eat, or to hear things which no Jew ought to hear, and in cases where medical skill cannot avail, and God, who alone is the physician, has appointed him to die, let the Israelite at least have the consolation in his dying hour, of hearing the words, 'Hear, O Israel, the Lord our God is one Lord' [emphasis in original].[32]

## THE CHURCH IN JERUSALEM

> On the altar [of the church in Jerusalem] there was no image to be seen, but instead there stood two tablets of black marble on which the Ten Commandments were engraved in gold lettering and in the Hebrew language. On one of the chairs ... I found a Jewish prayer book containing the ancient traditional liturgy with a few verses omitted here and there ... This was the way they worked quietly and with ease upon the heart and mind of the New Christian, and by continuous and smooth-voiced whisperings to guide and accustom him to their religion and creed.[33]

As previously stated, the delays, which were caused by the need to obtain a *firman* for the erection of the church, were finally overcome in the autumn of 1845, so that those who were engaged in its construction should have been able to continue with their work at full speed. Yet additional difficulties cropped up from time to time such as the rise in costs and the shortage of building materials and manpower. However, in spite of these hindrances, the work advanced at a reasonable rate. A significant boost was given by the generous donation of £2,600 transferred by Jane Cook (1776–1851), which made it possible to complete the construction of the church building on Mount Zion.

At the beginning of 1847 it was already possible to obtain a visual impression of the building in progress, and, according to the report by Critchlow, the construction overseer, 'The Church may be seen from all sides of the city ... it is higher than any building near it, except the Castle of David.'[34] Even the interior furniture work for the church was progressing as expected and, at the suggestion of the architect, this was being made by expert workmen in England. The furniture items were loaded and dispatched from the port of London in the summer of that year on the deck of a ship leased especially for that purpose. The interior decoration of the building was accorded careful attention so that Jews would feel comfortable in it. Therefore the planners avoided setting up the image of the crucifixion and other clearly recognisable Christian symbols. The work was evidently done with such extreme zeal that it drew criticism from visitors to the church. For example, Albert Rhodes, the United States consul in Jerusalem, stated that this pandering to the taste of the Jewish public would eventually lead the Anglicans to become Jews rather than Jews to become Anglicans.[35]

On Sunday, 21 January 1849, the seventh anniversary of the entry of the first Protestant bishop in Jerusalem, the London Society church was dedicated and was named Christ-Church. Among the participants at the dedication ceremony of the impressive edifice were the British consuls in Jerusalem and in Jaffa, the Prussian consul in Beirut and representatives of the various churches in Jerusalem.[36] The distinctly perceivable relationship between the church and the bishopric deceived certain travellers as to the ownership of this church. Regarding this confusion, the society journal quoted a well-known traveller, John Aiton (1797–1863), who had visited Jerusalem in 1851, and in response to his words the editor wrote:

> Dr Aiton has apparently fallen. Christ Church itself is not connected with the Bishopric, being the property of the London Society, and supported by the funds placed at its disposal. The Bishopric alone, and apart from the Mission, is 'sustained at the joint cost of the English and Prussian government'.[37]

EDUCATIONAL INSTITUTIONS IN JERUSALEM

The plague of foreign education is spreading throughout our land. All levels of society have been caught and trapped in the net of the instigators: poor and rich, free-thinkers and ultra-orthodox ... for this education raises serpents in our midst, sets up amongst us a legion of instigators and rejecters, men and women apostates who will stand against us in a face to face battle over the Land of Israel ... We must not belittle nor turn a blind eye to the hundreds of victims of foreign education and say that 'our hands have not shed this blood'.[38]

## *The House of Industry*

On 21 December 1848, the House of Industry – the institution for vocational training in Jerusalem, formerly called the School of Industry – was dedicated in its newly reorganised form. The building used for this institution once housed the College, and was located in the Christian Quarter within the walls of the Old City near Damascus Gate. It was headed by Paul Isaac Hershon (1818–88), a Galician Jew who had converted to Christianity in Jerusalem and was one of the first students at the College. The institution was meant to train potential converts of both sexes in various types of craftsmanship so that they could support themselves after they were ostracised by the Jewish community. In its new form, the institution also contained a dormitory for its pupils, who were trained by expert instructors of the London Society in Jerusalem.[39] Besides carpentry and woodcarving, which were the special métiers offered in the earlier School of Industry, other skills were taught so that they could become 'tailors, shoemakers, watchmakers, silversmiths, &c.; whilst every evening they receive instruction in reading and writing, in German and English (most of them being German Jews) in arithmetic, &c., but especially in the word of God'.[40]

At the end of 1849 the building was renovated and in a short while the number of pupils increased to such an extent that it became overcrowded. Coincidentally, the opportunity arose to acquire part of a nearby building, which belonged to the consul of Sardinia in Jerusalem. John Nicolayson quickly completed the transaction, if only because the transfer of property from one European subject to another posed no problem. During the course of the negotiations, the philanthropist Jane Cook endowed a fund of £10,000, which produced an interest of £300 annually for the use of the institution, and immediately after doing this she also provided funds to purchase the entire building of the former Sardinian consulate. In September 1852 the two annexes of the institution were connected together by a stone archway above the street.[41]

A year after the establishment of the House of Industry, improvements were also made in the programme of studies, when the services of Conrad Schick, the Basler Pilgermission emissary, were employed. Schick, a native of the village of Bitz in the kingdom of Württemberg, a 'building consultant' and a Palestine researcher who was skilled in many occupations, had arrived in the country, as noted earlier, as an emissary of Christian Friedrich Spittler, founder of the Basler Pilgermission.[42] The extremely parsimonious Spittler soon left Schick in such penury that he was forced to find employment in the London Society institutions. Before leaving Basle, Schick was given a list of instructions that defined his assignments in Jerusalem, and in one of them it was stated:

> The brothers [Schick and his travelling companion Ferdinand Palmer] will be glad to assist the Bishop [Gobat ...] and the House of Industry (the institution for vocational training of the London Society for Promoting Christianity Amongst the Jews) as far as their strength and circumstances allow ...[43]

For this reason, the transfer of this German missionary to this institution in particular was not totally unexpected. Schick taught etching and woodcarving at the school, and so developed a branch of industry still existing in Jerusalem today, producing *objets d'art* from olive wood, which were eagerly bought by travellers and pilgrims. Schick guided his pupils in preparing wooden models of Jerusalem and neighbourhoods, which were formed under his direction in the House of Industry. Most of these models were based on the scientific discoveries of the Palestine Exploration Fund and his own discoveries as one of its members.[44] The large number of models planned by Schick and created by his pupils, some of them being of the temple and its contents, also became an attraction for the Jews in the city. They satisfied their curiosity by visiting one of the London Society buildings, where the models were displayed, and receiving the explanations given by one of its members. Conrad Schick remained in the services of the London Society in Jerusalem for over 50 years, during which time he was officially put in charge of, among other things, all the society's property. The German missionary, an honorary doctor of

Tübingen University, who contributed so greatly to the building and research of Jerusalem, died on 23 December 1901, and was buried in the Protestant cemetery on Mount Zion.

## The Boys' School

In 1857 the London Society decided to do something for the Jewish youngsters in Jerusalem, and sent William Bailey and his wife to set up a school for boys. This institution was located in a building to the south of Christ Church, the very first building to be constructed by the London Society in the city. Before the church was completed, the main hall of this building was used as a chapel for the Protestant community in Jerusalem and, when the school was founded, it served as the dining hall. At first, the Baileys were faced with fierce opposition from the Jews and the first class they opened contained a very small number of pupils, but by the time Bailey left in 1875 the institution had 50 pupils.[45]

In 1861 William Bailey gave the first two pupils lodgings in his home, which later on became a dormitory. One of the boys, Nathan Coral, eventually became the headmaster of the school and lived in the room he had occupied as a student.[46] At the end of 1860, a few months before Bailey did so, Johann Ludwig Schneller of the Basler Pilgermission had also lodged the first two orphan boys in his home. Although the target population for Schneller's Syrian Orphanage was, of course, far easier, Schneller was highly talented and reaped such success that the London Society could no longer compete with it. Schneller's enterprise won worldwide fame and recognition, while Bailey remained unknown.

## The Inquirer's Home

The Inquirer's Home opened in May 1862 as a hostel for those wishing to join the Protestant Church and to be admitted to the various institutions of the London Society in Palestine. Applicants were first given a three-month trial period while staying at the Inquirer's Home. During this time they were exposed to intensive Christian instruction and at the end, after their true intentions were verified, they were accepted into one of the society's institutions. In due course they were baptised, or, if they did not pass the test, rejected.

In the 1880s the institution was transferred to a location near

Damascus Gate inside the city walls, most probably the building used for the House of Industry and far from the watchful eyes of the rabbis in the Jewish Quarter. Jacob Nissim Coral (1832–91) managed the Inquirer's House for most of its period of existence. In the summer of 1897 Hastings Kelk bought a building near the Church of St Paul that belonged to the Church Missionary Society and opened a hostel for Jewish women along the same lines as the Inquirer's Home, thereby filling a need of many years' standing.[47]

*The Jewesses Institution*

It appears that missionary activity among young girls and women in Palestine faced particular problems typical of the East, but to which missionaries in the West were unaccustomed. Thus the percentage of women converts was relatively small and there were two reasons for this. The first was the exceptionally young age for marriage among Jewish girls, and their early entry into a restricted family life. The second was the scant attention given by the Jewish community to the education of their daughters, so that, for most of them, their entry into any educational institution, far less a missionary one, was never envisaged.

The Jewesses Institution founded by Caroline Cooper (1806–59) was established in 1849 as the private enterprise of a single woman, and it functioned as such for an entire decade. At the beginning of 1859, about a year before Cooper's death, the institution was handed over to the London Society and they appointed Mrs F. James to be its director.[48] The institution comprised three sections:

1.  A vocational school where Jewish women learnt skills related to sewing and embroidery.
2.  A girls' school which accommodated scores of girls, some as boarders and some as day pupils. Later on, the day school and dormitory were separated and housed in different buildings.
3.  The bazaar – a small enterprise which employed Jewish women in handicrafts, the products being sold in Palestine and in countries abroad.[49]

JAFFA

During the period under discussion, the London Society mission station in Jaffa did not expand much in size. Most of its activities centred upon the sale of sacred texts and the public reading of selections from them in order to stimulate discussion and generate interest in the gospels. For this purpose the converted Jew J.E. Sinyanki settled in Jaffa in 1847 and began working among the Jews in the city. In December 1852 the London Society adopted a series of resolutions with the intention of reinvigorating the missions in Palestine. Among these resolutions was the official relinquishing of its holdings in Jaffa, but the Book Depôt continued to exist until 1859.[50]

Throughout the 1860s and 1870s the London Society did not carry out any kind of missionary activity and preferred to support other existing missionary institutions in Jaffa. At the same time, it took advantage of chance opportunities to acquire land for future use. The London Society lent support to the school in Jaffa established in 1863 by Peter Martin Metzler (1824–1907),[51] a member of the Basler Pilgermission, whose work was continued by the Scotswoman Jane Walker Arnott (1834–1911). The school offered education to boys and girls of all faiths – Christians, Jews and Muslims – and was partly supported by the London Society, which sent regular subsidies to the establishment and paid the fees of the Jewish pupils during all the years of its existence.[52]

In the second half of the 1860s Joseph Barclay, the head of the Jerusalem mission, took advantage of the fact that certain choice plots of land were up for sale in Jaffa, and made an extensive purchase for a future mission station. The areas of land that had become available were part of the American Colony established in the autumn of 1867 by a group of settlers from the state of Maine, headed by George Jones Washington Adams (1811–80). When the settlement attempt failed, the Americans sold most of the land to the Basler Pilgermission, which dealt with, among other things, trading in real estate. In December 1867, through the mediation of Peter Metzler, Barclay bought a plot of land situated in the American Colony for £150. It had a wooden house standing on it, which later served as the Jaffa mission house.[53]

At the beginning of 1869, members of the Templar Society from Haifa began showing an interest in the land belonging to the American Colony in Jaffa, and conducted negotiations with Metzler for the purchase of that land in order to build a second German Colony.[54] This may have spurred the London Society members in Jerusalem to buy more land in Jaffa, since at the beginning of March 1869 Barclay paid £22 for an additional plot adjacent to the one he had recently acquired. After the purchase, under Barclay's orders, Calman P. Padua, a Jewish convert and a member of the London Society, visited Jaffa. He recorded in his diary a recommendation to the London Society to buy another plot of land bordering on the area it had acquired and sloping westwards (up to the road known today as Eilat Street). In June 1869 the recommendation became reality and this piece of land was bought for another £22.[55] Owing to the general decline affecting the London Society in those years, no extensive activities took place in Jaffa. Yet the society had wisely carried out the property transactions that enabled it to set up institutions and to respond quickly when the need arose at the beginning of the 1880s.

SAFED

From November 1846 the Jewish convert James Cohen of Jerusalem served as the London Society representative in Safed and conducted matters at a slow pace. It was only towards the beginning of 1848 that greater expectations arose with regard to the only missionary in the city, prompted by two petitions sent by the Jewish population in Safed and referring to the London Society and James Cohen himself. The first petition was sent to the London Society centre in Jerusalem and consisted mainly of a request to send the Jewish community a society member who was also a qualified doctor to care for its wellbeing. The second petition, which was signed by hundreds of Jewish residents, was addressed to Queen Victoria and contained a description of the dire straits in which the Jews of the city found themselves by virtue of being subject to the malevolence of their Arab neighbours without having anyone to protect them. The signatories begged the Queen to nominate, as Her Majesty's consul in Safed, the London Society representative, James Cohen: 'This excellent man has been residing amongst us in these holy places for some time, and his eyes beheld the extent of our sorrows by reason of the oppressive and intolerable captivity which we endure.'[56]

Neither of these two petitions was successful, and in the London Society annual report of June 1849 it was declared, without going into detail, that because of organisational changes the Safed mission station would no longer be staffed. A few years later, the matter was clarified orally at a conference of missionaries in Jerusalem, though not published. In a report that summed up the conference it was stated that at the beginning of 1849 Cohen was mired in heavy debts and 'other embarrassments' and was dismissed from the ranks of the London Society.[57]

In November 1849 the missionary David Daniel (d.1897) arrived to introduce a new dimension to missionary activity in Safed. The London Society once again recognised the importance of having a mission station in the city, and decided to set up a permanent centre, which would be the nucleus and focal point of attraction for the Jews in the northern part of the country. For this purpose, the society members in Jerusalem organised a visit to Tiberias, Acre, Haifa, Tyre and Sidon.

The difficulties which faced the London Society members in Safed after the reopening of their mission station, and the initial involvement of Consul Finn in missionary matters there, are manifest in an incident which occurred in Safed in the spring of 1850. One of the Jews in the city, R. Jonah, wished to join company with the society members and announced his intention to convert. In reaction to this, a number of Jews gave him and his Christian companion a severe beating. The Turkish governor threw the assailants into jail, but since they were British citizens he did not pass sentence, but waited for Her Majesty's consul in Jerusalem to arrive and judge the case himself. In the meantime, the Jewish community exerted heavy pressure upon the recent convert and demanded insistently that he give his wife a divorce and leave the city immediately. When they proved unsuccessful, they imposed a ban of excommunication upon Jonah, who had taken refuge in the Mission House. Ten days later, Consul Finn appeared and began to investigate the matter thoroughly.[58] At the end of his examination, Finn demanded that in exchange for the release of the prisoners, who were charged with violent assault, the rabbis of the community would issue a written declaration containing a commitment:

> That they would proclaim in all their synagogues that no Jew or Jewess, young or old, should for the future attempt either to beat, cast stone on, or molest in any way, the Missionary, or any Jew, who should hereafter differ with them in his religious views.[59]

Three weeks later, Jonah could no longer withstand the weight of public censure and returned to his wife and the Jewish community. But some years afterwards, he again changed his mind and left Safed to join the Protestant Church. He eventually found a place among the London Society members in the mission station in Constantinople.

In 1852, owing to their declining health, Daniel and his wife left the mission station in Safed, and a year later they left Palestine. A Jewish convert and native of Safed maintained the mission station for a few years until it was closed down completely. However, the Safed mission was not abandoned. Regular visits were made over a period of three decades by most of the missionaries in Jerusalem. In 1867 an opportunity arose to acquire about two acres of land with a few buildings on them. The London Society used this plot when the mission station reopened again in the 1880s, this time on an impressive scale.[60]

THE BARCLAY PERIOD

Samuel Gobat died on 11 May 1879. On 19 June, Benjamin Disraeli (1804–81), the British Prime Minister, suggested that Joseph Barclay, who had served during the 1860s as head of the London Society mission in Palestine, should be appointed as Protestant bishop in Jerusalem. After some hesitation, Barclay agreed to the nomination, and his appointment was outwardly received with satisfaction by the London Society leaders as expressed in the following statement:

> Your Committee looked with considerable anxiety to the appointment of his successor ... Great was their satisfaction when that choice fell upon one of your former Missionaries, the Rev. Dr. Barclay, who for ten years laboured with much blessing and acceptance in the Holy City; Whose piety, zeal, and learning eminently qualify him for the office of a Bishop in the Church of God.[61]

However, when the need arose to assist the bishop in covering the cost of his lodgings in Jerusalem, as the London Society had been doing for the past 40 years, they refrained from doing so because of past antagonisms, mainly the ill will generated by Barclay's refusal to serve as head of the mission in Jerusalem in 1876.[62]

On 15 January 1880, Barclay sailed from Portsmouth and on 3 February he entered the gates of the Holy City. The society members, unlike their leaders in London, received him with great enthusiasm. Unfortunately, the bishop was not able to leave his own distinctive mark upon the missionary enterprise in Palestine. A year and a half later, after a brief illness, Barclay died in Jerusalem on 22 October 1881, and was buried in the Protestant cemetery on Mount Zion.

During the course of 1882 rumours began spreading that Germany had no intention of appointing anyone to replace the late bishop. These rumours proved to be based on fact, when in July of that year the German Ambassador in London sent a letter to the British Foreign Minister inviting him to discuss the cancellation of the 1841 agreement for founding the bishopric.[63] At the heart of the German dissatisfaction was the feeling that the German Protestant community in Palestine was neglected by the bishop in comparison with its British sister community. Anxiety over such a possibility had already been reflected in the agreements for the establishment of the joint bishopric 40 years earlier, when the King of Prussia insisted on the formulation of the paragraphs stating that strict attention should be given to ensure that maximum cooperation between the two churches was preserved and that 'due consideration be give to the independence of the Evangelical Church and to the distinctive character of the German people'.[64] German apprehensions were realised during Bishop Gobat's lengthy period of office. The Evangelical community was not considered a full partner in establishing the Protestant way of life in Jerusalem, and was discriminated against, especially in the prayer services at Christ-Church. The lack of equality was particularly evident during this period in which the bishop, having been chosen by the Prussians, was naturally expected to give consideration, first and foremost, to the community that had elected him. Over the years, the feeling of deprivation continued to fester among the members of the Evangelical Church in Palestine, and later on, when the position of Germany became stronger among the European nations and the German community in Palestine gained greater influence, this feeling became even more acute.

The German intention not to nominate a bishop implied the abolition of the joint Protestant bishopric in Jerusalem for Prussia and for Britain. The rumours of this intention perturbed the London Society leaders, who tried to reverse the situation and rejected the charges that this establishment had failed.[65] In their view, the Jerusalem bishopric, unlike similar establishments in the larger European cities, was from the very outset cast in a different mould, and therefore it was not justified to expect it to be 'sending forth armies of Missionaries destined to convert the East to the true faith, and to found dozens of new sees in dependence on the mother bishopric of Jerusalem. Illusions of this sort, however natural, were scarcely reasonable.'[66]

Once the rumours about the closure of the joint bishopric became sufficiently confirmed, the leaders of the London Society declared that Germany's abandonment of this establishment did not necessarily imply its total collapse, and wished to continue maintaining an exclusively British episcopate in Jerusalem. They assumed that it would still be possible to retain its framework, since half the funding for the bishopric had come from the British partner, and most of this was supplied by the London Society. In addition, the beginning of 1883 had brought a floodtide of Jewish immigrants, and hundreds of them filled the missionary institutions to maximum capacity as well as filling the hearts of the missionaries with great hope, and therefore they gave full vent to their feelings: 'We ask is this a time to abolish the Jerusalem Bishopric?'[67]

Nevertheless, the intention of Germany to cease its support for the joint establishment was accepted by London Society circles with a certain degree of understanding, and they listed, point by point, Germany's own reasons for abolishing the partnership:

> The German community, which in 1841 scarcely existed, is now a very large one; that a plan of giving a Bishop of the English Church a sort of jurisdiction over other Protestant communities has not promoted union; that the [German] Lutheran Protestants do not derive the same degree of advantage from the Bishop's presence, as the members of his own [Anglican Church] communion do; and that the interests of Germans are not looked after by the Bishop, but by the German Consul. In a word, it is urged that after forty years' trial the scheme, so far as the Germans are concerned, is a failure; notwithstanding the wise and considerate administration of Bishop Gobat ...[68]

The contacts between Britain and Germany, which commenced in July 1882 with the aim of rectifying the balance of power within the joint framework of the Jerusalem bishopric, were long and drawn out. In a letter dated that same month and addressed to Lord Granville, the British Foreign Minister, the German Ambassador in London, Georg Hebert Münster, clarified the motives of his government in regard to the cancellation of the agreement. He stated that, besides the need to release the growing German community in Palestine from the fetters of the Anglican Church and give it a deserved independence, the fulfilment of the agreement was, from the very start, not in line with the vision and expectation of the late King of Prussia, Friedrich Wilhelm IV.

Nearly a year passed before the Archbishop of Canterbury responded to the German demands and, in his conclusion to a long and detailed letter, which he sent to his Foreign Minister, he expressed the hope that some way could be found to remove the objections of the German government and to continue to maintain the joint bishopric. Ten months later the German ambassador in London noted in response that his government would be willing to reconsider the continuation of the partnership on two conditions. The first was the cancellation of the veto of the Anglican Church to the appointment of a bishop by the German Kaiser. The second condition was that the bishop appointed by Germany would not have to obtain the approval of the Anglican Church or be committed to its principles.[69]

Two years went by, during which time letters were exchanged between the various parties in London and Berlin. Only in February 1886 did the head of the Anglican Church announce his decision to 'forthwith rescind' the agreement signed in 1841 to establish the joint bishopric. Another year passed in discussions as to the manner in which the partnership between London and Berlin in Jerusalem should be terminated. At the beginning of 1887 the British Foreign Minister summed up the matter in a brief letter to the German Ambassador in London, and declared that in spite of the formal break-up of the partnership, the Archbishop of Canterbury was willing to grant the request of Germany to continue maintaining the harmony between the two peoples in Christ-Church, Jerusalem.[70]

## RESURGENCE

We see that the period was characterised by a steady decline in the activities of the London Society in Palestine, resulting from local conditions. The major change was in the trend led by Bishop Gobat, in which the main focus of missionary work was directed towards the Arab population in Palestine. This trend prevented the London Society from developing properly, although it should be examined whether the international balance of power had influenced the continuous decline.

The British and the Germans were the most prominent Protestant factors in Palestine in the nineteenth century, and the equilibrium maintained between the two nations was a major component in the success of their institutions in the country. At the beginning of the century the London Society was the first to settle in Jerusalem while German nationals served as their emissaries. The touchstone of the balance of power between these two communities was the establishment of the joint bishopric for which Germany needed the goodwill of Britain. Even in the 1850s when independent German institutions began to strike root in Palestine, some of their emissaries gained their livelihood through positions obtained in British missionary societies. At the beginning of the 1870s the situation changed. The international standing of Germany strengthened after its unification in 1871, and so did the status of its community in Palestine, especially with the significant addition of hundreds of members of the Templar Society.

That same decade epitomised the failing powers of the London Society. During this period it did not manage to place even one prominent figure at the head of its enterprise in Palestine for longer than a year, and employed no fewer than ten missionaries successively in this position. Such a state of affairs could not be found in any other mission station of the London Society in Europe or in its centre in London; nor could its erosion in Jerusalem be attributed to economic reasons. In fact, in 1875, the budget of the London Society expanded to unprecedented proportions.

Perhaps the decline ought to be attributed, on one hand, to the diminished status of the London Society in Jerusalem, and to the empowerment of the German community on the other. Most probably, the German missionaries were preoccupied with their nationalistic concerns and preferred to work under a German flag. A similar tendency developed among the German Catholic emissaries in Palestine who deserted the traditional Vatican umbrella and began working for the cause of German interests in the country. Only a brilliant administrator such as Hastings Kelk could manage at the end of this period to rebuild the London Society missionary enterprise from its ruins, to instil new life into the mission station in Jerusalem, and to prepare it for the burst of Jewish immigration that inundated it at the beginning of the 1880s.

## NOTES

1. Lambeth, MS.3397: Calman in Jerusalem to Alexander's widow, 4 August 1846.
2. Abeken, *The Protestant Bishopric*, pp. 162–5: see there for correspondence that includes the King's proposal to Gobat and the latter's response; Stock, E. *The History*, II, p. 141. On Gobat's indecision regarding the offer by the King of Prussia see Thiersch and Gobat, *Samuel Gobat*, pp. 207–9. On Gobat, see Thiersch and Gobat, *Samuel Gobat*; Carmel, A. *Christen als Pioniere im Heiligen Land. Ein Beitrag zur Geschichte der Pilgermission und des Wiederaufbaus Palästinas im 19. Jahrhundert* (Basle: 1981), pp. 59–125. For a brief biography until his appointment as bishop see Abeken, *The Protestant Bishopric*, pp. 167–75. On the Church Missionary Society see below.

3. *Jewish Intelligence* (October 1846), p. 345: Gobat, from Beuggen, 15 August 1846.
4. Ibid. (September 1846), p. 316.
5. Thiersch and Gobat, *Samuel Gobat*, p. 289.
6. Ibid., p. 216.
7. *Jewish Intelligence* (January 1848), pp. 3–4: Gobat, from Jerusalem. This statement by Gobat also conforms to his basic conception of the mission's task, in opposition to that of the London Society members. According to his scale of priorities, the field of education would produce the best results rather than the field of medical care, which was a top priority of the London Society.
8. ITAC, Jerusalem Local Committee Minutes Book, I, No. 12 (9 December 1851): detailed report on the institution and its activities written by its director, Ferdinand Palmer. The school, which later bore the name of the 'Bishop Gobat School', was erected on the slope of Mount Zion near the southwestern corner of the Old City and outside its walls. Today the building serves as an American academic institution.
9. Most of the emissaries of the Basler Pilgermission in Palestine left the institute, and some of them were even active in the London Society. But the contribution made by Spittler and the institution he headed to the advancement of Palestine in various fields is well recognised. On this enterprise in general see Carmel, *Christen als Pioniere*; Eisler, E.J. *Der deutsche Beitrag zum Aufstieg Jaffas 1850–1914: Zur Geschicte Palästinas im 19. Jahrhundert* (Wiesbaden: 1997), pp. 17–25.
10. ITAC, Jerusalem Local Committee Minutes Book, I, No. 15 (10 October 1850): note on Fliedner's letter, and decision to allot £50 for the travelling expenses of two sisters. The former hospital compound in the Old City now houses a Maronite hostel. In later years the Deaconesses' enterprise flourished. In 1868 the sisters inaugurated 'Talitha Kumi', a prestigious school for Arab girls, and in 1894 they opened the gates of a new and excellently equipped hospital, both institutions being built outside the walls of the Old City. On Fliedner and the Deaconesses' enterprise in greater detail, see A. Carmel, 'Der Missionar Theodor Fliedner als Pionier deutscher Palästina Arbeit', *Jahrbuch des Instituts für Deutsche Geschichte*, XIV (1985), pp. 191–220.
11. For a detailed history of the Church Missionary Society, see Stock, *The History*. On its early activities in Jerusalem, see *Proceedings of the Church Missionary Society for Africa and the East*, 53 (1852), pp. 65–70; ibid., 54 (1853), pp. 60–1. For an interim report of the activities in Palestine, see *The Church Missionary Gleaner*, 17 (July 1890), pp. 105–6.
12. Bodleian, Dep. Cmj, d.54: pamphlet published in London in 1891 by the Church Missionary Society in the wake of harsh publications against it by the Anglican bishop in Jerusalem: 'C.M.S. in Palestine', pp. 4, 15.
13. *Jewish Intelligence* (January 1852), p. 2: Gobat, from Jerusalem.
14. ITAC, Jerusalem Local Committee Minutes Book, I: report of December 1851 consisting of 48 pages. For a concise formulation of the decisions signed by Reichardt see ibid., No. 20 (11 December 1851).
15. Bodleian, Dep. Cmj, d.59: instructions received from the society by Crawford before he set out for Palestine: 'Instructions of the Committee of the London Society for Promoting Christianity Amongst the Jews to the Reverend Henry Crawford on his Proceeding to Jerusalem – Delivered Jan[uary] 15/[18]52'.
16. Finn, J. *Stirring Times or Records from Jerusalem Consular Chronicles of 1853 to 1856* (London: 1878), II, pp. 64–72.

17. Nicolayson was buried in the Protestant cemetery plot on Mount Zion that he himself had acquired. On his grave the following words are inscribed:

> For twenty-three years a faithful watchman on the walls of Jerusalem, fearless in the midst of war, pestilence, and earthquake, a master of all the learning of the Hebrews and Arabs, founder of the English Hospital, builder of the Protestant Church: lived beloved, and died lamented, by Christians, Jews and Mohammedans.

In time the gravestone began to crumble and a special project to renovate it was undertaken in 1986 by Nicolayson's townsfolk in Denmark. The occasion was commemorated by a memorial tablet on the wall of his residence in No. 13, Klostergade, Lügumkloster, Schleswig. On this, see the articles in the Danish press: *Jyllards Posten* (20 June 1986), 'Guldbrudepar restaurerer gravemæle i Jerusalem'; *Jydske Tidende* (23 June 1986), 'Guldbrudepar fik usædvanlig gave'.

18. *Jewish Intelligence* (August 1879), pp. 218–19.
19. *Joseph Barclay, Third Anglican Bishop*, pp. 333–4; also ibid., p. 267.
20. Ibid., pp. 366–7, 400–1.
21. The following is a partial list of prominent figures among the nine missionaries who headed the London Society Mission in Jerusalem during the period indicated. In January 1871, James Neil (1841–1916) was appointed to succeed Barclay and served in this capacity until April 1874. He was replaced in February 1875 by O.F. Walton, who, in addition to his position as head of the mission, also acted as the pastor of Christ-Church. Walton left during 1876, and was temporarily replaced by Elias Benjamin Frankel (1826–1903). Somerset B. Burtchaell (1832–78), a native of Dublin, was called over from his residence in Italy to serve as the permanent replacement, but he died in June 1878.
22. St Albans, Applications and Appointments, Vol. A. No. 184. Hastings Kelk served until 1901, when he returned to London to become head of the London Society branch there. His position in Jerusalem was taken by Johnston Carnegie Brown (d. 1930), the pastor of St Paul in Brixton.
23. *Jewish Missionary Intelligence, the Monthly Record of the London Society for Promoting Christianity Amongst the Jews* (March 1908), p. 39. In 1886 Kelk stood at the centre of an embarrassing affair that mainly involved accusations laid against his moral standards. Kelk, who was married, was accused by Herbert Marriott, an Anglican clergyman from Beirut who spent about a year in Jerusalem, of an improper liaison with a young woman, Emma Carolina Fitzjohn (d. 1920), who directed the London Society's educational institution for girls in Jerusalem. During the first half of 1886 leaflets were published and letters were exchanged between the parties involved in the affair, until finally the London Society announced that it saw no blame in the conduct of Kelk, head of its Jerusalem Mission. On this subject, see Bodleian, Dep. Cmj, d.140: pamphlet published by Marriott on 12 May 1886 entitled 'Expose of an Extraordinary Appeal in Case of Scandal at Jerusalem'; ibid.: counter-pamphlet published by the London Society on 1 October 1886 entitled: 'A Few Facts Respecting Pamphlet Circulated by the Rev. Marriott, of Jerusalem'.
24. *Jewish Intelligence* (January 1949), p. 3: Gobat, from Jerusalem.
25. *Report*, 46 (March 1854), p. 55.
26. For a detailed account of the affair from the London Society point of view, see Bodleian, Dep. Cmj, c.110: document entitled 'L.J.S. Remarks of the

Committee upon Mr. Young's Letter relative to Mr. Simeon Rosenthal's Case'. On the position opposed to that of the Society, see ibid., d.149: 'Jerusalem: Its Bishop, its Missionaries, and its Converts, being a Series of Letters Addressed to the Editor of the "Daily News" in the Year 1858'.

27. *Daily News* (2 April 1858), p. 9.
28. Bodleian, Dep. Cmj, d.55: handwritten document entitled 'Jerusalem' among a collection of pamphlets.
29. *Jewish Intelligence* (January 1848), p. 13: Macgowan, from Jerusalem, 4 October 1847; ibid. (May 1848), p. 134: Macgowan, from Jerusalem, in a report from February; ibid. (November 1850), pp. 374–5: Macgowan, from Jerusalem.
30. On the Lepers Hospital and Dr Chaplin's contribution see Schwake, *Die Entwicklung*, pp. 603–33.
31. On St John's Ophthalmic Hospital and Dr Chaplin's contribution to it see, for example, King, E.J. *The Knights of St. John in the British Empire*, 3rd edn, (London: 1934), pp. 163–75; Izhaki, R. 'The Ophthlamic Hospital of the Order of St. John (1882–1948)', in *Cathedra*, 67 (1993), pp. 116–18 (Hebrew).
32. *Jewish Intelligence* (September 1854), pp. 284–6: Macgowan, from Jerusalem. In 1887 the Rothschild Hospital was transferred to its new location outside the city walls and the old building was taken over by the Misgav Ladach Hospital.
33. Frankel, L.A. *Nach Jerusalem! Reise in Griechenland, Kleinasien, Syrien, Palästina* (Vienna: 1860), p. 190 (Hebrew).
34. *Jewish Intelligence* (May 1847), p. 158: Critchlow from Jerusalem, 5 February 1847, 4 March 1847.
35. Rhodes, A. *Jerusalem As It Is* (London: 1865).
36. FO, 78/803, No. 2: James Finn to Palmerston, 22 January 1849, in Eliav, M. *Britain and the Holy Land 1838–1914: Selected Documents from the British Consulate in Jerusalem* (Jerusalem: 1997), pp. 150–1. Most of the visitors to the church lavished praises on the building, while only an exceptional few expressed their criticism. See, for example, Rhodes, *Jerusalem*, pp. 443-4, where it is mentioned that at the far end of the hall there was an organ, which did not appear very impressive and 'produces any thing but tuneful sounds'.
37. *Jewish Intelligence* (November 1853), p. 371.
38. Grajewski, *The Struggle*, n.p.: 'A Voice Crying!' (Hebrew).
39. Bodleian, Dep. Cmj, d.62: Detailed list of the pupils in the institution from the day of its establishment in December 1848 till February 1863. The list includes the names of its directors and all the instructors who taught there during this period.
40. *Report*, 42 (1850), p. 66; *Jewish Intelligence* (January 1850), p. 3: Gobat, from Cairo, 2 November 1849; ibid., p. 210.
41. Bodleian, Dep. Cmj, d.62: documents marked B.a.5. According to these, John Nicolayson purchased the building from Consul Adolfo Castellinard on 27 August 1849; ibid. c.125: list of acquisitions in June and July 1850. At the beginning of 1873 the House of Industry was enlarged again, and an additional floor was built above the roof. On the start of the fundraising campaign for the institution, see ibid., d.139: Alexander McCaul to the London Committee, Kent, 25 August 1854.
42. ITAC, unclassified documents: agreement for Schick's employment signed by John Nicolayson on 11 November 1850; ibid.: Jerusalem Local Committee Minutes Book, I, No. 34 (12 November 1850). On Schick, see mainly Carmel, *Christen als Pioniere*; Carmel, A. 'Conrad Schick's Road to Jerusalem', in *Zev*

*Vilnay's Jubilee Volume*, Jerusalem 1984, pp. 115–26 (Hebrew).

43. Spittler's instructions to Schick and Palmer, Basle, 14 August 1846 in Carmel, 'Conrad Schick's', p. 120.

44. PEF, The Schick Files; ITAC, Jerusalem Local Committee Minutes Book, II (22 June 1872); Lees, G.R. *Jerusalem Illustrated* (Newcastle-on-Tyne and London: 1893), pp. 154–63; Goren, H. and Rubin, R. 'Models and Maps of Jerusalem and its Buildings made by Conrad Schick', in H. Goren (ed.) *For the Sake of Jerusalem, Conrad Schick, Ariel, 130-131* (Jerusalem: 1998), pp. 79–92; S. Gibson, 'Conrad Schick and the Palestine Exploration Fund', ibid., pp. 64–8.

45. Gidney, *Sites and Scenes*, pp. 87–8.

46. In July 1888 Coral resigned and was replaced by George Robinson Lees (1860–1944). See ITAC, Jerusalem Local Committee Minutes Book, III, No. 201 (5 July 1888). At the beginning of 1895 the school was headed by the converted Jew, Aaron Charles Hornstein (1830–99). See *Report*, 81 (March 1889), p. 11: Appointments, Removals, &c., of missionaries from 1 April 1888 till 31 March 1889.

47. *Jewish Missionary Intelligence* (September 1897), p. 137; W.T. Gidney, *Mission to the Jews: A Handbook of Reasons, Facts and Figures* (London: 1897), p. 100.

48. ITAC, Jerusalem Mission Minutes: detailed copy of Cooper's offer to transfer the school to the London Society ownership, which includes revisions that she requests the society to make in the transfer agreement and her decision to accept the agreement, 3 December 1858; Bodleian, Dep. Cmj, c.250: transfer agreement for ownership of the institution from Cooper to Crawford and Macgowan on 21 February 1859; ibid., c.125: rental records of May and October 1859.

49. Keller, ILJ.04, Plans and Prospects of the Institution for Jewesses at Jerusalem: Caroline Cooper, Jerusalem, 5 September 1856.

50. ITAC, Jerusalem Mission Minutes: Register No. 23 of the General Committee Meeting in London, 1 December 1852.

51. On Metzler, an unknown missionary, see Eisler, J.E. *Peter Martin Metzler (1824–1907). Ein christlicher Missionar im Heiligen Land* (Haifa: 1999).

52. In 1912, after the death of Jane Arnott, the property and management of the institution, which by then included three schools – a boarding school and a day school in Jaffa, and a third school out of town – were transferred at Arnott's request to the Church of Scotland. See Bodleian, Dep. Cmj, d.57: report of the Walker-Arnott Tabeetha mission at Jaffa for the year ending 1912; *The Church of Scotland, Home & Foreign Missionary Record* (1 March 1875), pp. 299–300.

53. On the American Colony, see Holms, R.M. *The Forerunners* (Independence, MO: 1981); Eisler, *Der deutsche Beitrag*, pp. 77–83.

54. On the history of the Templar Society and the causes for the move to Jaffa, see A. Carmel, *Die Siedllungen der Württembergischen Templer in Palästina 1868–1914*, 3rd edn (Stuttgart: 2000).

55. Bodleian, Dep. Cmj, c.127: ownership documents J4, J8; ITAC: ownership documents J4, J8.

56. Margoliouth, M. *A Pilgrimage to the Land of My Fathers* (London: 1850), II, pp. 264–7.

57. ITAC, Jerusalem Local Committee Minutes Book, I, No. 15 (9 December 1851): extract from the summary on Safed.

58. FO, 78/839: Finn to Palmerston, 23 April 1850, in Hyamson, *The British Consulate*, I, No. 114 and Appendices, p. 166.

59. ITAC, Jerusalem Local Committee Minutes Book, I, No. 15 (9 December 851): from the summary on Safed; *Jewish Intelligence* (July 1850), pp. 251–6: from Daniel's diary in Safed, 3 April 1850 till 14 April 1850, 9 May 1850, 22 May 1850; ibid. (June 1851), p. 222: annual report.
60. Bodleian, Dep. Cmj, c.125: document marked K.1.1, testifying to the acquisition in Barclay's name, dated 30 November 1867, and his declaration that the property actually belongs to the London Society. A copy of this document can be found in ITAC: ownership documents.
61. *Jewish Record* (June 1880), p. 24.
62. *Joseph Barclay, Third Anglican Bishop*, pp. 424–5.
63. Bodleian, Dep. Cmj, d.53: collection of documents submitted to the British Parliament in July 1887 entitled 'Correspondence respecting the Protestant Bishopric at Jerusalem' (Germany, No. 1, 1887): Münster to Granville, London, 17 July 1882.
64. Von Mirbach, E.F. (ed.) *Das deutsche Kaiserpaar im Heiligen Lande im Herbst 1898* (Berlin: 1899), p. 26.
65. Voices were also raised in Britain that necessitated the break-up of the bishopric. See Bodleian, Dep. Cmj, d.54: chapter entitled 'The Three Anglican Bishops in Jerusalem' in *The Church Quarterly Review* (July 1884), p. 327, where it is mentioned that 'the See should die out' since the whole project had failed entirely. One of the reasons put forward by the journal was that none of the three bishops who had served so far in this position was sufficiently qualified to manage the institution. On the same subject, see the article ambiguously entitled 'The Dead See' in the *Guardian* (16 February 1887), p. 252.
66. *Jewish Intelligence* (May 1883), p. 101.
67. Ibid., p. 103.
68. Ibid., p. 102.
69. Bodleian, Dep. Cmj, d.53: collection of documents entitled 'Correspondence respecting the Protestant Bishopric at Jerusalem' (Germany No. 1, 1887): Münster to Granville, London, 17 July 1882; ibid., 24 January 1884.
70. Ibid.: letter of the British Foreign Minister, Henry Stratford, 1st Earl of Iddesleigh (1818–87), London, 8 January 1887; see also the declarations of the Archbishop of Canterbury, the Archbishop of York and the Bishop of London on 18 February 1887 in St Albans: pamphlet published as a report on the activities of the bishopric in Jerusalem, entitled *The Primary Charge of the Right Reverend George Francis Popham Blyth, D.D. Bishop of the Church of England in Jerusalem and the East* (London: 1890), pp. 71–3.

# 4

# 1892–1896

HIGH HOPES

[The new Jewish immigrants] wandering to and fro like walking shadows pass through the streets of our city, and their condition is frightful with thousands doomed to starvation and the future lies before them in blackest colours, and who can tell how they will end? The Mission Houses, which have always been a snare and pitfall for the dwellers in Jerusalem, now find a broad field of action, and with wide open arms they welcome these miserable brethren of ours, giving them work while preaching foolish sermons to them, and many of these wretches will be entrapped because famine and deprivation have driven them mad; for the net is spread out before the eyes of these unfortunate people and they will lie in ambush for their souls.[1]

When the first reports began to filter into London about the pogroms among Russian Jewry, the subject was also raised in the society journal. The editor expressed deep sympathy for the Jews who were going through such a terrible crisis in various parts of Eastern Europe, and he speculated that the pogroms and the frenzied exodus of the Jews were a sign from God. At the beginning of 1882, articles in the journal began to provide the first details, and this showed that a realisation of the enormous scope of the pogroms had been grasped by the London Society leaders. The events were used to strengthen the beliefs on which the existence and activities of the London Society were based, and they were given an ideological interpretation by its official spokesman. The committee appointed by the society to investigate the pogroms in Russia thought, as did may other friends of Israel, that these sufferings presaged:

… the beginning of a fulfilment of the prophetic Scriptures foretelling the return of the Jews to their own land … The Missionaries of the Society rejoice at the protest which Christians everywhere are making against these outbursts, as being not only abhorrent to our common humanity, but also alien to the true spirit of Christianity.[2]

The profound emotions among the society's supporters were initially expressed by their taking an unequivocal stand. Their realisation of the grievous state of the Jews in various parts of Europe, and especially in the Russian Empire, led them to openly declare their sympathy for the Jews for 'the indignities and suffering they are undergoing at the hands of the relentless and enraged population'.[3] But, besides these strong feelings, practical measures were also taken. They set up a £100,000 fund to give initial assistance to the Jewish refugees from Russia to leave their country. The appeal by many Jews to receive protection in mission stations in Europe strengthened the sense of missionary zeal among the London Society members.

The Jewish public responded to the outstretched hand of the London Society with mixed feelings. On the one hand, they did not modify their traditional stand of rejecting all contact with missionaries. But, on the other, some of them expressed positive feelings about the contribution of the missionaries to the welfare of the Jews in Palestine and for the fact that they sometimes even saved lives. The initial signs of the change in attitude by the Jews towards the work of the missions, at the time when the first refugees fleeing the pogrom in Russia began to arrive in Palestine, are to be found in a letter sent by Zebi Hermann Friedländer (1830–86), a native of Schneidemühl in Prussia (today called Pita in northwest Poland). Friedländer converted at the age of 22, joined the society in 1866, and two years later was sent as a London Society missionary to Tunis. In November 1872 he arrived in Jerusalem and then, during the first wave of Jewish immigration, he began working with Hastings Kelk and became the most important emissary of the society in Palestine. According to some sources, Friedländer served as personal secretary to the British romanticist and lover of Zion, Lawrence Oliphant (1829–88), who is described in the following manner:

> As it be beholden upon us and every man of Israel to thank and bless the wonderful deeds of the lord Oliphant, so it is our duty to reveal that the channel through which this lord conveys his good mercies is an abomination to us, the children of Israel! This channel, the emissary of the delegation whose net is spread out to snare souls from Israel and make them stray from their faith, is an apostate Jew who conducts the affairs of the instigators in our city, who was charged to draw the souls of Israel to himself, and all his wish and

desire is to have transactions with the Jews and to find stratagems to deal with them.[4]

Friedländer's letter written in July 1882 mainly shows his surprise at the friendly manner in which he was received by the newly arrived Jews. The pleasant relationship that the missionaries had with the new immigrants derived from two sources. The first was the crisis that the latter had undergone during the pogroms in Russia and the deprivation they experienced when they arrived in Palestine so hastily and empty-handed. Since the missionaries offered them immediate solutions both physically and spiritually, they gained the appreciation of a large number of immigrants. The second source was the familiarity of the refugees with the missionary phenomenon in the country of their origin, where the emissaries were received with greater tolerance. Another aspect of the contact between the missionaries and the immigrants was that, in the wake of those hundreds of new immigrants who chose to take refuge in the mission houses, a large number of the Palestinian Jews who had previously feared to take this step were now ready to enter the London Society institutions in Palestine. Friedländer wrote that during his stay in Jaffa he received many letters from refugees staying in the city who asked for his advice and assistance. The missionary warned that, in spite of their explicit wish to join the London Society institutions in Jerusalem, the society should be very cautious in deciding who should be granted refuge, since the available funds were being stretched to the very limit.

The society members were struck with amazement at the sight of hundreds of new immigrants in dire distress filling the church courtyard in Jerusalem and placing themselves in the hands of the missionaries. Some of the society leaders in London expressed doubt as to their ability to finance this necessary change in priorities and to allocate the additional resources needed for the missionary works in Palestine. Many papers were drafted on this problem and some even termed the arrival of such large numbers of Jews from Russia and Eastern Europe a serious crisis. The means available at the mission station in Jerusalem dwindled until it began to collapse under the financial strain. At the same time the missionaries realised that the opportunity that had come their way was 'absolutely unprecedented in the history of the Mission'. They set out on a fundraising tour among the friends of the Jewish people, asking them for help in this favourable hour to spread the gospel among a large and easily persuaded number of Jews now to be found in Palestine.[5]

The London Society members, Hastings Kelk, the head of the mission, and Friedländer, his assistant, who had experienced first-hand contact with the Jewish refugees now massing at the doors of the society institutions, presented a united front and were determined to increase the utilisation of their maintenance funds even at the cost of accumulating enormous debts. The London Society leaders were taken aback at the first overdrafts run up by the Jerusalem missionaries and sent a delegation of senior officials to examine the situation at first hand and to review the policy of their members in Palestine regarding the allocation of resources.

W. Ord-Mackenzie (1816–98) and Frederick Smith, who headed the delegation, faithfully performed their assignment and brought back to London a full and comprehensive report. They first stated that the motives behind such a large number of Jews seeking assistance from the mission were the utter destitution in which they found themselves and the indifference they encountered among the local Jewish community. They then went on to describe some of the characteristic aspects of the newly arrived immigrants. In their view, the social status of most of the refugees in their country of origin had been above average and they were highly educated. Many had held respectable positions, and none had been forced to live on charity until they were violently dispossessed of home and property in Eastern Europe.

The stated objective of the investigating delegation was to examine whether the missionaries in Jerusalem had acted hastily when they undertook the care of such a large group of refugees and to see if they had exaggerated in their spending or if there had been another plan of action that could have been adopted instead of the one they had chosen. The leaders of the delegation agreed unanimously that given the circumstances and pressure of events, Friedländer and Kelk had had no choice but to do as they had done, that is, to provide for the physical needs of the refugees with money, clothing and food on the one hand, and for their spiritual sustenance through meetings, study and prayer on the other. Had the missionaries in Jerusalem acted otherwise and neglected their duty in this matter, the following results would have occurred:

1. Damage to the public image of the Mission as an institution of charity.

2. Starvation of most of those who wished to join the Mission.

3. Sacrifice of a golden opportunity that had presented itself to preach the truths of Christianity.

As an appendix to the report from Jerusalem a letter was attached, signed by 37 adult immigrants representing, according to them, over 200 Jewish souls:

> We, the undersigned Russian Refugees, desire to offer, from the depth of our broken hearts, a sacrifice of thanksgiving for the love shown to us by your Agents here ... If the Divine Providence had not raised up your Ministers, we should have perished – we with our wives and little ones, long since in the streets of Zion ... We hope that our Heavenly Father will prosper the plans entertained by your Agents, to settle us in peace on the inheritance of our ancestors, so that we, fathers and children, may rejoice, and everlastingly remember all the kindness and mercy extended to us by your Missionaries, and all the world will have to acknowledge that the first foundation for the redemption of Zion has been laid by your Agents.[6]

The flourishing of missionary activity in Jerusalem raised the hopes of the missionaries to new heights. As the society leaders wrote in one of their reports, this was the time for 'the reaping of the harvest for which the previous sixty years ... were the sowing time'.[7] However, besides the satisfaction expressed in many articles that filled the society journal, a central place was given to an urgent call for financial support and manpower. The general feeling was that a huge number of potential converts on a scale never before known by the London Society would be irretrievably lost for lack of funds. The activists in London, aided by Friedländer, who had come to London from Jerusalem expressly for this purpose, launched a campaign during 1883 to raise funds in order to meet the enormous needs in Palestine. When the London committee met to respond to the lack of means, it formulated a new ruling, apparently because of essential differences of opinion among the top ranks of the society, that no support should be given to adult Jews from the current budget. The way to fill this need must be through setting up a separate fund – the Temporal Relief Fund – that would be handled by a special committee of society members of the higher ranks.[8]

In the years 1890–1, a renewed stream of Jewish immigrants arrived in Palestine as a second surge in the first wave of immigration. Hastings Kelk, the head of the Jerusalem mission, foresaw that the increase in the number of refugees would create difficulties in the supply of basic food items. As in the earlier wave of immigration in 1881–2, there appeared a large numbers of people interested in the words of the gospel. The attitude of the immigrants towards the missionaries continued to improve, and the path leading to the hearts of the Jews in Palestine was more easily trodden. As the missionaries themselves expressed it, 'The seed is more widely sown, and we must hope that some may bring forth fruit.'[9] The London Society quickly adapted the range of its activities to the tidal wave of immigration that swept over it, and decided to increase the number of its missionaries in Palestine to 29.

THE BLYTH PERIOD

In the spring of 1887 George Francis Popham Blyth (1832–1914) was nominated as the Anglican bishop in Jerusalem and the East. Blyth was born in Beverly in the county of Humberside in the northeast of England. He was educated at Oxford and worked for 21 years in India and Burma. In 1887, after returning to England via Palestine, he was offered the episcopate in Jerusalem.[10] The patron of the London Society, the Archbishop of Canterbury, explained the motives for this appointment. In the prelude to his speech, he reported that since Germany had decided, with the assent of Britain, to cease her support of the joint bishopric in Jerusalem, a decision had been reached in Britain to continue financing the office of the Anglican bishop with British means alone. In response, the London Society felt it necessary to clarify that it had not been consulted about the decision to continue maintaining an exclusively Anglican bishopric and to appoint a new bishop in Jerusalem. However, as a missionary society subordinate to the church, it had no choice but to assist in the revival of the episcopate and to give its blessing to the appointment of the bishop.

The Archbishop of Canterbury appealed to the London Society leaders to assume part of the financial cost for the bishopric, and they agreed to do so. They set up a special fund for this purpose, and allocated £300 annually from the fund, which, together with a similar sum donated by the Church Missionary Society, filled the financial gap created by the withdrawal of the Germans. In their summation of the decision to place the above amount at the disposal of the bishopric, the London Society leaders stated in the protocol that their committee acknowledged the promise made by the Archbishop of Canterbury that in appointing the new bishop in Jerusalem the Church of England recognised the valuable contribution of the society, and that the bishop chosen would cooperate with it in the mission activities.[11]

Once the bishop was elected and the society had taken responsibility for half the cost of the bishopric, its leaders felt that their position was sufficiently strengthened to lay down a few conditions. At first, they indicated their pleasure at the warm appreciation expressed towards the society in the formal letter of appointment for the bishop: 'On the Society's work in accordance with those Evangelical principles which have always hitherto marked its operations, and from which the Committee have never consciously deviated, and, by God's grace, never will.' They then made the assumption that, by his very decision to continue maintaining the bishopric, the Archbishop of Canterbury now recognised once more the importance of the society's work and the need to appoint a bishop who would cooperate with it. In conclusion, the missionaries carefully pointed out that the fundamental principle of the society was that their work among the Jews would be sustained in the future as well.[12]

Bishop Blyth arrived in Palestine in May 1887 with well-defined missionary conceptions. Within a very short time he began an attempt to subject the London Society members and their institutions, as well as its sister organisation, the Church Missionary Society, to his own authority.[13] At the beginning of 1888 Blyth made the proposal to give Christ-Church, the manifest symbol of the London Society in Palestine and its source of pride, a touch of grandeur by transforming it into an Anglican cathedral with the addition of two wings on the east and west sides, and the erection of a tower to a height of 100 feet (30 metres). His aim was to turn the church compound into a collegiate deanery, as was the practice in Britain, and to nominate a dean to head it. To his proposal Blyth attached the plans drawn up at his request by Conrad Schick as well as his explanatory remarks of the sketches, a work plan, timetable and proposed costs.[14]

At a meeting held at the beginning of February 1888, the London Society rejected this plan outright and stated that, although they respected the bishop's endeavours, the idea contradicted the modest style of the church founders.[15] By taking a stubborn stand to preserve the simple and pleasant aspect of the church building, they signalled that they were the sole owners of Christ-Church and that they intended to remain so in spite of the plans made by the Anglican bishop in Jerusalem. Their refusal aroused strong criticism in England, which centred upon the disappointment at the way the Anglican Church was represented in the Holy City, and surprise at the disregard shown by the London Society for the wishes of the bishop in Jerusalem. The critics went as far as to advise their readers to transfer their contributions for the London Society to other missionary societies and in effect to cut off its financial resources. T.S. Ellerby, the London Society representative in Toronto, Canada, responded to this criticism in the name of the society and answered each charge separately. With regard to turning the church into a grand cathedral, the Canadian missionary intimated that divine beauty was to be found in the believers themselves, and in his view they should deck themselves with humility, with faith, hope, and charity, and with all the graces of the gospel.[16]

Blyth did not spare the rod even in his relationship with the Church Missionary Society. The fact that it had been given all the mission stations and educational institutions that had once belonged to the late Bishop Gobat induced the new bishop – who had no control over the church or over any other missionary or educational institution, and not even over a single missionary – to publish a strongly worded statement of accusations against this society as well. In its own detailed statement, the Church Missionary Society stressed the fact that it had been in existence in Jerusalem for 35 years before the bishop's arrival, and that the bishop owed his very presence in Jerusalem to it and to the London Society, which carried the main financial burden of his residence in the city.[17] It seems probable that the contentious feelings of the new bishop, without a church of his own, towards the London Society and the Church Missionary Society led him to erect a monumental edifice of his own – the Anglican College of St George dedicated in 1898, and to found a new missionary society called Jerusalem and the East Mission.[18]

## THE NEW HOSPITAL IN JERUSALEM

The Mission! The Mission Hospital! The Mission Doctor! These are the words that now fill the mouths of our brethren, the dwellers in our city. They ask each other: What has happened today at the Mission Hospital outside the city? Who went to consult their doctors sitting for a few hours a day in their clinics within the city? And suchlike enquiries of various kinds, for the feelings of our brethren have grown mightily against the instigators … who for many years past have lain in wait for Israel in Jerusalem to snare the souls of them with their nets.[19]

9. The New Hospital in Jerusalem; it is now 'The Anglican School'

10. The dispensary in the New Hospital

In the mid-1870s, during the month of June, rumours began to spread in Jerusalem and London concerning the need for a new hospital because of the dilapidated state of the old hospital building and the increasing rate of occupancy in that period. But the initial practical step to set up this new institution was taken only in August 1889 by an English woman who anonymously donated £1,000 to the building fund.[20] In the meantime there was a change in hospital directors. The veteran director, Dr Thomas Chaplin, resigned his position on 1 January 1886 and was replaced by Dr Percy Charles Edward d'Erf Wheeler. He was later joined by Ernst William Gurney Masterman (1867–1943), born in Hall-Rotherfield, Sussex, who was a surgeon appointed to work in the hospital and who arrived in Jerusalem in December 1892.[21]

In September 1889, the first decisions were made regarding the site for the proposed building. The London Society Committee in Jerusalem warmly recommended that the hospital be built outside the city on a stretch of land already acquired in 1863 on which the society's recreation site, called the 'Sanatorium', would later be built. They envisaged the new institution as incorporating all the hospital facilities, including the dispensary and staff quarters, near the hospital wings. The old hospital building inside the city walls would be retained for use as outpatient clinics and a dispensary.

The plans for the new hospital were entrusted to a British architect who was also a member of the London Society, A. Beresford Pite (1861–1934), who completed the assignment at the end of 1891.[22] The basic principle that guided Pite in his plan for the hospital was the setting up of each unit and department of the institution as a separate building connected to all the others by covered walkways. This was to allow for maximum ventilation for every department on all sides of the building and to maintain absolute isolation in order to prevent the spread of infectious diseases from one wing to another. The innovative principles in planning the hospital were drawn up after much thought and extensive touring by the planner among similar institutions in Europe. At the dedication ceremony of the building, Beresford Pite described the planning process:

> Three years ago funds were sufficient for an inspection to come out and survey the spot. I visited about twenty different hospitals at that time. The principles of the erection of the present hospital are simple, the main object being to cure patients with as little medicine as possible, and give them as much light and sunshine as we can. We all notice how many windows and doors the building contains.[23]

In December 1892 it was announced that after a long wait, the Turkish authorities had rejected the request to build the hospital because of its close proximity to a Muslim mosque. Consequently, Sir John Henry Kennaway (1837-1919), president of the London Society and a member of the British Parliament, presented a request to the Under-Secretary of State in the Ministry for Foreign Affairs to find out through Her Majesty's ambassador in Constantinople why the Sublime Porte was delaying the grant of a *firman* to build the new hospital. Besides the British ambassador in Constantinople, Dr Thomas Chaplin, the former director of the hospital, also tried to exert his powers of persuasion, and set out on a four-month lobbying tour, visiting Jerusalem and Constantinople. His efforts bore fruit, and in the summer of 1893 the Secretary of the British Embassy in Constantinople sent Chaplin a telegram informing him that the Supreme Court of the Turkish Empire had ordered the granting of a *firman* to permit the erection of the hospital in Jerusalem. At the end of August the *firman* was granted and a copy reached Jerusalem on 21 September. In November the London Society sent Pite to complete the plans and to adjust them to the licence and limitations of the *firman* with the intention of beginning construction work on the hospital building at the beginning of 1894. It appointed Theodor Sandel (1845–1902), an architect from the German Colony in Jerusalem, as supervisor of the construction work. The cornerstone was laid on 6 March 1895 by Thomas George Baring, Earl of Northbrook (1826–1904), most probably the nephew of Sir Thomas Baring, the London Society president who had served from 1815 to 1848.[24]

The new hospital for the Jews in Jerusalem, the flagship of the London Society in Palestine and the institution in which most of the funds and attention were invested, was dedicated on 13 April 1897. Taking part in the festive ceremony were some of its leaders in England, Thomas Chaplin who was the hospital director for 25 years, consuls of foreign countries, heads of churches in Jerusalem, representatives of the Turkish government, all the London Society members in Palestine; but not a single Jew was present! During the ceremony the guests were served in a large pavilion erected in honour of the occasion by the travel agency of Thomas Cook (1808–92) and were pleasantly entertained by the orchestra of the Schneller Syrian Orphanage. All the speakers praised the fine modern building and the work done by the British planner Beresford Pite and the builder Theodor Sandel.[25]

The fact that not a single member of the Jewish community in Jerusalem took part in the events held for the dedication of the hospital in Jerusalem was not a matter of chance. Its opening aroused fierce opposition led mainly by an association called 'Bnei-Israel' (Sons of Israel), founded in 1897 in reaction to the erection of this medical institution. The association, which acted by common consensus of nearly all the Jewish communities, was given significant assistance by the Alliance Israélite Universelle and by the widow of Baron Moritz Hirsch (1831–96), Clara Hirsch (1833–99), and during the period of its activity it provided dispensaries and free medication for the welfare of the Jews in Jerusalem. Its avowed objective was to 'work for the unity of the congregations and for the improvement of the general situation'. However, it mainly engaged in violent attempts to prevent the hospitalisation of Jews in the new London Society hospital.[26]

It was not long before the Jewish sentinels positioned at the gates of the hospital took violent action, which caused the people in the medical establishment and the guards (*kawass*) of the British consulate to react. A few days later in the wake of the riots, both Her Majesty's ambassador in Constantinople and the Foreign Office in London took up the entire matter.[27] It seems that the appeal made by the head of the Jerusalem mission to the Jewish community, in the journal *Ha-Zevi* which had published a summary of the clarifying conversations held between him and the rabbis of the community, contributed to a calming of spirits. Hastings Kelk said that he had no complaints against the rabbis, who were merely fulfilling their duty according to their faith, and dissuading the public from using the medical services of the society, but that he objected to the use of force.[28]

The activities of the Bnei-Israel organisation can be understood from a petition submitted to the British consul in Jerusalem by certain Jews who were in opposition to it:

> We come in the name of thousands of sick and unfortunate people, amongst whom are also some English subjects. We come to the English Consul to whom it is already well known what the society Bnei-Israel have done in Jerusalem. They have forbidden the Jews to enter the English Hospital or to employ the English doctor. The reason they give us is that it is against religion, and with this swindle they have contrived that the Rabbis shall help them with the 'Cherem', but we Jews know how far that is from the truth – religion is not their object – but only to beg money from Europe. We have already announced this to the Pasha last week, but he has done nothing. We sent a letter to the Pasha and begged him not to allow people to place themselves as spies before the English Hospital and doctor's House. We showed him how necessary the English

Hospital is in the town. First, because the doctor is a good one, and we have no such good doctor as he – the doctors in the Jewish Hospital have no experience. And secondly, they have not such a Dispensary. In their Dispensaries there are only lads, who hardly know how to read the prescriptions. Many young women and children are dying now, and it is the fault of the doctors. We believe that in Europe such doctors would not be allowed to practice. But what can we do? The Bnei-Israel are so strong and behave in such a savage way, that they say if any one allows himself to be treated by the English doctor they will beat him, and do him all kinds of harm, for they will pay money to the Government, so that no complaint against them will be listened to.[29]

Besides the violence employed against those visiting the medical institution and sometimes against its employees, the members of the Bnei-Israel used other means to eliminate the 'plague' called the Mission Hospital. The fact that the institution was built outside the walls of the Old City and that it was not possible to maintain a close supervision over those entering its gates merely gave them added incentive for their actions. For example, the Bnei-Israel organisation induced the Great Bet Din (Supreme Law Court) of the Jewish community to publish in writing a sharp warning – one of many – that no Jew should use the services of the new hospital. The official declaration was as follows:

> We heads and leaders of the holy congregation of Jeshurim of the Sephardim and Ashkenazim Committees have unanimously decided to order a decree according to our rite, that it is unlawful for any 'Shochet' to kill either beast or fowl for the use of the afore-named Hospital, likewise it is unlawful for any Israelite to sell, provide, or permit to be sold any Kosher meat to the aforesaid Hospital. This prohibition applies to the sellers who sell directly or indirectly, and whoever transgresses these our commands, if he be a Shochet, whatever he killed will be considered 'Nebela' (beast that dieth of itself), and if he be a butcher, he will not be trusted to sell Kosher meat, and supply them (the hospital), he will be dealt with according to our laws.[30]

Towards the end of the nineteenth century the London Society added other buildings to the hospital to complete the original plan. In the spring of 1898 it instructed the hospital builder, the architect Sandel, to continue with the construction of the Doctors' House at the site assigned for that purpose in the left wing of the hospital. On 11 July 1901 this institution was completed together with the dedication of another wing of the hospital in the name of the philanthropist Richard Cadbury (1835–99) of Birmingham, UK, who had passed away in Jerusalem. Thus the construction of the grand medical institution, which took a place of honour among the monumental nineteenth-century buildings in Jerusalem, was finally completed.

OTHER INSTITUTIONS IN JERUSALEM

## *The Sanatorium*

The low level of sanitation within the walls of the Old City of Jerusalem, which had frequently caused many of the missionaries and their families to fall ill, increased the need to find a site close to the city to serve as a sanatorium where those who required it could find rest and recuperation. At the same time, the London Society leaders wished to acquire some land to be used as a site for the summer camps organised by the missionaries for pupils of the boys' school and the House of Industry in the city. They located a large compound of six acres to the west of the city near the road leading to Jaffa, and in January 1863 its purchase was completed. those who chose not to sleep in tents outdoors. (This building still stands at the far end of the compound in the rear courtyard of the compound.)[31]

In the summer of 1882, when the first wave of Jewish immigrants flooded the London Society institutions, the boys in the holiday camp had to vacate the compound and allow scores of Jewish refugees who had taken shelter with the missionaries to occupy the tents. About 100 Jews were employed at various jobs on the site itself, improving the access roads to the Sanatorium, raising the surrounding walls higher, and some were employed in archaeological excavations. The employment of the Jews naturally roused the anger of the Jerusalem rabbis, who protested against this and, at the same time, expressed their contempt for the type of work being done there:

> … money is of no value to the missionaries, and stones can be found in abundance on the land it possesses, and their compatriots have drawn the poor people of this community into its work of carrying stones from one place to another, and by their wages they have paved the way in their hearts to forget God and to give up their religious faith.[32]

For their toil, the Jews were provided with lodgings on the site and a small wage while being tested for their readiness to work and to listen to the words of the gospel. The work was supervised entirely by Abraham Leo Oczeret (1854–86), a converted Jew and native of Jerusalem.

*The House of Industry*

Towards the end of 1881, Conrad Schick left his position as director of the House of Industry and was replaced by Herman Friedländer, who held this post until August 1885. During that time, Friedländer was accused of being responsible for financial irregularities and was suspected of having personally appropriated the payments received for the sale of articles produced by the House of Industry. Harsh words were exchanged between him and the London committee, which ended in his leaving the ranks of the society in July 1886.[33] The activities of one of the most prominent missionaries in the entire history of the London Society ended in a scandal that did not enhance its honour.

In the summer of 1885 James Edward Hanauer (1850–1938), a native of Jaffa, was nominated as head of the institution.[34] Two years later, in the second half of 1887, the institution was moved to its new and airy quarters outside the city walls:

> Leaving the Damascus Gate, the Northern Gate of Jerusalem, and going along the Damascus road for about half a mile, or a little more, after passing a beautiful grove of olive-trees, and leaving to the right the interesting 'Tombs of the Kings', we find ourselves opposite the large, fine building, now known as the House of Industry.[35]

The transfer of the institution brought several advantages. The new building was far more spacious than and a great improvement on the former one, housing all the workshops under one roof. Even the rent for the building paid to the Muslim owners was considered very low. Yet it seems that the greatest advantage was in the distance placed between the pupils living in the institution and the hard-core Jewish community found inside the city walls, who objected to the very existence of this institution, and even more so to Jewish apprentices living there.

In May 1891, E.G. Hensman replaced Hanauer as director of this vocational institution. A year later, the institution was again transferred, and was installed in the society buildings that had previously served as an institution for Jewesses in the city. It was then that the olive woodcarving work flourished:

> In the Society's House, a stock is kept of choice Olive-Wood Articles, made by the Converts in the House of Industry, Jerusalem. These articles are very suitable as presents and gifts; also for Sales of Works and Bazaars – in which case, a considerable reduction in price is offered.[36]

At the end of that decade, on 21 December 1898, the House of Industry, which was one of the most important and well-known enterprises of the London Society in Palestine, celebrated its jubilee, the 50th anniversary of its founding.

### Girls' Dormitory

Towards the end of the 1880s the girls' school increased in dimension, as did other London Society institutions. The appropriate manner of dealing with this situation was to separate the two main sections of the educational institution – the school and the dormitory. Discussions were conducted in the second half of 1887 regarding the construction of a suitable building for the dormitory, and in the end the London committee decided to erect such a building within the Christ-Church compound. However, the sanitary conditions in the school within the city became so impossible that there was a danger of a plague outbreak, and the London Society leaders in Jerusalem recommended the immediate transfer of the girls to the buildings on the Sanatorium site outside the city. Since the London committee insisted on constructing the dormitory in the church compound inside the city, its members in Jerusalem quickly sent out proposals for its construction on the Sanatorium site, which had been in their possession for 25 years.

A few reasons for this were attached to the proposals:

1.  The erection of the dormitory outside the city walls would not reduce the number of girls who might study at the day school within the city area, since the number of Jews living outside the city justified the establishment of a special educational institution there.
2.  The division of the Jewish communities between the Sephardim inside the city and the Ashkenazim outside it would make it possible to create two homogeneous educational institutions.

3.  According to the medical reports, the present site near the church was a health hazard, and even substantial improvements would be useless.
4.  Certain houses belonging to the society could be sold and other institutions moved away to finance the building in the Sanatorium site.
5.  The establishment of the institution in the projected location within the church compound would be exceptionally expensive, and the building would be facing the barracks of the Turkish soldiers in the military fortifications near the Citadel.[37]

A year passed and no decision had yet been taken about the site for the institution for girls wishing to study in a dormitory facility. The society members in Jerusalem tried every possible way to persuade their colleagues in London to approve their proposals. In March 1889, Conrad Schick formulated a proposal to build a girls' school on the Sanatorium site with a new hospital next to it. Schick also attached to his proposal an estimate regarding the construction costs. Three months later the London committee agreed to the proposal and approved the erection of an educational institution outside the city, and at the same time they submitted a request in Constantinople for a *firman* to build it.[38]

It took two more years, until March 1891, for the *firman* to be received and for Conrad Schick to be able to go out to the construction site. After the foundations were laid, a festive cornerstone ceremony took place on 23 May, Queen Victoria's birthday, with the participation of most of the Protestant community in Jerusalem. The Anglican bishop, Popham Blyth, and the British consul, John Dickson, inserted within the foundations of the entrance gate to the building two scrolls with the names of the community members in Jerusalem and those of the society leaders in London. On 3 November 1892 the new school for girls was opened with an impressive ceremony.[39]

## SAFED

Ben-Zion Friedman [*sic*] ... sauntered about through the alley ways of Safed with a swaggering gait. He had a luxurious apartment in the new building of the Mission House and added another wing to it. In his courtyard there were all sorts of strange things that no eye had ever beheld. There were swings and cradles hung between one tree and another, cages of colourful birds, a small monkey tied to a chain, and a parrot that spoke English … The people of Safed have never seen such wonders before. The courtyard seemed like an enchanted garden. In the afternoon hours the apostate and his tall wife, dressed in silks, and a few other English people could be seen sitting at their ease in the shade of spreading tree, at a table covered by a cloth of shiny whiteness, drinking tea and nibbling cakes, while servants waited upon them, and there was expensive china and gold and silver dishes scattered over the table, and Ben-Zion was contentedly smoking a thick cigar and laughing and enjoying himself. 'A righteous man suffers while the evil man benefits' – this phrase began to gnaw at the hearts of many … this apostate had entered the city like an evil wind, and there was no shield or protection from him.[40]

At the end of 1880 a large missionary delegation from Jerusalem, led by Hastings Kelk, went on a tour to examine the possibility of increasing its activities in the Galilee region. At the beginning of the new year, after visiting Haifa, Acre and Tiberias, the group stayed over for a few days in Safed. There they became aware of the sufferings of the settlers in the new agricultural colony of Safed Jews – Gai-Oni (today known as Rosh Pina). Since this productive experiment of their fellow citizens did not find favour in the eyes of the Safed rabbis, they placed a ban upon them and withheld their share of the charity funds. The distress of the settlers induced them to beg Hastings Kelk to register their lands in his name and thus obtain the protection of the British consular agent in Safed.

Kelk refused, but reported that some of them had shown an interest in the gospels and praised the pioneering settler movement, which encouraged a sense of self-reliance. During his stay in Safed, Kelk was favourably impressed by the spirit of tolerance flowing across the city and recorded that:

> *I would urge with all my powers the importance, the necessity, of taking up the work at Safet [sic] and Tiberias as early as possible.* Fanaticism has died away, and there is an earnest desire for education and some movement towards inquiry into the truth of Christianity … In considering the question how might this work be done, it seems to me plain that education, schools, must occupy a foremost place. And I believe a mission might be worked at comparatively little expense. If a school were opened in each place, there would be great facilities afforded for working it easily and well. In Safet we have already a house, which would for the time afford accommodation for the school and its master [emphasis in original].[41]

Kelk's visit to Safed in January 1881 and his optimistic reports from there, again stirred the interest of the London Society to renew its activities in the Galilee. The first practical measures were already taken in that same year, but sudden changes in the order of priorities delayed the opening of the mission station until 1884. The missionary Jacob Lotka (d. 1907), who had been expected to arrive there in 1881, was sent urgently to respond to the sudden state of distress among the Jews of Persia. Even Abraham Oczeret, who had been sent from Paris at the end of 1882, found himself delayed in Jerusalem, because of the flood of Jewish immigrants needing attention, instead of going on to Safed. It was only after the missionaries had responded to most of the urgent needs of the immigrants that Oczeret, together with Dr M.J. Franklin, also a converted Jew, was free to deal with the Safed project.[42]

In March 1884, a distinguished delegation set out from Jerusalem to facilitate matters for the opening of the Safed mission station. Among the members of the delegation were Hastings Kelk, the head of the London Society mission in Jerusalem, Dr Thomas Chaplin, director of the mission hospital in Jerusalem, the new missionaries Abraham Oczeret and Ben-Zion Friedmann (1852–1916), and the converted Jew Samuel Wiseman (1835–1920), who was the translator for the missionary society in Jerusalem. The delegation stayed in Safed for two days, rented another house for the mission station, and returned to Jerusalem. On 21 May, the society leaders in Jerusalem sent off Dr Franklin and Abraham Oczeret to take up permanent residence in Safed. Franklin served as doctor of the new mission station for only a few months until the society severed its connections with him in October 1884.

After his departure, Franklin's place was taken at the beginning of 1885 by N. Shadan (d. 1885), a native of Safed, who was put in charge of the medical department. Until his sudden death, Shadan did some good work, which lent credit to the mission. In March 1886 his place was filled by Dr Faris Sahyun, an Arab Protestant from Syria and a medical graduate of the American College in Beirut, who became the director of the medical department of the London Society mission in Safed.[43]

The sporadic manner in which the missionaries in Safed had worked until then, which could be said generally of all the London Society members in Palestine, was often calamitous. We must, of course, attribute this mode of behaviour also to the frequent changes and disturbances in its activities, which did not contribute to the stability needed for sensitive missionary work. It was diametrically opposed to the methods of the rival German mission in Palestine, which acted 'slowly but surely' and thus, perhaps, succeeded in deepening its impression.

In mid-1886 Abraham Oczeret fell ill, and Hastings Kelk, who had come for a visit to Safed, sent him to recuperate in Vienna. The converted Jew Ben-Zion Friedmann left Jerusalem to take his place for a short while, and then returned. Friedmann was a native of Russia who had immigrated to Palestine with his father many years earlier, lived for two years in Safed, and was even ordained there as a rabbi. He made friends with the society members and under their influence went over to the mission station in Jerusalem. From there he continued on to England to complete his studies at their institutions.

In December 1878 Friedmann was baptised, and in November 1882 he returned to Palestine and gained a reputation as a missionary who was especially liked by the Jews of Jerusalem. He was also highly esteemed in London Society circles, and more than once it was said of him that his characteristic, forthright style indicated that a great future was in store for him.[44] Only Ben-Zion Friedmann, who knew the Jewish community in Safed very well and devoted himself entirely to his work, managed, during the course of his 30 years of activity in the city, to turn the mission station into an institution worthy of its name. In August 1887 he had returned to Safed to become the permanent director of the mission station in the city.

Accompanying Friedmann to Safed was Elias Christopher Bardt, a converted Jew and an apprentice pupil of the School of Industry in Jerusalem. In spite of the fears of Friedmann's superiors that he might be received with hostility by his old acquaintances after they found out he had converted to Christianity, he was welcomed with warmth by his former comrades and he began to push forward the mission's concern. The colourful touch that his personality gave the city was noted by a citizen of those days:

> In the darkness of the night which spread through the narrow streets of the city of Safed, a great sorrow is to be found among the pious and the faithful. Standing beside the missionaries is that infuriating apostate, Ben-Zion Friedmann, who has succeeded in banishing souls from Israel. At midday, when the sacred city of Safed is bathed in the holiness of the Sabbath, the chimes of the Christian church bells would echo down the street to the door of the saintly Ari [Rabbi Isaac Luria]. The uncleanliness has grown stronger in the holy city.[45]

The mission station in Safed comprised at that time the mission house, the medical department and dispensary of Dr Sahyun, and the Book Depotfor which Bardt was responsible. In addition to all this, Friedmann set up a school for the Jewish girls of the city, and appointed his wife, Margaret Isabella James (1847–1927), to be its headmistress. In May 1889 Friedmann managed to conduct the first baptismal ceremony for a Jewish girl of 17, a pupil of the school. At the end of that year he was joined by his sister, Gisella Friedmann, a native of Fastov near Kiev. She stayed in Safed until 1891, when she was sent to England, where she was baptised and completed her education in London Society institutions. In May 1892 she returned to Safed and became a teacher at the school. When Margaret James retired, Gisella took over the position of headmistress until she left Palestine in June 1914.[46]

During 1890 Dr Sahyun was forced to leave the Safed mission, and he was replaced by the elderly Jerusalem missionary Alexander Robert Iliewitz (1815–95).[47] Iliewitz was a converted Jew who had arrived from the Mission Station in Bucharest in 1858 and served in the Mission Hospital in Jerusalem as Dr Chaplin's assistant. In spite of his advanced age, Iliewitz did wonders in Safed and his feats of accomplishment were described in a Jewish journal:

> The new doctor Iliewitz, an apostate Jew, who not long ago arrived here from Jerusalem, daily visits his patients in the house assigned to them, and also performs the duty of 'visiting the sick'. He works with diligence, and even in the middle of the night he will ride upon his donkey to visit the sick in their homes without charge. The man is old, and cannot go on foot, so he must ride everywhere that he has to go. Medicinal herbs for healing are also provided without money.[48]

In June 1893 Dr Ernst Masterman replaced Iliewitz, who returned for a few months to Jerusalem and then retired at the end of the year. As soon as Masterman arrived he sent the London Society leaders his impressions of the importance of Safed as a mission station. The main point he made was the urgent need for a real hospital. Its vital importance was based on his own estimate that there were 30,000 inhabitants in the city (actually, there were only 10,000 at that time), half of whom were Jews, and according to him:

> There is not one single Hospital in the whole town. Such a state of things does not exist elsewhere in Palestine. Practically, all the large

towns in the country have well-appointed Medical Missions; but these are no good to those really ill in Safed, as a journey even to so near a place as the Scotch Mission [Hospital] in Tiberias, can only be made by difficult mountain roads … Tiberias (4,000 inhabitants). Here the Scotch now have a Hospital, and are building a new and substantial one on the shores of the lake … In Nazareth (7,500 inhabitants), the Edinburgh Missionary Society has a long-established Medical Mission, with a small Hospital. At Nablous (20,000 inhabitants) [should be 13,000] the C.M.S. has a flourishing Medical Mission, only recently started, but with a Hospital and a salaried nurse. At Haifa (8,000 inhabitants), I understand our Bishop has a small Hospital attached to his Medical Mission. At Jaffa (23,000 inhabitants) there is, as you know, a long-established Medical Mission Hospital, with a large staff of nurses. The Roman Catholics also have a fine Hospital. At Hebron (10,000 inhabitants) Mrs. Meredith has also Hospital premises, and a Scotch doctor … is now at Constantinople taking his diploma preparatory to taking charge. The Jews are also building a small Hospital there. I quote the above to show that these towns (though all smaller than Safed [*sic*]) have well-appointed Medical Missions, with Hospitals; while we in Safed, though having so long established a work there have no Hospital, in spite of the fact of the needs being much greater.[49]

This strongly worded report reached London and attracted a great deal of attention. As a result of its publication, explicit instructions were sent out to obtain a *firman* for building 'a small hospital' on land belonging to the London Society in Safed. However, the success of the medical enterprise in the city led to a change of plan, and attempts were made to locate an additional plot of land to build a more spacious hospital. In order to carry out this project, Dr Walter Henry Anderson (1869–1937), a native of Burton-upon-Trent, England, was appointed to head the medical department so that Masterman would be free to return to his duties in Jerusalem. As soon as he arrived, in April 1894, Anderson took up his position with great energy and declared that he saw his position in Safed as his vocation in life. His first recommendation was to open a small hospital of six beds immediately, and at the same time to continue in the efforts to set up the large hospital that was projected. The London Society approved of his proposal and at the end of 1895 he rented a building to be used as a hospital for a period of three years, which was opened in February 1896.[50]

*The Scottish Mission in Safed*

A number of Scottish missionary societies were engaged in missionary work among the general population in Palestine, including the Jews. One of these – the Mission of the United Free Church of Scotland – joined up with other missionary circles in Safed as a natural extension of its activities in Tiberias.[51] The founder of the Scottish Mission in Tiberias was Dr David Watt Torrance (1862–1922) of Glasgow, who had settled in Tiberias in 1885. The oppressive heat of the summer months forced Dr Torrance to spend the season in Safed, where he rented a house. He very soon realised the importance of this city, which justified setting up an independent Scottish mission. Dr Torrance knew about the work being done by the London Society in Safed, but thought that the Scottish mission should not ignore the vital need of a presence there and that there was place in the city for another mission station. In his words, there was place for 'not only a second, but a third and a fourth'.[52]

The intrusion of the Scots in Safed began to raise complaints among the London Society ranks immediately following the publication at the end of 1888 of the first indications that the Scottish mission intended to set up a summer station, which would be active during the summer season. The secretary of the London Society quickly sent a letter to the committee of the Scottish society to refresh their memory regarding the understanding that he believed had existed between the two missionary societies, in which the Scottish missionaries saw Tiberias as 'their' territory while the English missionaries considered Safed 'our' territory. Simultaneous activities by two similar organisations in the same city would be construed by the Jewish population as rivalry which would harm the common missionary effort.[53]

The secretary of the Scottish mission did not delay in responding with a well-reasoned letter. He began by saying that in 1883, when the Scottish mission decided to work in Palestine, Safed was not yet staffed by the British missionaries. In spite of this, in view of the British interest in Safed, the Scots began working in nearby Tiberias and chose the Galilean village of Peki'in as a refuge in the summer season. But, after it became clear that it was not possible to use Peki'in for this purpose, Dr Torrance decided to stay in Safed instead. Since in recent years, the doctor found the conditions in the city to be insupportable during the hot summer months, sometimes bordering upon a situation of life or death, the Scottish mission decide to improve his living conditions there and to strengthen their base in Safed. Nevertheless, they declared that they would endeavour to play fair with their British colleagues.[54]

These letters were the opening shot in a lengthy series of written exchanges between the two missionary societies, which dealt with the attempts to gain precedence in Safed. The letters sent by the Scottish side were concerned with putting forward suggestions in a delicately formulated manner that the British concentrate their efforts in the area of Judaea and allow the Scottish mission to work in the Galilee region.[55] The London Society rejected these hints outright and hurriedly declared that it did not have the slightest intention of deserting the mission station in Safed.

At the beginning of the 1890s the arguments over principles became a quarrel over territory, involving the control of some land and buildings that would either allow or prevent the expansion of the missionary institutions belonging to the British and Scottish missions in Safed. In 1895 the conflict reached a climax. Legal stratagems were employed on both sides with the aim of gaining a hold upon land adjoining both mission stations in the city, and the written exchanges became increasingly caustic. For example, the Scottish representative in Tiberias complained about the tone of the letter sent by Dr Anderson, the British doctor in Safed, and even threatened that the position taken by the London Society members would cause a 'scandal' in the British Isles.[56] At the same time, the leaders of the societies in London and Edinburgh conducted a dialogue between themselves and even met together to resolve the dispute. However, the conflict ended in the summer of 1895, when the Scots managed to acquire the contested plot of land. Apparently, this local triumph in the struggle for precedence in Safed, though it was not settled at that time, already heralded the total control of the Scottish mission over London Society property in the city by 1921.

## JAFFA

The direct cause for the renewal of the London Society missionary activities in Jaffa was the wave of Jewish immigration at the beginning of the 1880s. In July 1882, Friedländer arrived at the port city of Jaffa and met a group of Jews who had just arrived from Russia and felt that their vocation lay in agricultural settlement. To avoid direct confrontation with Jewish leadership in Jerusalem, he did not send these immigrant enquirers directly to the society institutions there, but hinted to them that there was a converted Jew living at the mission house in Jaffa who extended help to immigrants.[57] This man, Moritz Hall (1835–1914), who had not yet been accepted into the ranks of the society, wished to assist newly arrived Jews on a private basis. Hall was one of the most prominent figures in the Jaffa of those days, and is described in the diary of his neighbour, Mordechai Ben-Hillel Hacohen, in the following manner:

> An old-timer of the neighbourhood [the German Colony in Jaffa] was Hall, father-in-law of Baron Ustinov [Plato von Ustinov (1840–1918), the grandfather of Sir Peter Ustinov], who had planted the large garden and built the Hotel [du Parc]. This man, Hall, was a converted Jew, a native of Poland, who had become a Christian when he was young, and became an emissary of the Mission in the land of Cush [Africa], the state of the Abyssinians [Ethiopia]. There he married a native woman, came to Palestine and settled there, becoming one of the founders of the colony … [58]

When the harsh realities of life in Palestine began to take their effect upon the immigrants, some of them started congregating around Moritz Hall's door. He went up to Jerusalem to consult the members of the mission station and it seems that, at this juncture, the ties between him and the London Society were formalised. As a result of this meeting he returned to Jaffa and borrowed a few tents from Baron Ustinov, his son-in-law, and he pitched the tents in the courtyard of the mission house to accommodate 30 people.[59]

The recognition of Jaffa's importance as a gateway through which the immigrants passed, and the shattered dreams of the Jewish masses who clustered within the courtyard of the mission house where Moritz Hall lived, led to the London Society's decision to renew its activities in the city. In April 1883, Leopold Paul Weinberg (1839–1915) arrived in Jaffa. He was a native of Russia and a converted Jew, and he began working out of his own home. The Jaffa missionary spent some of his time on the docks of Jaffa port, where he met thousands of Jewish refugees and Christian pilgrims, in most cases on board ship before they reached the shores of Palestine.

Weinberg broadened his field of activity, and in that same year he visited the new Jewish colony, Petach Tikvah, and was given a warm welcome. The work of the missionaries in general was done with greater ease in Jaffa, and in the 1890s they termed the manner in which they were received in the city as an 'open door'. The explanation given for this was that the city, which was not one of the four holy cities in the Land of Israel, was not allotted any of the traditional charity funds sent by the Jews of the Diaspora. Thus the commitment of the Jews in Jaffa to the rabbis of the Jewish community in Palestine, who had control over the distribution of the funds, was far weaker, and made them less hesitant about contacts with the missionaries.

The mission house was located in the German Colony north of Jaffa, near the 'Baron's Garden' – a charming botanical garden established by Baron Ustinov in his courtyard, in which there even was a small zoo. This became an attraction for all the Jaffa residents, and Weinberg took advantage of the fact that so many Jews were drawn there during the weekends to interest the visitors in the words of the gospel. Since this was the German Colony with a Protestant ambience, 'The Jews behave more politely.' It made Weinberg's work far easier, and he even set up an evening school in the mission house, which was attended by scores of Jewish citizens in Jaffa.[60] In the mid-1880s the activity of the Book Depot within the city was renewed, and many Jews who did not want the trouble of going all the way to the mission house in the German Colony visited Weinberg at the Book Depot. The institution was situated 'just in the midst of the bazaar, where the greatest part of the traffic goes on; and the people going backwards and forwards to the beach, pass that way'.[61]

At the beginning of the 1890s a renewed wave of immigrants intensified Weinberg's missionary activity, and the completion of the railway line to Jerusalem gave the city of Jaffa an added importance. For this reason, and in order to reinforce the mission station, James Edward Hanauer was transferred from Jerusalem to Jaffa in December 1893. In the following spring Hanauer sent a secret report on his activities in the previous three months, and transmitted his impressions of the Jewish population in Jaffa, which was so different from that of Jerusalem. Jaffa, as the transit station to and from Palestine and also the business and administration centre for the members of the Jewish colony settlements in the area, was inhabited by Jewish immigrants who belonged to that section of the population known as the new Jewish community. As Hanauer expressed it:

> I have found here a good many belonging to a class with whom I have hitherto very rarely come into contact, men who have received a good secular education in German schools and whom it is not easy

at first to distinguish from well-educated Germans. I have had conversations with several of these, but though they are polite and refined, and would not mind if they were (I even suspect some of them wish to be) taken for Christians, they are very far indeed from the Kingdom of God; and though one cannot class them with the openly profane and irreligious, yet they are certainly sceptics, who doubt the Divine inspiration of their own Scriptures.[62]

The arrival of a missionary of Hanauer's rank in Jaffa gave a boost to missionary work and placed this London Society mission station in the centre of another dispute, one among many others, which arose between the society and the Anglican bishop, Popham Blyth. On the day after Hanauer's arrival at his new residence in Jaffa, a letter was sent to the society's centre in London containing a proposal to set up an additional building in Jaffa on the basis of a plan drawn up by Conrad Schick, the Jerusalem architect and a member of the London Society. The plan was to renovate the stable adjoining the mission house in the German Colony and to convert it into a prayer hall and classrooms. (The building no longer exists, and it is now the site of a private parking lot in Tel Aviv.) A month later the society approved the project and also allotted the sum of £75 for its completion.[63]

The intention of the London Society to establish a prayer hall in the heart of the German Colony in Jaffa aroused much interest. When the construction work began, and it was discovered that technical obstacles would increase the building costs, most of the residents of the colony gave the project extensive support. The work was overseen by Bernard G.P. Heilpern (1846–1909), a converted Jew and London Society member, who was a Thomas Cook travel agent. Besides managing the construction work, Heilpern also volunteered to raise funds from his many client travellers arriving in Jaffa. Moritz Hall volunteered to provide the doors and windows, and Bishop Blyth sent a personal donation.[64]

In October 1894 the work was completed, and the new building was called 'Daughter of Zion' since the small community in Jaffa was a sub-community to the one on Mount Zion, Jerusalem. However, the prayer hall was not opened to the public because of a fierce dispute that broke out between Hastings Kelk, head of the London Society mission in Jerusalem, and the Anglican Bishop Blyth. The frequent clashes that occurred between the two institutions and between the two individuals were in this case caused by the bishop's demanding ownership of the new building. Apparently, Blyth made use of his donation of funds for the

11. The Book Depot in Jaffa

construction of the building, and tried through demanding ownership and other claims to drive a wedge between Kelk in Jerusalem and his colleagues in Jaffa, and in this way to take control of the entire mission station.[65] The bishop also took advantage of the fact that most of the building costs were covered by the residents of the German Colony, and he managed to gain the allegiance of certain people, such as Heilpern himself, in support of the demand to register the ownership in the name of the residents. The dispute soon carried beyond the borders of Palestine, and the London Society leaders made a clear-cut decision that the building would remain under its sole control and ownership. Oral and written exchanges were conducted over a period of time until finally a compromise was accepted in which the land and the prayer hall remained the property of the society, while the interior furnishings belonged to the Anglican community in the German Colony. The first prayer service conducted there on 21 November 1894, officially put an end to the controversy, but a bitter aftertaste remained in the relationship between the London Society and the Jerusalem bishopric.[66]

12. The Mission House in Jaffa

Hanauer continued doing valorous work in Jaffa, yet throughout his stay in the city he longed to return to the Jerusalem that he loved so much. The talented missionary made use of the opportunity provided by the periodic visit of Dr Thomas Chaplin on behalf of the London Society, and submitted a specific request to return with his family to the society's centre in the Holy City. A few months later, in April 1900, the society recognised the importance of his return to Jerusalem and acceded to his importunity. As his replacement in Jaffa, they sent Joseph Jamal (1852–1932), a native of Jerusalem and a member of a Greek Orthodox family who had been educated at the Bishop Gobat school and by the bishop's direction had worked at the Lepers Hospital in Jerusalem before joining the London Society.[67]

During 1902 the Book Depôt, the most prominent among the Jaffa Mission institutions at that time, was moved to a more central location near the large Jewish hotel situated on the road leading from the railway station to the city. In that same year, one of the London Society leaders, E.H. Lewis Crosby, visited Jaffa in the framework of his periodic tours among the mission stations in the world. He was impressed by the importance of the city as a missionary centre, and his main recommendations were to increase the pace of missionary work among the women in the city by sending out women missionaries, and also to set up a medical institution as a branch of the hospital in Jerusalem.[68]

On the eve of World War One, the London Society continued to conduct regular missionary activities in Jaffa concurrent with those in the mission stations of Jerusalem and Safed. The importance of the city as a gateway through which most of the Jewish immigrants passed was, as already stated, the main motive for its conducting activities especially there. At the end of the war, when the society's activities were reduced and the mission station in Safed was completely closed down, the society deliberately bought property in Jaffa. Apparently, the impression of the hordes of immigrants converging upon the mission station in the city before the war was still vivid in the minds of the missionaries. And so it came about that the London Society bought Baron Ustinov's Hotel du Parc (today a youth hostel and a community centre at the corner of Orbach and Bar Hoffman Streets), which is still used by the society as one of its holdings it continues to maintain in Israel.

HEBRON

Regular visits to Hebron were conducted each year. In 1886 a respectable delegation, including Hastings Kelk, the head of the mission in Palestine, Dr d'Erf Wheeler and other missionaries reached town. The group rented two rooms and remained in the city for a while. The main conclusion resulting from this visit was that the time had come to set up a permanent mission station in Hebron. In August 1889, another delegation of missionaries from Jerusalem rented a house in Hebron with the intention of turning it into a permanent base. The building, which was rented from a' well-respected Muslim, was located at the entrance to the 'Kasba' (labyrinth of houses) in the Jewish Quarter, yet the society did not manage to maintain a constant presence in the city. During a visit to Hebron at the beginning of 1893, the missionaries made use of the mission house placed at their disposal, and in October they paid another visit in the course of which they relinquished possession of this building because of poor sanitary conditions. In January 1894 they rented two rooms in a building that stood a little way outside the city, with the intention of buying it up entirely so as to save expenses. In spite of the distance of their new residence from the city centre, the missionaries expressed their satisfaction that the building was situated on an easy route to Jerusalem, that the water supply was good, and that, on the opposite side of the road, an important rabbi resided. They added that in the past six months, new and well-constructed buildings had already been set up in that area, and the missionaries thought it quite probable that in time a large Jewish neighbourhood would develop around the new mission house in Hebron. In their view, the society leaders should decide on appointing a representative to stay in the building on a permanent basis.

During 1894, additional visits were frequently made, and the mission house was used extensively. In August 1895 new hope arose when a society member, Louisa Jane Barlee (d. 1917), settled in Hebron. She remained in the city for six months, during which time she felt disappointed at the low level of response to her efforts from the Jewish population and was constrained to return to Jerusalem.[69]

Disappointment did not weaken the resolve of the society members in Palestine. From May 1900 regular monthly trips were made to Hebron, during which the missionaries occupied the building belonging to the society and were mainly engaged in offering assistance to the Jews of the city who needed medical care. Every four weeks, at noon on Monday, the emissaries would leave Jerusalem for Hebron, returning on Wednesday evening, which gave them two full mornings to work among the Hebron Jews. At the beginning of the twentieth century, the Scottish Mission established a strong presence in the city. As a result of this, and because of the firm attachment of the Hebron Jews to their own faith, the society confined itself to its regular visits and no longer tried to retain a hold upon the city.[70] The failure to set up a permanent mission station in Hebron emphasises even more strongly the feeling of impotence that sometimes overcame the London Society. Here, a short distance away from its power centre in Jerusalem, and after a time span of 50 years, it still was not astute enough to establish a permanent hold in the important Jewish centre of Hebron.

## THE AGRICULTURAL SETTLEMENT OF ARTOUF

When the people of Jerusalem began to extend their borders and to establish agricultural villages, an apostate called Friedländer used a 'modern' subterfuge to draw the Jews to apostasy: He bought the Arab village of Artouf in the mountains of Jerusalem, near Bab-el-

Wad, for the purpose of settling Jews there and converting them. Not a single person among the new settlers in Artouf became a Christian. It seems that agricultural work made their bodies healthy and also strengthened their souls ... and the missionaries abandoned the attempt.[71]

Another aspect of the high tide that overwhelmed the London Mission in Palestine following the wave of Jewish immigration in 1882, was the attempt to imitate the settlement enterprise of the Jewish community and to establish a missionary agricultural colony for the new immigrants. However, this was not the first time that members of the society had tried to set up an agricultural settlement in Palestine with the purpose of ameliorating the conditions in which the Jews lived and at the same time drawing them closer to the Christian faith. Already, in 1845, John Meshullam (1799–1878), a converted Jew and a native of London, had bought some land from the village of Artas south of Bethlehem. He and his family, together with other settlers, maintained an agricultural farm there as a private enterprise for several years.[72]

In 1855 a few members of the London Society, once again outside the society framework, began looking around in order to purchase a piece of land near Jaffa on which to found a 'model farm' intended as a habitation and source of living for converted Jews. Among the promoters of this venture and the person who bought the land in the autumn of 1856 was Albert Augustus Isaacs (1826–1903), then serving as assistant secretary of the London Society. Isaacs was a native of Berry Hill, Jamaica, and the son of a converted Jew who owned a coffee plantation there. He appointed Paul Hershon, who had been director of the House of Industry ten years earlier, to be in charge of the agricultural farm. Other missionary members of the society in Jerusalem also participated, including Erasmus Scott Calman, Ferdinand Christian Ewald, and David Albert Hefter (1819–96), a native of Dembrowa in Galicia. This 'model farm', which was run in a manner similar to the Society's House of Industry in Jerusalem, deteriorated in time and was later purchased by members of the German Templar Society.[73]

The idea to establish agricultural settlements for the first wave of Jewish immigrants was originally conceived by the society member Hermann Friedländer. At the end of a comprehensive report which reviewed the preparedness of the mission station and the abilities of his colleagues in Jaffa and Jerusalem to measure up to the challenge of the masses of Jewish refugees milling about the society's institutions, Friedländer expressed surprise at the attitude taken by the society towards Jewish settlements in Palestine. He listed the many applications made by immigrants disappointed with the false promises of the Jewish settlement institutions who had turned to him, and asked why the London Mission did not buy land and settle the newly arrived Jews on it. His report went on to note that he was aware of the general reluctance of the mission society to engage in 'secular activity' such as agricultural settlements, but he explained that in his view, through proper training and strict examination of the potential settlers, it would be possible to achieve success in the missionary field as well. The stumbling block was the lack of funds to realise his plans, and he therefore ended his report with a fervent question: 'Should not every Christian make an effort to further such an end?'[74]

In the summer of 1882, when the thin trickle of Jewish immigrants from Eastern Europe turned into a massive wave that flooded the society's institutions in Jerusalem, its leaders sanctioned the publication of an independent journal, *Tidings from Zion* dealing solely with the mission's affairs in Palestine, and its leading articles covered matters concerning the Jewish refugees. In all the issues published month after month, the idea for establishing an agricultural colony was circulated, and in time it began to take actual shape. In September, Friedländer addressed the crucial question as to the political problems that might be created by the project for a Christian colony. His opinion was that, in contrast with the plans for Jewish settlement, the missionary project was more suited to the interests of the Sublime Porte since it was meant to provide a solution for the distress of Jews already in the country and did not encourage further immigration.

A month later, Hastings Kelk, the head of the mission in Jerusalem, joined in the efforts to persuade the readers of the necessity for this project and offered practical suggestions for its fulfilment. He proposed setting up an aid society for Jewish immigrants, which would engage in raising funds for establishing a few colonies in which converted Jews, as well as those still faithful to their original beliefs, would live together in mutual tolerance. His suggestion was to buy plots of land in small batches from private hands and thus not arouse the anger of the Turkish authorities, which forbade carrying out extensive settlement projects. Towards the end of 1882 Kelk expressed confidence in the success of the envisaged project of the Jerusalem Mission and referred to their plans as a *fait accompli*. He utilised the journal to make a direct appeal to the reading public to contribute generously towards the purchase of suitable land. Settlement difficulties encountered by

Jewish organisations at the beginning of 1883 only increased the conviction of the missionaries of the necessity of establishing a Christian colony. Further support for this could be found in the fact that the original plan of Lawrence Oliphant to settle Jews in the Gilead region could not be realised.[75]

In the spring of 1883 the Jerusalem missionaries Kelk and Friedländer received two concrete proposals to buy land for the intended colony, and therefore thought that one of them should go to London to explain their needs at first hand. In April, Friedländer was summoned by the society institutions to London and his intention was to present the proposal for the establishment of a missionary colony to settle Jewish refugees. At the same time, he would ask the society to settle the outstanding debts of the mission station in Jerusalem and to transmit additional sums to cover future expenses. In July 1883 the London committee reached a decision as follows:

> That the Revs. A.H. Kelk and H. Friedländer be informed, that whatever sympathy they may show towards any colonisation scheme, the Committee feel very strongly that their position as Missionaries of the Society engaged in spiritual work, renders it not only inadvisable, but impossible for them to undertake any responsibilities or official position whatever connected with the same; but the Committee are prepared to take into consideration the spiritual charge of Jews located in any such colony in Palestine.[76]

The refusal of the London Society to take official responsibility for the colonisation project was resolved by setting up a separate fund. This would administer colony affairs and raise funds independently of the society, just as temporary aid funds had been set up before for other urgent needs. The organisation founded was called the 'Jewish Refugees' Aid Society' and its objectives were to buy land, to settle Jewish refugees on it and to enable them to subsist independently in the land of their forefathers, with the hope that the kindness bestowed upon them would make them more open to the influence of the Christian mission.[77]

It appears that the care of the immigrants in the projected colony was deliberately entrusted to a separate organisation, which was named so as to give no indication that it was a missionary society. On the front page of *Tidings from Zion* of November 1883, in an article on the establishment of the new colony, a 'Special Notice' inset in a vivid red colour was added, stating that, although the article might lead the readers to believe that the new colony was connected with the London Society, this was not the case.[78] Although the committee that headed this new society in Palestine included among its members some of the more prominent personalities then living in the country, they were not expected to be called upon to make actual decisions. These members were Noel Temple Moore (1833–1903), the British consul in Jerusalem; Johannes Zeller (1830–1902) of the Church Missionary Society; Dr Selah Merrill (1837–1909), United States consul in Jerusalem; Dr Thomas Chaplin, director of the London Society hospital in Jerusalem; Conrad Schick; Hastings Kelk, head of the London Society mission in Jerusalem; and Hermann Friedländer. Yet, in actual fact, the mission colony was owned by the London Society and administered by its members. All attempts to minimise this fact were of no avail.

In the spring of 1883, before approval was received from the society institutions in London, Friedländer already began to select suitable candidates from among the hundreds wishing to join the future colony. On 20 October, the House of Industry conducted the first founding session of the settlers, at which 60 heads of families were present. At this session a discussion was held about the regulations that had been set down by the society but that were repeatedly rejected by the settlers. Finally, at the end of the discussion, 46 families signed the revised version of the regulations and expressed their readiness to go out to the colony site immediately. The following is the set of regulations as they appeared in a Hebrew journal:[79]

1.  Each settler must pay 5 per cent every year from the total which the above Society expended for the house and land which is allotted to him.
2.  The settlers must give a tithe (10 per cent) of all the produce of the land to the agent appointed by the said Society, and the Society must pay the tax on the land to the government as law and custom of the state demands.
3.  The settlers must work the land by their own hands with the help of their families. Only in particular cases and with special permission of the agent, will they be allowed to employ foreign workers.
4.  All those wishing to be settlers must state truthfully before the Committee here in Jerusalem whether they have any cash funds or other property, and its value, so that the Committee can estimate how much they need in advance to buy seed, animals and other implements required for tilling the soil.
5.  Until harvest time, the Committee will extend a loan of 2.5

piasters a day for each person in the household of any settler who is totally impoverished and has nothing to feed himself and his family.

6. All loans from the Committee to the settlers either for items needed for work or for subsistence, must be repaid by the settler to the agent appointed by the Committee, and the agent will set the periods of repayment according to his judgement of the situation for each member of the colony.

7. The settlers may purchase their allotment of land for permanent possession by paying its price over a period of twenty-one years, after which this land will be their inheritance forever.

8. If a settler has already begun paying the price of his land for a period of some years, and wishes to leave his land before the twenty-one years have expired, the Committee must return his money after all the debts owed to the Committee have been deducted.

9. The settler is forbidden to engage in trade or purchases in the colony for anything besides his work on the land, unless he has permission from the agent.

10. Any quarrel or dispute between settlers will be brought before the agent who will either arbitrate or present the matter to the Committee here in Jerusalem.

11. All rules and regulation set down by the agent for the cleanliness of the homes and courtyards ... the maintenance of the houses and yards and the repair of the roadways, must be observed by the settlers in total compliance.

12. Any complaint or grievance by a settler against the agent will be stated clearly in a letter addressed to the Committee in Jerusalem through the secretary of the Committee, Rev. [Hastings] Kelk.

13. The Committee in Jerusalem has the sole power to reclaim the land allotted to the settler if he causes any dispute among the settlers or because he does not abide by the rules and regulations of the agent and the Committee. The settler must pay all the debts he owes the Committee and he will make no claim or demand for his labour and toil during the past years.

14. All children of the settlers from the age of six to fourteen are obliged to attend the school which will be opened in the colony ...

15. If a member of the colony becomes impoverished because of a long and fatal illness and is reduced to extreme penury, all the settlers must help and support him as advised by the agent and four other settlers chosen by him.

16. The colonists must aid and assist all the widows and orphans as stated by the agent and the four settlers chosen to oversee such matters …
17. The Jewish Refugees' Aid Society will act speedily to build hospitals for men and women, but the settlers must pay for the doctor themselves, and also for the equipment needed inside the hospital.
18. The Committee will do its best to find an experienced doctor among the settlers who is proficient in medical knowledge, and will provide the budget to pay the fees for each visit.

The land on which the colony was established had belonged for the past few years to the Spanish vice-consul in Jerusalem, Alexander Spagnolo, and was part of the lands of the Arab village Artouf, on which the village of Naham, in the vicinity of Bet Shemesh, stands today. An agreement was signed on 20 October 1883 between Spagnolo and the missionaries Kelk and Friedländer for the transfer of ownership of 1,250 acres to the Jewish Refugees' Aid Society for the price of 45,000 francs (about £1,800).[80] Four days later, on 24 October, the agreement came into force and the establishment of Artouf, the London mission colony in Palestine, was publicly declared. About half of the new settlers together with scores of pupils from the House of Industry and the Inquirer's Home came down on foot from Jerusalem to the site of the colony in order to establish the claim and to perform the ceremony for settling the land.

In the first stage, the colony contained 150 Jews, and each family received a plot of about 40 acres, which was used mainly to grow wheat and barley. At the same time the farmers became owners of livestock – a cow and a pair of oxen of a good breed – installed in a central stable, in addition to acquiring a share in the chicken pens and beehives.[81] The settlers first lived in long wood cabins, but it soon became clear that the extreme heat made the living quarters in the colony unbearable. Even the missionaries from Jerusalem avoided staying at the site itself because of the difficult conditions, and chose to pay only weekend visits to the settlers. Activity at the site very soon slackened, and the only official persons remaining there permanently were the directors of the colony. The fact that these directors were frequently replaced testifies to the difficulties in making the colony a place for stable residence. Moritz Hall, who had in the meantime joined the ranks of the London Society, directed the colony during the first year.[82] On the first anniversary of the establishment of Artouf, Hall left and was replaced by W. Gallatin, who remained at his post until the summer of 1887, when he was dismissed and replaced by Reuben Tchertkoff. He was a surgeon by profession, a converted Jew and a native of Russia who had come with his family to settle in Artouf from its founding day, and accepted the position of colony director at the beginning of July 1887.

By the summer of 1888 there was some improvement in the condition of the colony since the long-awaited permit for the construction of permanent housing was finally received, and the London Society members began to raise funds for this purpose. At that time there were rumours about the future railway line that was to run between Jaffa and Jerusalem. A main way station was planned for a site near Artouf, which would make access to the colony easier.[83] The sense of renewed hope was felt beyond the confines of this small Anglican community, reaching as far as Hebron. In May 1889, 12 Jews of Hebron who had families to support sent a letter to the chairman of the Artouf committee pleading to be included in the agricultural project:

> To the most charitable and noble Secretary of the Refugees'Aid Society.
>
> Dear Sir,
>
> Relying upon your boundless pity, we take courage to present this petition to you in order to represent to you the distress from which we all suffer. Our souls are famished, our offspring and infants ask for bread, and in our hands there is neither bread nor water, nor is it in our power to earn even one piece of silver. Having, dear Sir, heard that you possess lands which you give to be tilled, planted and sown, we desire to become tillers of the ground, in order to enjoy the labour of our hands. Place before your eyes the great and good work which you will do in reviving so many souls by the works of your pity.[84]

This petition was viewed by the society circles with a suspicion that proved to be well founded when the missionaries next visited Hebron. In the autumn of 1890 it became clear that the petition was submitted to put pressure upon the rabbis of the town to grant the 12 signatories some building land in the city of Hebron itself.[85]

In the summer of 1890, after many delays, the construction of permanent housing for the Artouf settlers was begun. From the very outset there were difficulties in obtaining workmen because of the competition created by the railway construction and the high prices being paid by its builders. Therefore, it was only during

1892 that the building of six stone houses was finally completed. But in spite of the relative improvements in the conditions for access to the colony and in living quarters, the number of settlers dwindled. In 1893 only four families were still living in Artouf and by 1894 only one single settler was left. The missionaries in Jerusalem found it hard to find additional candidates, even though the land and the living quarters placed at the disposal of the farmers were free of charge. The London Society ceased its fundraising and sent three of its leading members to review the situation and decide what could be done. After a close examination of the recently created situation, the three men recommended that the London Society close down the colony and sell all its assets. The society members in Jerusalem then contacted representatives of the Jewish community in Bulgaria and in September 1895 they signed an agreement with its accredited agent, Yitzhak Aryeh, to transfer the Artouf colony with all its assets to the Bulgarian community for the sum of £3,500 to be paid in instalments into the London Society account.[86] In the summer of 1900 the balance of £1,750 was paid, with two thirds of the amount transferred to cover the expenses for building the new hospital in Jerusalem and the remaining third to the fund for setting up a hospital in Safed.

The failure of the Jewish colony at Artouf sponsored by the London mission in Jerusalem resulted from the lack of Jewish resolve to put down roots in the place as time went by. Besides the difficult objective conditions in the colony, and the new settlers' lack of training in agricultural work, which was typical for every Jewish settlement enterprise in nineteenth-century Palestine, the failure of Artouf had two other causes. The first was the policy of the London Society, which did not provide for a fixed monetary allowance. The settlers were engaged in agricultural work and transferred the produce to the management in exchange for which they received their wages as well as a modest stipend to supplement their income. This arrangement was based on the society's previous experience, in which Jews who received a fixed monthly income remained subservient to it and did not become independent workers.

The second cause was in the method used for conversion in Artouf. The Jews of the colony were located far from the Jewish city centres and were not under the influence of the Jewish community leaders, and therefore could be approached directly and without hindrance by those preaching for conversion. This led to an increasing rate of desertion. The hopes of the society leaders for the success of their settlement attempt, as well as their expectations for mass conversions, were disappointed. However, as customary with them, on summing up the enterprise they noted that there was no evil without some good, and that the transfer of the colony to the Bulgarian Jewish community conformed to the aims of the society, which were to support the settlement of Jews in Palestine and to make them economically independent.[87]

## VISITS TO THE JEWISH SETTLEMENTS

After the establishment of the first Jewish settlements in the 1880s, periodic visits were paid to them by society members from Jerusalem. When the mission stations in Safed and Jaffa became well established, the missionaries there also paid frequent visits to the settlements and they soon divided up their areas of responsibility. The settlements of Judaea and the southern Sharon region were patronised by the Jaffa mission station, while those of the Galilee region down to Zichron Ya'akov were visited by the missionaries from Safed.[88]

For instance, in March 1887 a delegation headed by Ben-Zion Friedmann visited Ekron. The missionaries were very impressed with the flourishing colony and were received with friendliness in spite of their report of a strong sense of Jewish spiritual power among the settlers, surpassing not only other Jewish settlements but even that of the Jews in Jerusalem. In June 1889 Friedmann visited Zichron Ya'akov and attributed the pleasant welcome he received in the settlement, as compared with his previous visit there, to the replacement of the Baron's officer in charge. At the beginning of 1894 Friedmann visited this settlement once more and noted the possibility of more extensive missionary activity there. He thought it might be worth while opening a book depot and entrusting it to a society member who was serving as a missionary in nearby Haifa.

Generally speaking, the missionaries were received in the Jewish settlements in a pleasant manner and were offered hospitality. This was possible because most of the settlers had only recently arrived from Europe and had been exposed to missionary visits in their countries of origin so that they showed tolerance towards them in Palestine as well. The London Society members gave great importance to their visits, but they appear to have made a wrong assessment of their prospective success. In spite of the friendly welcome they received, their attempts to draw the settlers towards the Christian faith were ineffective, and the London Society was unable to find a foothold even temporarily in any one of the settlements.

The missionaries made frequent visits even among the Jewish settlements near Jerusalem and Jaffa. In the 1880s, when the Jewish community in Jerusalem began increasingly to move outside the walls and to build new residential neighbourhoods, the society emissaries continued to visit them regularly. In most cases they were received by the Jews in these suburbs with greater ease, which could be ascribed to the physical distance from the zealous core of religious extremism in the Jewish quarter.

## THE RESPONSE TO JEWISH IMMIGRATION

The period opens in turmoil with the arrival of multitudes of Jewish refugees in Palestine. This called for a response that contradicted the normally accepted principles of the London Society. In its earlier contacts with Jewish communities in Europe, the society cautiously entered their neighbourhoods, gained their trust and made guarded attempts to convert a few individuals in the community. Unlike in Europe, the staunch allegiance of the Jews in Palestine to their faith and their isolation from foreign influences sometimes entailed the granting of financial benefits to a few Jews in total opposition to the declared policy of the society.

The hundreds of immigrants who crowded, at their own initiative, around the doors of the society's institutions in Jerusalem and Jaffa, without any need for persuasion, required an instant response. The enormous potential and the desire to take advantage of this unique opportunity made it necessary to allocate immense resources to the mission stations in the country, including the transfer of funds directly into the pockets of the immigrants. The Society was fortunate in having a talented representative in Jerusalem who succeeded in coping with the situation and taking in most of those seeking refuge. Acting for the first time contrary to the society's policies, Kelk and his assistant Friedländer exhausted the funds in the account and even went into debt to assist the immigrants, walking a tightrope that nearly led them into a state of financial betrayal of trust with their superiors in London.

The dramatic events made it necessary to make a reassessment of society policy and a distribution of authority between the management in London and those working in Palestine. The mission affairs in Palestine were conducted by three bodies. Once a year the London committee met in full session for a few days, listened to the reports of its emissaries throughout the world and laid down the main lines of action to be taken by the society in the coming year. Once a month a group of personages who formed the executive council made detailed, practical decisions and responded to the immediate needs of the mission stations in Palestine. And, once a week in Jerusalem, the local committee comprising senior missionaries met to conduct the current affairs of the community and of the mission institutions. The links between the society management in London and its members in Jerusalem were very close and included an almost daily exchange of letters. Generally, most of the decisions were made in London, and the head of the Jerusalem mission's freedom to act was very limited.

Another event that occurred during this period that demonstrates the relationship between London and Jerusalem was the founding of the agricultural colony, Artouf. The establishment of Jewish settlements, the stream of immigrants rushing towards the mission institutions and the necessity of responding to their needs brought about the initiative to establish an independent missionary colony. In principle, the society was opposed to the establishment of agricultural colonies for its converts and held to this principle even when the proposal was sent from Jerusalem. Once more, it was Hastings Kelk who, by the force of his personality and his administrative abilities, managed to bypass this policy and to set up a separate body which both placated the London Society and provided the answer for the immediate needs in Palestine.

## NOTES

1. *Havazeleth* (1894), p. 168.
2. *Jewish Intelligence* (March 1882), p. 53.
3. Ibid.
4. Taubenhaus, E. *One Man's Way: A Dreamer and Fighter in the City of the Kabbalists* (Haifa: 1959), pp. 131–2 (Hebrew).
5. *Jewish Intelligence* (October 1882), p. 258: letter by Friedländer in Jaffa at the end of July 1882; ibid. (March 1883), p. 50.
6. Ibid. (August 1883), pp. 206–7.
7. *Report*, 77 (March 1885), p. 96. The use of the 'agricultural' metaphor in order to describe their hopes was apparently a result of the fact that at that time the agricultural colony that the missionaries had established at Artouf was flour-

ishing, and its success then raised the anticipations of the London Society members in Jerusalem. On the Artouf enterprise, see below.

8.   *Jewish Intelligence* (July 1883), pp. 177–9. The fund ceased its functions in May 1884, and the source of financial support for the immigrants was henceforth the current budget of the mission station in Jerusalem.

9.   *Report*, 84 (March 1892), p. 107.

10.   It seems that Blyth had almost foreseen his appointment to the bishopric. In the summer of 1885, in a letter to the secretary of the London Society regarding the need for expanding the educational enterprises and their residential facilities in Jerusalem, he already referred to the problem of the living quarters provided in Jerusalem for the bishop to be elected. See, Bodleian, Dep. Cmj, d.55: Blyth to William Fleming (1829–1900), 22 June 1885; on Blyth, see mainly E. Blyth, *When We Lived in Jerusalem* (London: 1927), pp. 1–12; Lambeth, MS.2233: brief account of the bishop and his work in *Palestine Post* (6 April 1937).

11.   Bodleian, Dep. Cmj, d.55: reprint of the London committee resolutions regarding the renewed establishment of the bishopric, dated 22 April 1887. At the same time, the Church Missionary Society adopted similar resolutions. Its directors were willing to contribute their share in the financial support of the bishopric on condition that the new bishop be elected with their approval and cooperate with their members in Palestine. See ibid., d.53: memorandum classified as 'private and confidential' entitled 'The Jerusalem Bishopric: Memorandum by the Secretaries of C.M.S.', dated 10 January 1887.

12.   *Jewish Intelligence* (June 1887), p. 91.

13.   St Albans: a pamphlet published as a report on the activities of the bishopric in Jerusalem, entitled *The Primary Charge of the Right Reverend George Francis Popham Blyth, D.D. Bishop of the Church of England in Jerusalem and the East* (London: 1890), pp. 2–3; another pamphlet in the series, entitled *The Second Triennial Charge of the Right Reverend George Francis Popham Blyth, D.D. Bishop of the Church of England in Jerusalem and the East* (London: 1893), p. 8.

14.   Lambeth, MS.2232: sketches by Conrad Schick and an addendum in his handwriting entitled *Notes of the accompanying drawings*, Jerusalem, 13 January 1888.

15.   Bodleian, Dep. Cmj, c.30: protocols 1886–1889, resolutions dated 3 February 1888, 11 February 1888.

16.   Ibid., d.55: response to the attacks upon the London Society, entitled 'A Reply', Toronto, 26 March 1888. The minimal change that Hastings Kelk agreed to make to improve the appearance of the church was to install church bells in its tower in addition to the small one which, by order of the Turkish authorities, was placed in 1854 on an adjacent building and not on the church itself. See *Jewish Missionary Intelligence* (August 1898), p. 114, where there is a quotation from Conrad Schick in the *Palestine Exploration Fund Quarterly Statement*, July 1898.

17.   Bodleian, Dep. Cmj, d.54: pamphlet published in 1891 by the Church Missionary Society in response to harsh publications against it by the Anglican bishop in Jerusalem, Popham Blyth: 'C.M.S. in Palestine' pp. 1–2.

18.   Lambeth, MS.2232: history of the Jerusalem and the East Mission entitled 'List of Bishop Blyth's Foundation with Dates', pp. 94–153. Popham Blyth resigned his position as Anglican bishop in Jerusalem on the eve of World War One, and died in England a few months later. A quotation from the letter of resignation dated 23 May 1914 can be found in the *Guardian* (4 June 1914).

19. *Havazeleth* (1897), p. 288.

20. *Jewish Intelligence* (August 1889), p. 113. It seems that the donor was Lady Victoria Evans-Freke. See ibid. (October 1889), pp. 158–9: letter dated 24 August 1889.

21. Wheeler studied medicine in Madras, India, and received his MD only at the beginning of 1892 after he had already served as director of the hospital in Jerusalem. See St Albans, Applications and Appointments, Vol. A, No. 171. On Masterman, see *Report*, 85 (March 1893), p. XI: Appointments, Removals, &c., of Missionaries from 1 April 1892 till 31 March 1893.

22. Bodleian, Dep. Cmj, c.250: Pite's original plans from the Royal College of Arts in London; ITAC: pamphlet entitled 'Fifty-two Years Medical Work in Jerusalem', pp. 38–44, where there are additional sketches with detailed annotations of the various sections of the building in an article by Dr Wheeler, Jerusalem, 7 March 1892.

23. *Jewish Missionary Intelligence* (July 1897), p. 105: detailed description of the building sections and their functions as addendum to the panoramic photograph of the hospital. See ibid. (January 1898), pp. 8–9.

24. Ibid. (September 1895), p. 145; ibid. (May 1895), p. 73.

25. Bodleian, Dep. Cmj, d.25: invitation to the inauguration events of the new hospital, signed by Hastings Kelk and d'Erf Wheeler. The building was supposed to have been inaugurated earlier, but because of the illness of Dr Wheeler, the director of the new hospital, who was staying in Damascus to recuperate, the official opening was postponed; ibid.: programme of the inauguration ceremony; *Jewish Missionary Intelligence* (July 1897), pp. 101–10: detailed report on the conduction of the ceremony and the speeches.

26. On the Bnei-Israel Association see mainly Grajewski, *The Struggle*, n.p., 'The War of the Bnei-Israel Association against the Activities of the Mission' (Hebrew); Shirion, I. *Memoirs* (Jerusalem: 1943), p. 40 (Hebrew).

27. On the stormy demonstrations and bans against the hospital see FO, 195/1984: a series of exchanges between John Dickson (1847–1906), British consul in Jerusalem, and Philip Henry Wodehouse Currie (1834–1906), the ambassador in Constantinople, and other documents in Hyamson, *The British Consulate*, II, No. 385–90, pp. 505–14. On the watchers stationed by the Jewish community leaders at the gates of the hospital to prevent Jewish patients from entering the institution, see FO, 195/2028: Percy d'Erf Wheeler, director of the hospital to Dickson, 14 July 1898 in Hyamson, *The British Consulate*, II, addendum to No. 393, pp. 516–18.

28. *Ha-Zevi* (24 June 1897).

29. *Jewish Missionary Intelligence* (March 1898), pp. 40–1.

30. Ibid. (August 1897), p. 115: the decree translated into English, signed by the Chief Rabbi.

31. Bodleian, Dep. Cmj, c.125: transfer of ownership documents marked F. Sanatorium; ITAC, Jerusalem Local Committee Minutes Book, I, No. 73 (18. November 1862).

32. Frumkin, I.D. *Selected Writings of Israel Dov Frumkin* (Jerusalem: 1954), p. 129 (Hebrew).

33. Friedländer was accused mainly for his pretence of spending large amounts of money for the benefit of the Jewish refugees and for the current upkeep of the mission station, which were in fact not spent at all. When Friedländer was recalled to London and met the society accountants, he refused to provide explanations for these accusations as well as for the suspicions against him

that he sold art objects produced by the House of Industry and retained the proceeds. On this affair, see the collection of personal documents: Bodleian, Dep. Cmj, d.140: internal certificate produced by the leaders of the society summarising the accusations, entitled 'Resignation of the Rev. H. Friedländer', dated August 1886; ibid.: letter of warning by Fleming, secretary of the society, to Friedländer urging him to respond to the accusations, dated 22 June 1886; ibid.: copy of the resolution by the society directors dealing with the acceptance of Friedländer's resignation, dated 9 July 1886; ibid.: detailed letter from Friedländer to Ralph W. Harden, secretary of the London Society branch in Dublin, dated 9 September 1886, in which the former responds point by point to all the accusations raised against him; ibid.: Harden to Friedländer, 30 September 1886; ibid.: Friedländer to Harden, 4 October 1886. Friedländer left the ranks of the London Society and tried to return to Palestine as an independent missionary and to take advantage of his ties with the Jewish community. On this subject, see Bodleian, Dep. Cmj, d.140: pamphlet for support and fundraising on behalf of Friedländer, entitled 'Extension of Mission Work among the Jews in Palestine', published on 12 August 1886. Friedländer died in 1886, but the affair did not end there. In May 1891 a claim was submitted to the head of the London Society mission in Jerusalem for the debts incurred by Friedländer during his period of employment by the society. The claimant was not reimbursed, but the discussions regarding the demand for payment occupied the parties for another year. See ITAC, Jerusalem Local Committee Minutes Book, III, 29 May 1891, Nos 351–3; No. 354 (31 March 1892).

34. On Hanauer, see detailed autobiographical notes, ITAC, Diary Notes – Reminiscences, pp. 1–27; St Albans, Applications and Appointments, Vol. A, No. 117.
35. *Jewish Intelligence* (August 1890), p. 122.
36. Ibid. (November 1889), p. 175; ibid. (December 1889), p. 178; ibid. (January 1890), p. 6. Woodwork was carried out in the institution's workshop for outside customers in Palestine and abroad. Later on, the pupils made certain items for the German hospice, Auguste Victoria, on the Mount of Olives, and were even awarded a certificate of appreciation from Kaiser Wilhelm II.
37. ITAC, Jerusalem Local Committee Minutes Book, III, No. 187 (12 April 1888).
38. Ibid., No. 237 (7 March 1889); ibid., No. 167 (20 June 1889). In London, approval was given for the erection of the school on the eastern side of the Sanatorium, nearest the city, while the western side was designated for the future hospital building. In Jerusalem they tried to change this decision, giving the following arguments. If the hospital were built on the west side, the western winds would blow from it towards the school and harm the pupils. Moreover, near the eastern border of the compound there was a large Turkish building that would be a hindrance for the schoolgirls. The Turks were planning to build a hospital of their own near the western border, and would certainly not allow the construction of another hospital adjacent to it, and therefore it was preferable to erect the school there. The western side was situated on the Jaffa Road, making the school more easily accessible. See ibid., No. 268 (29 May 1891). The objections finally prevailed, and the institution was indeed erected on the western side of the compound.
39. Ibid., No. 350 (29 May 1891). The school building was destroyed in 1951 and the Mercazi Hotel was built on its site.
40. Bar-Yosef, Y. *Ir Ksuma* (Tel-Aviv: 1958), II, p. 8 (Hebrew).

41. *Jewish Intelligence* (January 1881), pp. 8–9. The house was built inside a vine-yard on the slopes of the Castle Hill overlooking the Jewish quarter. The land was acquired by Joseph Barclay, head of the Jerusalem mission, during his visit to the city in November 1867. See *Joseph Barclay*, p. 308: Diary of a Journey to the Galilee, 5 November 1867.
42. ITAC, Jerusalem Local Committee Minutes Book, I (16 May 1848).
43. Ibid., III, No. 5 (1 January 1886).
44. St Albans, Applications and Appointments, Vol. A, No. 51. On Friedmann more extensively, see the eulogy after his death in *Jewish Missionary Intelligence* (April 1916), pp. 47–9. Friedmann died on 1 January 1916 and was buried, as were some of his colleagues, in the courtyard of the Safed mission. Later on, when the mission house was destroyed, and the Mercazi Hotel was built on its site, the gravestones were transferred to a fallow field on a slope north of the entry road to the city. Several gravestones, among them those of Friedmann and his wife, are still lying there.
45. Taubenhaus, *One Man's Way*, p. 358.
46. Bodleian, Dep. Cmj, d.71: biography of Gisella Friedmann.
47. ITAC, Jerusalem Local Committee Minutes Book, III, No. 81 (19 May 1887), where doubts on the diligence of Dr Sahyun are listed in detail. The asser-tions and explanations that followed filled the pages of the London committee protocol file for a long while. Two years later, Dr Sahyun became involved in the murder case of a Jewish child in Safed. The doctor, who testi-fied during the investigation, gave the impression that he supported the view of the city governor rather than that of the Jewish community. On this subject, see ibid. Nos 249–63 (27 May 1889). These events did not, of course, add to the prestige of Dr Sahyun, but his departure was actually caused by a new Ottoman regulation that invalidated his licence to practise medicine.
48. *Hamagid* (9 January 1890), p. 13: article from Safed.
49. *Jewish Missionary Intelligence* (October 1893), p. 146. The population figures given in square brackets are taken from Ben-Arieh, Y. 'The Landscape of Palestine on the Eve of the Zionist Colonization', in I. Kolatt (ed.) *The History of the Jewish Community in Eretz-Israel since 1882: The Ottoman Period* (Jerusalem: 1989), pp. 75–141 (Hebrew).
50. *Report*, 86 (March 1894), p. XI: Appointments, Removals, &c., of Missionaries from 1 April 1893 till 31 March 1894.
51. The affiliation between the London Society and the Scottish mission began in the early nineteenth century. In September 1810 a group of people in Edinburgh had already volunteered to help the London Society through a penny-a-week campaign and the collective transfer of the donations to London. This group worked according to a system common to other societies in Britain in the nineteenth century called the 'Penny Society'. A year later, a branch of the London Society was opened in Leith, Scotland (Leith was a village near to Edinburgh, which was incorporated into the city in 1920). These two societies cooperated in order to assist the mother society in London. In 1818 all the supporters of the London Society gathered in Edinburgh at a joint conference and announced the establishment of the 'Edinburgh Society for Promoting Christianity Amongst the Jews', which would act in close affiliation with the London centre. In that same year another society was established in Glasgow for the same purpose and was called the 'Glasgow Society for Promoting Christianity Amongst the Jews'. In 1838 a conference was held under the patronage of the Church of Scotland,

which was aimed at uniting all Scottish mission societies that were concerned with Jews, and a year later these societies were merged and began to work together. On this subject, see mainly *Record of the Church of Scotland* (January 1902), pp. 26–7.

52. Ibid. (December 1902), p. 553; Livingstone, W.P. *A Galilee Doctor, being a Sketch of the Career of Dr. D.W. Torrance of Tiberias* (London: [1922]), pp. 84–5.

53. Bodleian, Dep. Cmj, d.63: William Thomas Gidney (1853–1909), secretary of the London Society, to the Scottish mission committee, 6 October 1888.

54. Ibid.: W. Affleck, secretary of the Scottish mission, to Gidney, 24 October 1888.

55. In the margin of the letter there is a handwritten notation by its British recipients that the letter implied 'early hints of pushing us out' of the Safed holdings; ibid.: J.H. Wilson to the London Society, 5 August 1892.

56. Ibid.: John Soutar to Anderson, 11 April 1895.

57. ITAC, Jerusalem Local Committee Minutes Book, II (7 February 1882).

58. Hacohen, M.B.-H. *My World* (Jerusalem: 1928), IV, p. 62 (Hebrew).

59. *Tidings from Zion*, I (17 July 1882), pp. 3–4: Friedländer to Kelk.

60. *Report*, 77 (March 1885), p. 103; ibid., 82 (March 1890), p. 117.

61. Ibid., 81 (March 1889), p. 108; ibid, 83 (March 1891), pp. 112–13.

62. *Jewish Missionary Intelligence* (July 1894), p. 102

63. Bodleian, Dep. Cmj, d.57: collection of documents entitled 'Copies of Minutes and Extracts from letters with reference to the Mission House at Jaffa – belonging to the London Society for promoting Christianity amongst the Jews': Hastings Kelk in Jerusalem to the secretary of the society in London, 13 December 1893; ibid.: resolution of the society directors and the sub-committee for Finance, 11 January 1894.

64. ITAC, Jerusalem Local Committee Minutes Book, II (24 April 1875). Later the chapel served most of the residents of the German Colony. Besides the converted Jews, the Templar residents also assembled there, returning to the folds of the Protestant Church until 1904 when they erected a church of their own nearby.

65. Bodleian, Dep. Cmj, d.57: Kelk to the secretary of the London Society, 15 November 1894. Kelk wrote explicitly that, 'The Bishop is now always on the watch to do something against us, and he thinks he has now found an opportunity.'

66. Ibid.: resolution of the London committee, 21 December 1894. A few weeks after the end of the affair, Kelk summed it up in a letter to London in which he wrote, 'I am sorry to say I do not trust the Bishop's word'; ibid.: Kelk to the secretary of the London Society, 10 January 1895.

67. St Albans, Applications and Appointments, Vol. A, No. 201. Hanauer served in Jerusalem for eight years and in March 1908 he was appointed as head of the Damascus mssion station for a few years. In 1920 he returned to Jerusalem, wrote one of the most charming books about the city, and remained there until his death in 1938.

68. Bodleian, Dep. Cmj, d.26: report by Crosby, 13 May 1902.

69. *Report*, 88 (March 1896), pp. 94–5.

70. On Scottish activities in Hebron see Bodleian, Dep. Cmj, c.105: report of their representatives there, entitled 'Deputies' Report', pp. 3–10; on the relations between the two societies after the Scottish based themselves in Hebron in 1900, see ibid., d.57: letter from Edinburgh to the secretary of the London Society, 7 October 1901.

71. Rivlin, A.B. *Jerusalem, the History of the Jewish People in the 19th Century* (Tel-Aviv: 1966), p. 97 (Hebrew).

72. On this episode and about Meshullam, see Minor, C.S. *Meshullam! Or, Tidings from Jerusalem* (Philadelphia: 1851); Perry, Y. *Mount Hope. Deutsch-Amerikanische Siedlung in Palästina 1850–1858* (Haifa: 1995).

73. Since the 'model farm' was a private initiative of society members and was not established in any of its frameworks, it is not a subject for this research study. On this enterprise, see Bodleian, Dep. Cmj, d.62: Annual Reports: 'Report of the Palestine Model Farm and Industrial Institution for Jewish Converts' for the years 1870–75; Isaacs, A.A. *A Pictorial Tour in the Holy Land* (London: 1863), pp. 5–9.

74. *Tidings from Zion*, I (15 August 1882), pp. 3–13. One of Friedländer's supporters was the pastor William Henry Hechler (1845–1931), who was for a short while a member of the London Society. Hechler was involved in a plan for settling East European Jews on the land acquired in Syria by the Syrian Colonization Fund. The fund was headed by Lord Shaftesbury, who was then president of the London Society, and Elizabeth Ann Finn, wife of the second British consul in Jerusalem, who was the daughter of Alexander McCaul. Hechler is better known as the person who assisted Herzl in his contacts with the German Kaiser. On this, see below.

75. Ibid., I (15 February 1883), p. 125. On his plan for settling Jews in Gilead, see Oliphant, L. *The Land of Gilead* (Edinburgh and London: 1880).

76. *Jewish Intelligence* (July 1883), p. 179.

77. St Albans, first annual report of the Jewish Refugees' Aid Society, 1884, p. 3.

78. *Tidings from Zion*, II (15 November 1883), p. 65. A year later, in the June 1884 issue, the settlement in Artouf was already called the 'offspring' of the London Society in Palestine.

79. *Havazeleth* (1883), pp. 9–11. See there for the regulations in Rashi script with remarks by the editor.

80. ITAC, unclassified documents: transfer-of-ownership agreement signed by the parties, dated 20 October 1883. For the list of ownership deeds see ibid.: Wiseman in Jerusalem to Chaplin in London, 22 December 1884.

81. St Albans, article by James Edward Hanauer describing the Artouf settlement accurately and in thorough detail after his visit there in September 1886, in a collection of annual reports of the Jewish Refugees' Aid Society.

82. On Moritz Hall, Hacohen writes, 'He and his fellow missionaries eventually bought Artouf to found a Jewish settlement and to disseminate among them Christian beliefs. The settlement was founded, but what they had intended doing did not succeed … ' See Hacohen, *My World*, IV, p. 62; Klausner, J. *Awakening Nation: The First Aliya from Russia* (Jerusalem: 1962), p. 318 (Hebrew).

83. St Albans, sixth annual report of the Jewish Refugees' Aid Society, 1891, p. 6. The railway line was completed in 1892 and the station near Artouf is located today at the nearby town of Beth Shemesh.

84. The letter dated 12 May 1889 and signed by twelve Hebron Jews is addressed to Beresford Pite, head of the Jewish Refugees' Aid Society. See *Jewish Intelligence* (September 1889), pp. 133–4.

85. Ibid. (September 1890), p. 140. The stratagem of sending this declaration eventually succeeded in gaining their desired allocations of land in Hebron for the undersigned.

86. St Albans, eighth annual report of the Jewish Refugees' Aid Society, 1895, pp.

4–6. See there for the account of the sale. In December 1895 the first families from Bulgaria arrived and established the settlement of Hartuv. On this see mainly Ben-Artzi, Y. 'Hartuv – A Forgotten Colony in the Judean Mountains', in *Horizons: Studies in Geography* (1977), pp. 123–39 (Hebrew); Ben-Artzi, Y. 'The Story of Hartuv', in *Zev Vilnay's Jubilee Volume* (Jerusalem: 1984), pp. 351–8 where further sources are given (Hebrew).

87.   It seems that even before its foundation as a settlement, Artouf could be given a significance that went beyond the act of colonisation itself. In February 1883, when the enterprise resulted in the publication of several articles in a number of journals, Baron Edmond James de Rothschild (1845–1934) already surmised that behind the campaign to set up Jewish settlements in Palestine 'there lurked the sinister forces of English missionaries'. See the quotation from Rothschild's letter to Baron Moritz Hirsch, dated 1 February 1883, in Schama, S. *Two Rothschilds and the Land of Israel* (London: 1978), p. 76. The idea to set up an agricultural colony reappeared on the agenda of the London Society several decades later, as a result of the failure of its converts to support themselves through their work during the winter of 1934. In the article that presented the plan, which was never carried out, no mention was made of Artouf, nor was it even hinted at. See *Jewish Missionary Intelligence* (February 1934), pp. 16–17.

88.   ITAC, unclassified documents: see comprehensive report on the history of each Jewish settlement. Handwritten and undated.

# 5

# 1897–1914

Hitherto, the Jews have been a people 'scattered and peeled, robbed and spoiled,' wandering on the face of the earth without common leaders, without a country and without national cohesion. To-day, this state of affairs seems to be coming to an end. The Jewish race is organising itself in such a way that we believe that we are actually seeing ... a movement amongst the 'dry bones' of Israel, bone is united to bone .... This national movement amongst the Jews is destined to make missionary work amongst them more difficult.[1]

Towards the end of the nineteenth century, with the birth of a Jewish national organisation called the Zionist movement, the London Society began to follow the development of events. Already in June 1897 the society journal made a reference to the Zionist Congress, which was to take place in Basle two months later. After the session of the First Zionist Congress, the journal devoted special attention to the proceedings of the conference. In the October 1897 issue, the editor published the opening address and full speech of Theodor Herzl (1860–1904) and from then on, month after month, additional speeches were printed. The speech of Max Nordau (1849–1923) was printed in the November issue, a selection of articles from the world press in the December issue, and, in the following years, extensive reports were given of the Zionist congresses that were held.

This novel phenomenon of Jewish national revival was received by the society leaders with great enthusiasm. A few months after the First Congress, in an article entitled 'Zionism', the editor of the journal gave a profile of the Zionist leader – 'The best known name in the Jewish world today is that of Dr Theodor Herzl' – and listed the main points he made in his book, *The Jewish State*. In the course of the article the editor expressed the attitude of the London Society to Herzl's ideas:

This idea, however, has grown and received considerable impulse at the Basle Congress last August, and is now known as 'Zionism.' It is of a political nature rather than a religious character. Whatever we may think of Dr. Herzl's scheme, whether we consider it Utopian or practical, a likely contingency or a mere dream, it is, at any rate, great and imposing, and we cannot help admiring the creative genius of the man.[2]

In those years the London Society circulated among its converted members a letter for their perusal. This contained a proposal for sending a collective message to Herzl of ten paragraphs, singing the praises of the man and his deeds, and laying before him an offer of assistance in attaining his Zionist goals. The signatories first declared that their conversion to Christianity did not prevent them from showing strong sympathy for their brethren. They called themselves 'Messianic Zionists' and stated that their special status as Jews by race and Christians by faith placed them as a bridge between the two communities. The very fact that they supported the establishment of a Jewish state would influence the nations of the world to come to the assistance of the Jewish people.[3]

The impression made by the Zionist revival movement upon the London Society continued to find expression in the years that followed. In the context of reports on the Fifth Zionist Congress in Basle, the society journal stated that the new Zionist movement could no longer be ignored:

Zionism is a new power in the world and has come to stay. Its object is the arrangement of the national future of the Jews. Consciously, or unconsciously, Zionists are working out God's purposes for His ancient people, namely, their return to the land of their forefathers. The proceedings of the Fifth Zionist Congress ... may be regarded as another step in the onward march of events.[4]

This spirit pervaded the corridors of the London Society for many years, and, whenever discussions arose about the secularity that predominated over this Jewish organisation, the society leaders felt it necessary to point out that the main aim of this secular Zionist movement was to regain a hold on the land of Israel in order to fulfil the vision of the return of the chosen people to its homeland.[5]

With the consolidation of the Zionist movement and the establishment of its institutions, the mutual relationship between the London Society and the Jews of Palestine took on a slightly different aspect. The second wave (1904 and onwards) of Jewish immigrants, some of whom belonged to the secular stream of Judaism, viewed the missionary phenomenon in a different manner from their tradition-bound brothers. Because of the distressed situation in the country, many of them were in need of the services offered by the London Society mission stations, mainly those in Jerusalem and Jaffa – as had been in the case of the Jews of the first immigration wave. It seems, therefore, that, in the first decade of the twentieth century, opposition to the missions lessened. However, this tendency did not deceive the society leaders, who recorded in their journal that, although the spirit of tolerance had replaced the fierce opposition to the mission, this should not be overestimated, since the source of this new spirit lay in the growing apathy of the Jews towards their religion. The place of religious faith was being continually occupied by Zionism and its nationalistic overtones.

And, in fact, the familiar coldness of attitude continued to be shown by Jewish leaders towards the representatives of the London Society. But now it was the secular Zionist establishment that joined the traditional warfare conducted by the rabbis and religious leaders against the mission people in their attempts at conversion. The leaders of the Zionist movement were afraid of missionary activity and viewed it, besides as being a recognised harm, as an offence against the national feelings of the Jews in the land of Israel. For the first time a common front of the religious and secular establishments was ranged against the London Society, and it created an ambivalence of attitude among the missionaries towards Jewish settlement in Palestine. The society members understood this expected problematic situation as being merely another obstacle in their path. Yet, at the same time, they did not disregard the ideology that underlay the London mission, which claimed that the Jewish people had a central role to play in the Second Coming of the Christian Messiah. The missionaries there-fore remained sympathetic towards the Jews as individuals while taking a stand against the religious and secular establishments.

Their position was made unmistakably clear in the society journal:

> It stands to reason that, if a people is organized, they are better able to cope with those forces that work amongst them, which they do not like. There is no need for us to hide the fact: the Jew, from the national standpoint, does not love the missionary. For he ignorantly imagines that one of the results of missionary propaganda is the denationalizing of individual Jews. We are most anxious, therefore,

to be in such a position in Jerusalem and Palestine to prove to the Jews that the converted Jew need not necessarily be denationalized. To do this effectively, the L.J.S. ought to have well-equipped mission stations dotted about Palestine, surrounded by whole-hearted Jewish converts who at the same time could prove themselves to be Jewish patriots.[6]

In its own words, the London Society recognised that Zionism was a 'secular nationalistic movement that opposed the mission'. Yet there was no evil without some good, and the missionaries found consolation even in this fact. Although the Zionists' opposition caused a partial desertion of Jews from the mission institutions, those who left the ranks of the society were in any case less firm in their Christian faith, so that this was a way 'to sift out the chaff'.[7]

The Zionist institutions in the Jewish community in Palestine wasted no time in trying to check the influence of the mission. Their clear stance with regard to this was published in an article entitled 'Missionary Activities in Erez Israel'. In the writer's opinion, the main reason for Jews taking advantage of the benefits offered by the missionaries was poverty. The resources of the Zionist movement were not limitless, and that some Jews were left without assistance could not be avoided. Also '*émigrés*' without means 'are drawn by offers of employment with immediate payment, and are especially attracted by the food and clothing also provided'. Although the number of Jews visiting the London Society institutions was not very high, the leaders of the Jewish community in Palestine took certain measures to curtail the mission's activity and to lessen its influence. These measures are listed as follows:

1.  The Zionist Commission Relief Department is endeavouring to find regular work for the girls who have been driven by unemployment to the missionary sewing workshop ...
2.  The Vaad Hair [Jerusalem Jewish City Board] has formed a special Sub-Committee to consider what steps can be taken to counteract missionary influence. This sub-committee has addressed a circular letter to parents of children who attend missionary schools, pointing out the seriousness of such action from the Jewish religious and national point of view ...
3.  In the matter of English instruction, the Vaad Hachinuch [Board of Education] has lately been improving its curriculum, only the lack of efficient teachers having prevented this previously ...

It will thus be seen that the Jewish Community, as far as its resources permit, is taking all steps to remove the slightest justification for Jews seeking benefits from non-Jewish sources.[8]

This period at the beginning of the twentieth century was a paradoxical one for the London Society. The growth of the Jewish population in Palestine, which had formerly meant the flourishing of the missionary enterprise, had been envisaged as offering a wider field for activity. Yet, for the first two decades of the century, because of fierce opposition, it was the very factor that reduced the society's activities to a bare minimum.

### INSTITUTIONS IN JERUSALEM

At the beginning of the twentieth century the London Society continued to prepare itself for a constant growth in the Jewish population of Jerusalem and for the necessity of responding to its increasing needs. It therefore enlarged most of its institutions in the three main areas of its activities: medicine, education and religion.

### *The Hospital*

> For many days the hospital which belongs to the Mission has been a stumbling block and an obstacle for the House of Israel. On the [bedside] table of the patients are laid the books of the New Testament and instigating material, and the inciters come and go visiting the sick and turning their hearts from the good way. On the prescriptions which they give the patients who lie in the hospital and for those who receive medical care and return to their homes, it is clearly printed that it is given by the 'Society for Promoting Christianity Amongst the Jews'.[9]

The increase in the Jewish population in Jerusalem was felt in the growing rate of occupancy at the hospital, and for this reason the opposition of the Jewish community grew stronger. Many provocative articles were published against the institution in the Hebrew journal *Havazeleth* in which the hospital conditions and the attitude towards the patients were described:

> Many have knocked upon its gates, and even the great ones of the congregation and its honoured members have not refrained from

the medication of the hospital doctors, either in the hospital or in their homes, and they receive the medical prescriptions as mentioned before and their faces have not blushed with shame. No man of Israel crosses the threshold [of the medical institution] of the Unitarians, the Franciscans or the [German] Sisters, who are also ready to heal the sick for nothing and without regard to religious differences … . They do not take the lawful meat from the Jewish butcher nor the Jewish servants to prepare food, for they have no deception in their hands, and our people know that these hospitals are not for us and keep away from them. But the Mission is deceptive, a wolf in sheep's clothing. They give lawful meat and lawful food to the patients. Should such deception be called a kindness by our people?[10]

The hospital in Jerusalem with all its different wards had to undergo several changes in order to adjust to the increase in the Jewish population. In October 1909, in the midst of this expansion process, a change of director took place. Dr Wheeler left his position to be appointed head of the London Society mission station in Manchester, and his place was taken by Dr Masterman, who had, until then, served as director to the medical department inside the walls of the Old City.

In the autumn of 1906, the outpatients' clinic of the hospital, which treated the Jews who did not need hospitalisation, reached the limit of its capacity, and it became necessary to enlarge this wing. Benjamin Sandel (1877–1941), the son of the German architect in Jerusalem who had overseen the construction work of the hospital, drew up the plans for the extension building at the cost of £640. The plans were approved by the society committee in London and those in charge were ordered to begin work immediately. On 15 February 1908 the new building near the gateway to the hospital was dedicated and the dispensary was transferred to it. The vacated space was occupied by the clinics for outpatients and the problem was resolved.

At the same time similar changes were made in the old dispensary and clinics inside the city walls, which were also crowded with visiting outpatients. The society took advantage of an opportunity to acquire the building that had once been used by Dr Macgowan as the residence for the hospital's director. The present occupant, Dr Masterman, had moved out in February to a residence outside the city, and his former home was renovated and adapted to house, quite comfortably, the dispensary and the clinics. On 16 April 1908 the new institution opened its doors to the Jewish public.

In the spring of 1909, Mrs Oxford of South Croydon, who had been travelling in Palestine, died at the hospital. In her memory, her husband decided to build an additional wing for children at the hospital, and gave the London Society half of the necessary funds. In the autumn of 1910 Mr Oxford himself died, and his children completed the project by funding the building of an additional floor above one of the hospital wings – the Meath Ward – where a children's and maternity ward was named for the Oxford family. This ward was dedicated by Bishop Blyth and the British consul in Jerusalem on 14 October 1911.[11]

*The Church*

On 20 January 1899, the events to mark the 50th anniversary of the dedication of Christ Church in Jerusalem were opened in the London Society centre. Among the speakers at the ceremony were descendants of the prominent persons in the history of the London Society in Jerusalem: the son of George Edward Dalton, the first doctor sent to Palestine in the mid-1820s (Dalton's son also became the stepson of John Nicolayson after the latter married Dalton's widow); the son of Michael Solomon Alexander, the first Protestant bishop in Jerusalem; and the grandson of Samuel Gobat, the second bishop in Jerusalem.[12]

In 1908 Ada Currey (d. 1913) visited Jerusalem. She was an artist specialising in wood sculpture, and, as a supporter of the London Society, decided to donate £2,000 to have the church enlarged and to place there some carved railings, which she had made herself. Beresford Pite, the British architect who had planned the hospital in Jerusalem, was appointed to draw up the plans for the new wing on the eastern side of the church, taking good care to make it match the original building in all its architectonic details. The extension would include two rooms to serve as classrooms and a hall for sacred rites, and in addition a niche with a stained-glass window. The cornerstone was laid in the spring of 1912, and a year later, on 25 March 1913, the new wing of the church was dedicated at a festive ceremony. Until today, a marble tablet symbolising the cornerstone of the new wing is set into the outer wall on the east side of the church and bears the inscription, in Hebrew and English,'The Ascension Day – 1912'.

*The Girls' School*

The School for Girls, which had originally been an integral part of the more comprehensive Jewesses' Institution founded by Caroline Cooper, went through alternating states of highs and lows during the course of its existence, just as it was with similar educational institutions in Jerusalem. For example, the number of pupils decreased when the Jewish school named after Evelina de Rothschild was opened in the mid-1860s.[13] And the numbers dwindled even further at the beginning of the 1890s, when the School for Girls was divided, and the dormitory for girls was built outside the city walls.

During 1900 the number of pupils in the School for Girls exceeded seventy. Since the sanitary conditions, which were already very poor, became much worse and caused frequent absences among the teachers and pupils owing to eye infections and high fever, the society in Jerusalem began considering the construction of a new building. Two German architects – Conrad Schick, a society member, and Theodor Sandel, a resident of the German Colony in Jerusalem – were asked to submit their suggestions for a building plan.[14] After examining the suggestions, the leaders of the Jerusalem mission station decided to build another floor on the roof of a building standing at the northern end of Christ Church courtyard to house the girls' school. The ground floor was to accommodate other society institutions: its front section facing west towards the street was to be a shop for olive-wood articles created by the House of Industry, and the ground floor area facing the church was to be used for the Book Depôt and the women's workshop.

At the beginning of May 1901, the London committee ordered Sandel to begin construction work immediately, and by the beginning of June even the required permits were received from the local governor.[15] A generous donation from a supporter of the project, the wife of the pastor Francis Paynter (1836–1908), made it possible to complete the work at the total cost of £1,200. On 21 January 1902, the day that marked 60 years since the first Protestant bishop entered Jerusalem, and 53 years since the dedication of Christ Church, the new School for Girls was inaugurated.

*Girls' Industrial House*

The main purpose for founding this new institution, in which Jewish girls could be trained in home industries, was the fact that girls in Jerusalem were married at an early age. The women who served as missionaries for the London Society regarded this as a wrongful practice that led to ignorance among the girls, as well as to the high rate of divorce in the Jewish community. They thought it was of primary importance to diminish the suffering of these young women who were thrust out of the family circle and thrown into the streets.

On 2 April 1903, the society opened the Workshop for Young Women on the ground floor of the new School for Girls in the Christ Church compound. In this institution a few girls over 13 years of age daily spent their time being trained in home maintenance, and were also given lessons in general subjects. For their work in sewing, ironing and other household employment they received a full salary.[16]

*Boys' School*

The large number of boys in the school situated at the southern end of the Christ Church compound, and the overcrowded hall that served as the dining room, induced the society leaders at the beginning of 1908 to include, within the fundraising campaign for their centenary celebrations, the project of renovating a building suitable for this purpose. Towards the end of that year, in the November issue of the society's journal, the head of the Jerusalem mission, Carnegie Brown, urged the readers to support this undertaking, and described in vivid detail the conditions that existed in the building which was to be renovated:[17]

> Anyone who has seen the room which is now used as a dining hall will not require us to say one word as to the need of a new one, but for the benefit of those who have not been here I may say a few words on the subject. Owing to the good reputation of the school among Jews of all nations we are always full to overflowing, and could easily take double the number. Every inch of room is therefore occupied, and the only place left for the dining hall is an old large room detached from the school, whose condition I will try to describe briefly … The walls … are saturated with moisture at all times, even the summer heat and all possible ventilation making little or no difference … It is so damp that anything left in it for a night or two becomes mouldy, and particularly in the winter the atmosphere is really that of an underground dungeon.

This emotional appeal brought response and in the summer of 1910, Bishop Blyth inaugurated the renovated building.[18]

*The Siloam Village Clinic*

Organised British missionary activity among the Yemenite Jews, who had immigrated in the 1880s and settled in the village of Siloam (Shiloah), was begun by the sister of Bishop Popham Blyth, who conducted meetings with the intention of assisting the Jewish women of the village. Miss Blyth invited the missionary Joseph Jamal to give lectures to those attending, and very soon his visits became regular. Jamal was well liked by the Jews of the village and he helped them to build an improvised synagogue and to hire a Jewish teacher. For a few years, Jamal made use of the knowledge he had acquired as director of the mission clinic and dispensary in Jerusalem to assist the Jews of that neighbourhood as well as he could, and at each visit he brought them basic medicines, mainly quinine.

During the year 1900, when the number of Yemenite Jews reached 3,500, the society rented a room in a building belonging to a Jew of that neighbourhood, and every Wednesday Dr Masterman received there many patients. When James Edward Hanauer returned from Jaffa to Jerusalem, he took over the responsibility for the Jews of Siloam village from Joseph Jamal.[19] Because of the inconvenient location of the building, the poor sanitary conditions, the dependence upon the Jewish owner who might at any time decide to break the lease agreement whenever ill feeling occurred towards the mission, and because it was not possible to store medical supplies for immediate distribution there, the society decided to rent an alternative building from a Muslim resident in a more suitable area on the village outskirts.

On 2 January 1901, the society opened a permanent medical clinic in that both Yemenite Jews and Arabs living in the village were regularly treated. It appears that this was the first time the London Society started giving medical assistance which was accompanied by missionary activity among a non-Jewish population. The declared motive for this aberration was the wish to avoid local opposition to activity among the Jews in such a small village, and also because of the miserable health conditions that led the villagers to beg for help. However, even in this exceptional case, the missionaries maintained the principle of giving priority to the Jews.

THE SAFED HOSPITAL

There in the quiet ordered wards
The patient drew new breath,
And nurses move like angel-guards
To face the power of death;
Here the beloved physician pleads
For room and helpers, till
They meet both souls' and bodies' needs,
Thou City on the Hill ... [20]

During the summer of 1907 Dr Walter Anderson, who was in charge of the medical department in Safed, was on leave in London and spoke at the annual session of the London committee. At the end of his speech on the situation at his Mission Station, he gave a clear analysis of the attitude of the Jewish community towards the missionaries in the city, and epitomised this in one sentence: 'A few years ago the difficulty with us was how to get at these fanatical people in Safed; now the difficulty is not how to get at them, but how to get away from them.'[21] Obviously, this statement contradicts the general trend that characterises the period, which is that Jewish opposition to missionary activity increased with the growing influence of Zionism over the Jews of Palestine. The fact that Safed then had an impressive medical institution, resulting from the surge in construction work into which the London Society was drawn, indicates that the main reason for building the new hospital must have been the warm support given by the Jewish community in the city for its erection.

Towards the end of the nineteenth century, the modest medical institution situated slightly north of the mission house became too cramped for the many visiting patients. The buildings, which had been bought in the earlier period of the mission station, were totally unsuitable, and the need arose for the purchase of land to construct a new building. By 1895 a suitable compound was located at no great distance from the Jewish quarter near the city exit. Opposite this compound was a piece of land bought by the Rothschilds on which, a few years later, a hospital was built to be named after them.

At the beginning of 1898 the society leaders noted that they were anxious to complete the construction of the hospital in Jerusalem so as to be free to assign funds for establishing a similar institution on a more modest scale in Safed. In the summer of that year, Dr Anderson managed to obtain a *firman* from the local

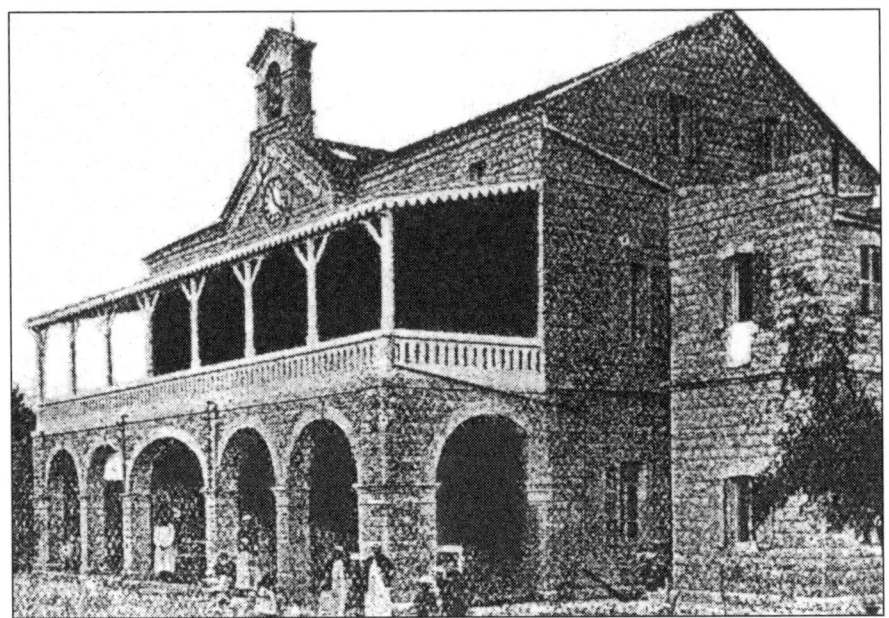

13. The society's hospital in Safed

14. The society's hospital in Safed; the site is now deserted

authorities to build a residence for his family in the compound intended for a hospital, with the hope of receiving, in time, permission for building the hospital itself. Anderson also reported to the London Society that at the end of June he had signed an agreement with the German building consultant in Haifa, Gottlieb Schumacher (1857–1925), for constructing the residence.

In the summer of 1900, the original fund that had been established for setting up a hospital in Safed was granted some of the money received from the sale of the Artouf agricultural colony. The London Society therefore ordered an immediate start on constructing a ward on the site intended for the new hospital for the treatment of patients not needing long-term hospitalisation. A year later, alongside the medical activities in the temporary hospital, the construction of a building for the outpatient clinics was completed, as well as an additional building for the doctor's residence in the new hospital compound. Prior to this, towards the end of 1899, Schumacher completed the first draft of his plans for the new hospital and transmitted them for review to the society leaders and in particular to Beresford Pite, who had planned the Jerusalem hospital.[22] Anderson and his colleagues took a long while before letting the construction work begin in order to discuss the exact location of the building within the existing compound. They also considered various options for altering Schumacher's plans and examined other price offers.[23] At the beginning of 1903 the building plans were finally approved at the cost of £3,000 and a *firman* was obtained for the erection of the hospital. At the same time, work agreements were signed with two Germans from Haifa, Gottlieb Schumacher, the building planner, and Friedrich Beilharz (1864–1937), in charge of construction. At the end of May the construction work commenced.[24]

At first progress was very slow, and Dr Anderson sent a letter from Safed complaining of the distress suffered at the temporary hospital, and stressing the urgent need for speeding up the process of building the permanent medical institution:

> I only wish I had the power vividly to bring before the Committee the misery of continuing to carry on the work in the present most wretched premises … At the present time I am obliged to perform surgical operations in the wards with a screen round the operation table! The so-called operation room defies description; the walls are reeking with damp, and the plaster falling off in all directions … If the new Hospital is not ready for occupation by the time winter has well commenced, I shall have to definitely advise the Committee to close that branch of the Medical work temporarily.[25]

At the beginning of the summer, Dr Anderson once more complained about the state of the temporary hospital and noted that the rental agreement for the building would expire in September. He claimed that, because of its dilapidated condition, the building would no longer serve his purpose even if the lease were extended for another year. Therefore he recommended renting another temporary building until the expected opening of the new medical institution in the summer of 1904, or, alternatively, to close down the medical ward completely.[26]

From another letter sent by Anderson to London, it appears that in the autumn of 1903 his April foreboding had proven to be true. The doctor preferred not to continue using the damp and decrepit building any longer, since, in his words, it was better, in the winter season, to place the patients outside the institution, under the open sky. Medical activity ceased and efforts were made to find another temporary building for rent while the permanent building was being completed. In spite of the difficulties, a measure of optimism is evident in Anderson's letter, which ends with a request for a special donation to build a clock tower for the new hospital so that it could be seen from a distance. Anderson chose to ask specifically for this item because there was not a single public clock of any value. The clock was to be installed on the front side of the hospital and would not only be of use to the institution but would benefit the entire city.[27]

On 31 May 1904, the new hospital was inaugurated in Safed. The four-storey building was equipped with the best medical improvements available and contained, besides hospital wards for forty men and women, a modern operating theatre and a kosher kitchen. At the dedication ceremony, for the very first time at an event of this kind, many of the Jews of Safed participated, since the hospital was the only medical institution in the city that also served the Jews in the Galilee settlements. The elderly vice-consul of Austro-Hungary and of Britain in Safed, Joseph Miklasiewicz (1823–1907), expressed generous praise in his speech: 'I express the sincerest wishes for the prosperity of the "London Jews' Society" asking it to maintain and increase their benevolent works, for the glory of God and the good of the people in this land.'[28]

This modern institution fired the imagination of the editor of the society journal in London. He published an article written by the hospital director, Dr Anderson, who described in great detail every aspect of the institution, taking the readers on a complete tour of the interior:

Upon entering we are at once struck by its brightness and English-like appearance. The floors are composed of white cement tiles, with a border of black. The walls are tinted a soft, pink colour. The modern English fireplace, with turquoise blue tiles and white enameled mantel-piece, at once arrests the attention of the English traveller, who has probably not seen the like since leaving the homeland.[29]

The Safed hospital soon gained a place of honour in the city and was crowded with Jewish patients. During the summer of 1905 the number of patients applying for medical care reached a new climax of 302 in one day. The value and importance of the institution in Jewish communal life can be gauged from a notice affixed to the gate of the synagogue in Safed expressing opposition to the Mission Hospital. However, the language here was different from the one typically used in the proclamation of bans against missionary institutions in Jerusalem:

> ... we are still very much under their power, as we are constantly in need of their help, because we have neither a hospital nor any good doctors. The one hospital we formerly had is, owing to many quarrels and dissensions, now closed. In consequence of this the Mission Hospital is now filled with Jewish patients, and the majority of the outside patients also are Jews. An evangelist preaches daily to all our brethren who come to consult the doctor, persuading them to embrace the Christian religion. All are compelled to be present, otherwise they would incur the doctor's displeasure. Let us not deceive ourselves by declaring that their efforts are vain and fruitless. Unfortunately Satan is too active and souls are caught in their net, among whom are many enlightened and sincere men ... . Thus last year ... a cherem [ban] was proclaimed against those who should consult the Christian doctor, but were not the rabbis themselves compelled to loose that which they had bound? Could our brethren obey the cherem? Would they not have died in their diseases? Therefore, dear brethren, if you are truly desirous to rescue the souls of our people from the missionary net, you ought to establish a committee comprising the important members of the various committees, and this committee should set to work with a will and energy to establish a Jewish hospital. Where there is a will there is a way! ... then only will we see no more of the face of the missionary who lies in wait for our souls.[30]

Anderson quoted this notice in a letter sent to London, and stated that it testified a thousandfold to the success of the hospital as part of the missionary activities in Safed. No longer was a ban imposed upon the hospital, which served so many Jews. Instead, there was an independent Jewish initiative to emulate the British institution and act for themselves.

The new hospital led to a surge in the level of the mission station's achievements.[31] The extent of its success can be derived from another Jewish ban publicly displayed in Safed in 1907:

> In our city the work of the mission is more than in any of the holy cities; the enticers labour day and night, and use every means to draw our brethren to them, especially the young. Their doctors heal all Jewish patients gratis, as if the Christian religion enjoins to pity *only* the Jewish poor, and by this means about fifty Jews (even of the most pious) listen daily to the addresses from the preachers, causing them to go astray ... We have to acknowledge that the mission sees blessing in its labours. Those young souls which receive benefits from them are drawn with cords of love, and the enticers are their friends and benefactors. Some young men have been already caught in their net, and we suspect that many more are ready to change their religion at the proper opportunity ... Truly we may say that these terrible missionaries have nowhere found such a field as in this city [emphasis in original].[32]

In the autumn of 1907 rumours spread through Safed that a large Jewish hospital was about to be built on the slope above the London Society medical complex. The missionaries received the news with mixed feelings. On the one hand, they were glad for the sake of the Jews, and for the fact that the Mission Hospital had succeeded in prompting the Jewish community to respond by setting up a similar institution. On the other hand, the missionaries thought it was unfortunate that the Jewish medical institution would be built near theirs and would, by its better location, obscure the Mission Hospital. They felt that it would suit them better if the Jewish hospital were erected at the other end of the city. But the land had been bought by the Rothschild family long before the London Society had acquired its own land, and therefore the members of the Safed mission received the news with understanding.[33]

## THE SAFED CHURCH

Apparently, the small Anglican community in Safed did not need a special building for a church when they set up the mission station in the city, but used the mission house as a meeting hall for gatherings and ceremonial rites. Only at the end of the century, when the number of community members increased as a result of the immigration wave from Europe, did Ben-Zion Friedmann rent a spacious room on the top floor of a private residence in the small Christian neighbourhood and call it a 'church'.[34]

At the beginning of 1908, in honour of the centenary for the establishment of the London Society, its leaders sent out a call to raise funds on an unprecedented scale for the construction projects in the mission stations around the world. Priority was given to the building of a church in Safed, since 'the Moslems there, of whom there are about 13,000 [should be about 5,000], have their many mosques; the Jews, numbering about 12,000 [should be about 7,000] possess several synagogues; but there is no English Church in Safed.'[35] The initiative for building a church came from London and met with objections from the missionaries in Safed. Friedmann and Anderson thought that it was preferable to allocate the funds to the construction of an entirely new building for the girls' school and even suggested setting up the educational institution on the land that had been assigned for a church. In the course of frequent exchanges of letters on this matter, a suggestion was made in London to build both the church and the school side by side on the same plot of land. The Safed missionaries rejected this possibility outright, since they claimed that no Jew with common sense would dare send his child to be educated in the courtyard of a church. Finally the problem was resolved – the School for Girls would be provided with a building rented especially for that purpose, and the church could be built on the site originally intended for it.[36]

In the spring of 1909 the London Society approached the German contractor in Haifa, Friedrich Beilharz, who had built the society hospital in Safed in 1904, and asked for a price offer for building the church. The assessments were made according to the plans of the French architect B. Rogoff, who had earlier been employed to draw up the plans for the hospital built by the Rothschilds in Safed. At the end of 1910 a *firman* was obtained for the church and during 1911 construction work was begun.[37] The site chosen was on the steep slopes of Castle Hill in Safed, a location which caused a significant overrun of the original budget. In the summer of 1914 the society made an emotional appeal to its supporters for assistance, explaining in detail the technical difficulties encountered by the builders, and the urgent need to devote further resources to this project. From the description given it seems that the construction on a slope required considerable

15. The society's church in Safed, 1913

16. The church in Safed; it is now an educational institute

earthwork to prevent the mud from being washed down during the rainy season. In addition, the builders were forced to dig the foundations very deep because the site was filled with the ruins of buildings from the Crusader period. They also decided to make further reinforcements for the building because the city was vulnerable to the earthquakes common in the region, and then to set up a wall around the church because of its proximity to the hostile Jewish quarter.[38]

The London Society did not manage to complete the building of the Safed church. World War One prevented the continuation of the construction work for a few years, and at the end of the war, when only 3,000 Jews were left out of the 7,500 who had lived there before, the society decided that there was no justification for maintaining an independent mission station there. Also, at the same time, the society had become involved in a legal dispute that was detrimental to its standing in the city. Its leaders therefore agreed to the offer of the Scottish mission to take over sole responsibility for missionary activity among the Jews of Safed, while the London Society would concentrate on Jerusalem and Jaffa. In 1921, as part of the agreement with the Scottish mission to transfer all the English property in Safed to them, the site of the church building was taken over by the Scottish church, which completed the project.[39]

HAIFA

From the start, Haifa aroused great interest among the London Society members. Most of the missionaries passed through this northern city on their journeys to and from the port of Beirut, and stayed over in Haifa during their visits to Jewish centres in the north of the country. For example, in 1872, James Neil, head of the Jerusalem mission station, was especially impressed with Haifa and thought it was worthwhile investing some effort in order to establish a mission station there. Neil listed the advantages of the city in comparison with other cities in the area, and noted that it could

> be peculiarly fitted for the residence of any missionary labouring in the Galilee. Tiberias is insufferably hot in summer; Safed's population are fanatical in the extreme; Acca [sic] has but few Jewish inhabitants; but at Haifa alone there would be found a considerable

17. The society's hospital in Haifa

18. The Mission House in Haifa

number of Jews, perhaps 600, and at the same time a large body of Protestant Christians [some of them of the German Templar Society].[40]

The first practical opportunity to obtain a foothold in Haifa turned up at the doorstep of the London Society at the beginning of the twentieth century, and is connected with the figure of David Christian Joseph (1836–1919). Joseph, a Polish Jew, was engaged in the jewellery trade, and on his way to the United States stopped over in England by chance. At the beginning of the 1860s he took an interest in the Christian scriptures, was converted in 1862, and in 1874 established a missionary centre among the Jews in London. After the death of his wife, he settled in Jerusalem, bringing his missionary institutions with him. In 1897 he moved to Haifa because of poor health, and founded the 'Carmel Mission' in the city. He rented some buildings to set up a small hospital for Jews, including a dispensary and a convalescent home, with a school alongside them. From one of the German residents, he bought a two-acre vineyard on the slopes of Mount Carmel at the outskirts of the German Colony, and later erected a few other buildings on it.[41]

During 1900 Joseph again fell ill, and thought that he would not be able to continue with his work in Haifa. He therefore began exploring the possibility that other missionary organisations would take over his work in the city, and in November 1900 he approached the London Society through his agent. The society leaders were very slow in responding, and in the summer of 1901 the offer was again placed before them in a letter sent by Ben-Zion Friedmann from Safed. During his stay in Haifa, on one of his periodic visits to the Jews in Zichron Ya'akov, the Safed missionary met with Joseph, and the two men examined the ways in which the institutions could be transferred to the society before Joseph went back to London. In the autumn of that year, while staying at his London residence, Joseph notified the London Society leaders that he had full confidence in Ben-Zion Friedmann, and therefore he was prepared to transfer all his property in Haifa to the society, free of charge, so that it could continue with his work there.[42]

In London, there was no great enthusiasm for the missionary institution that had fallen like ripe fruit into their hands, and nothing was done to establish a presence in that northern port city. The very opposite occurred. In 1902 the postbox of the society was filled with letters from the missionaries who had been working for Joseph, mainly containing complaints that the society was not paying their salaries any longer, and that it had deserted the mission and its workers. In that same year, Lewis Crosby visited Haifa during his inspection tour of the mission stations in Palestine on behalf of the London Society, and devoted most of his findings to this matter. Among other things, he estimated that the society could not make much use of the vineyard transferred to it, but he nevertheless stressed the importance of Haifa as a future missionary centre. Crosby claimed that the city had the best natural harbour in Palestine, and that, after the railway line to the east was inaugurated (as it was three years later in 1905), it would become a large and flourishing port city. In the meantime, the society inspector-general thought that one of the following options should be taken: to place a junior missionary in Haifa under the supervision of the mission stations in Safed or Jaffa; to place an additional junior missionary in Safed who would stay in Haifa and Zichron Ya'akov for a few weeks at a time; to relegate Haifa to the jurisdiction of the mission station in Jaffa or Jerusalem.[43]

In the meantime, while the London Society was still struggling to resolve the fate of the mission station in Haifa, Joseph recovered his health. In the spring of 1904 he returned to Palestine and demanded that the London Society hand back his property to him. Although the London Society refused, it allowed him to resume his work within the institutions it had retained. Joseph realised that the London Society had not fulfilled the agreed conditions that it would receive his property in exchange for continuing his work. Instead, it had dismissed his workers and transferred the medical equipment to its institution in Safed. The society did not staff the mission station in Haifa, either with its own people or with the missionaries whom Joseph had selected for it. He was particularly upset that the German missionary Martin Philip Schneider (1862–1933), who had worked for him, did not continue serving under the society, but had chosen to return to Germany. Joseph therefore decided to settle in Haifa, bought a plot of land adjoining the vineyard that he had given the society, and erected a building in which he conducted a small clinic for the society.[44]

In mid-1909, the London Society decided in principle to found its own mission station in Haifa, most probably because it became aware that a new Jewish neighbourhood, 'Herzlia', had been founded in the city at that time. Ben-Zion Friedmann in Safed welcomed this step, but regretted that the mission station would be placed under the protection of the Jerusalem mission station and be detached from that of Safed. He was right for several reasons: Haifa was the port for Safed and the settlements in the Galilee; there was a close link between the two cities and especially between the two Jewish communities; the missionaries in Safed maintained strong ties with the Jews of Haifa, and especially with the residents of Zichron Ya'akov; scattered between the two cities were Jewish settlements that were often visited by Safed missionaries, and Haifa and the settlements near it should not be deprived of these visits.[45]

In 1911 Joseph decided, for lack of funds, to rent his clinic to the Jewish doctor Elias Auerbach (1882–1971), who turned it into the first Jewish hospital in the city. The adjoining vineyard and the buildings on it were finally transferred to the London Society in 1913 for the sum of £400. In spite of the high hopes and Haifa's great potential, the London Society never maintained a real presence there. In this case, the failure of the London Society is the most glaring of all. In Haifa it was freely offered a ready-made mission station, which then had considerable assets, including a mission house, an educational institution and a completely equipped hospital. All it had to do was to continue paying the salaries of the local missionaries who worked there and were willing to go on serving under its authority. Considering the great importance given the city by the London Society emissary during his tour of inspection, it can only be supposed that this must have been a case of dispute with the head of the mission station in Safed over the delegation of authority, combined with a simple matter of missed opportunity, a situation that had affected the London Society several times during the nineteenth century.

## WORLD WAR ONE

World War One badly affected the London Society, as it did the members of other organisations of the Allied nations in Palestine, and in effect froze its activities. As soon as war broke out, the society leaders made it possible for all its emissaries of British nationality to return to England, because it feared for their safety, and most of them chose to do so. The Jerusalem mission station was left in the care of Paul Nyland, which was of Dutch nationality and was given, as were all other foreigners, the limited protection of the American consul in the city. He was in charge of all the converted Jewish missionaries who were residents of the country and did not hold British passports. The mission station functioned only on a limited scale during the war, since some of the Jews of Palestine were either forced or chose to leave. The

Turkish authorities very soon took control of most of the London Society institutions. The buildings were requisitioned for use by the Turkish army, mainly to provide accommodation for the soldiers and their horses.

One single ray of light that was seen by the London Society during World War One was the Balfour Declaration of November 1917. The society journal dealt extensively with this subject and even drew a parallel between Balfour's letter to Rothschild and the declaration of Cyrus:

> As the proclamation [of Cyrus, King of Persia] preceded the return of the Jews from captivity in preparation for the first coming of Christ, so the famous letter [of Balfour to Rothschild] was a step in the working out of God's purpose for the return of the people to the land in preparation for the second coming of our Lord.[46]

After World War One the London Society renewed its activities in Palestine and continues to be active to a certain extent until today.

OPPOSITION

The Jewish national revival that had brought the Jewish people back to its homeland inspired new hopes in the traditional support of the London Society. The leaders were overjoyed at the thought that their work would be done by the Jews themselves. They wished to take part in the Zionist enterprise and to assist it in order to hasten the Redemption. They sang the praises of Herzl, a friend of the London Society member William Hechler, and the personal traits of the Zionist leader, who was considered open-minded and a pluralist, increased the expectations of the missionaries. But, as time went on, they realised that the secular Zionist movement was also opposed to missionary activity for fear of injuring the national feelings of the Jewish public. Thus, at the close of this period, the society faced a double wall of hostility, the religious and the secular. In time, another unexpected partner in Britain joined the opposition. As years passed by, the Anglican Church and the Archbishop of Canterbury at its head preferred the good relations with the Jews of Britain to an identification with the mission society, which tried to Christianise the Jews, a pursuit that had become increasingly unpopular.

In 1992 this trend reached a dramatic climax in the history of the London Society, as expressed by a London correspondent of the Israeli *Ha'aretz* newspaper:

> The Anglican Mission which has been trying to bring about the conversion of the Jews will no longer be given the patronage of the Archbishop of Canterbury, Dr. George [Leonard] Carey. This is a violation of 501 [should be 150] years [since the entry of Alexander, the first Protestant bishop of Jerusalem in 1842] in which the head of the Anglican Church was the honorary head of the organisation. Carey, who was chosen a few months ago, yesterday gave a negative reply to the request that he become patron of the Church's Ministry Among the Jewish People [the current name of the London Society]. In his letter, the Archbishop noted that accepting this position as patron would undermine the trust he wished to build with the Jewish community. According to him, he did not wish to be governed by history. He aspired to do all in his power to build trust and friendship among the various faiths in Britain. One of the leaders of the missionary organisations, the priest, Tony Higton, called the decision by the head of his Church 'a shameful betrayal'.[47]

## NOTES

1. *Jewish Missionary Intelligence* (May 1918), p. 38.
2. Ibid. (March 1898), p. 35. William Henry Hechler, who was also among those attending the First Zionist Congress in Basle, followed in his father's footsteps by entering the ranks of the London Society. While serving at the British embassy in Vienna, he arranged for Herzl's meetings with the German Kaiser in Constantinople and in Palestine at the end of 1898, and even joined him during his visit to the country.
3. Bodleian, Dep. Cmj, d.26: undated.
4. *Jewish Missionary Intelligence* (February 1902), p. 17.
5. Bodleian, Dep. Cmj, d.158: pamphlet published in 1918 entitled 'Zionism, an Appreciation and Criticism', pp. 6–8.
6. *Jewish Missionary Intelligence* (May 1918), p. 38.
7. *Report*, 105 (March 1913), p. 81.
8. *The Zionist Bulletin*, 21 (31 December 1919), p. 4: 'Missionary Activities in Eretz Israel'.
9. Frumkin, *Selected Writing*, p. 131, from *Havazeleth*, 13 (1883), Issues 6–9.
10. Ibid.
11. *Report*, 102 (March 1910), p. 90.
12. Bodleian, Dep. Cmj, d.59: programme for the ceremony in London; *The Times* (21 January 1899): article on the Jubilee events.
13. The Jewish School for Girls was established in 1864. Three years later Lionel Nathan, Baron de Rothschild (1808–79), took it under his patronage and named it after his late daughter, Evelina.
14. Bodleian, Dep. Cmj, d.62: four detailed plans by Schick outlining the courtyard of Christ Church and the buildings around it, with proposals for the plan of the school; ibid.: Schick to Kelk, Jerusalem, November 1900; ibid.: Schick's proposals for alterations in the existing buildings, undated; ibid.:

Emily Georgina Birks (1853–1929), headmistress of the girls' school, to Kelk on the subject of Schick's plans, undated; ibid.: sketch of the buildings near the church with proposal of a plan for building extensions by Sandel.

15. Ibid.: Sandel to Wheeler, Jerusalem 6 May 1901; ibid.: Wheeler to the secretary of the London Society, 3 June 1901.
16. *Jewish Missionary Intelligence* (October 1903), p. 154.
17. The building, which was finally renovated in 1910, stood on the western side of the church courtyard. In 1997 it was renovated once again and a second floor was built above. The entire structure today serves as hostel for the London Society.
18. Ibid. (November 1908), p. 162.
19. On the immigration of Yemenite Jews and their settling in Jerusalem, see the extensive account in Nini, Y. *The Jewish Community in the Yemen in the Nineteenth Century and the Immigration to Palestine Until 1914* (Tel-Aviv: 1976) (Hebrew).
20. *Jewish Missionary Intelligence* (April 1909), p. 72: from a poem of praise to Safed by M.B. Moorhouse.
21. Ibid. (June 1907), p. 93: speech by Dr Anderson before the London committee, 3 May 1907.
22. Bodleian, Dep. Cmj, d.64: Pite in London to Anderson in Safed, 28 October 1899; ibid.: explanations for the building plans, Schumacher in Haifa to Anderson in Safed, 16 December 1899; ibid.: detailed estimate by Schumacher of the building costs, Haifa, 15 December 1899.
23. Ibid.: on the indecision regarding the site for the building see Anderson in Haifa to Chaplin, 27 May 1901; on the intentional delay see ibid.: Anderson in Safed to the secretary of the London Society, 1 June 1901; another price bid was received from a Haifa contractor who was also a member of the Templar Society, Friedrich Ehmann (1877–1926), see ibid.: Anderson to London, 2 May 1900; for additional explanations by Schumacher on the details of his plan, see ibid.: Schumacher in Haifa to Anderson in Safed, 25 February 1902; on the request for a *firman* and the different versions of the building plans, see ibid. d.26: report by Chaplin, 1901, pp. 14–17; ibid.: report by Crosby, 1902, pp. 5–6.
24. Ibid., d.64: agreement between Schumacher and Anderson, dated 6 June 1903; ibid.: Anderson in Safed to the secretary of the London Society, 5 May 1903; ibid., 14 January 1904.
25. *Jewish Missionary Intelligence* (May 1903), p. 71.
26. Bodleian, Dep. Cmj, d.64: Anderson to the secretary of the London Society, 2 July 1903.
27. Ibid.: request for ordering a clock for the hospital, see Anderson in Safed to Gidney in London, 30 October 1903; price bids and designs for the clock proposed by a company based in London, see ibid.: letters dated 27 October 1903, 2 November 1903, 10 December 1903. In 1905, the floor tiles of the hospital were damaged, and this caused altercations between Anderson and Schumacher. See ibid.: correspondence from May till November 1905. At the height of the dispute, Anderson threatened to apply to the Kaiser for arbitration, and Schumacher replied:

> If you really believe that H.M. the German Emperor has nothing more to do than to decide whether your floors have to be replaced or not, you may address His Majesty. I shall not join your step ... There are far more serious and grave questions pending between our 2 nations than those regarding the Hospital floors at Safed.

See ibid.: Schumacher to Anderson, 16 August 1905. After the dispute was resolved, Anderson summed up the matter in a letter in which he expressed his opinion of the German architect: 'I have regarded Dr. Schumacher [as] anything but an honourable man.' See ibid.: Anderson to Francis Lemoine Denman (d. 1939) in London, 9 November 1905.

28. Miklasiewicz served as the go-between for the society in Safed throughout the 1860s and 1870s, when the mission station was deserted and he even resided in the mission house on a rental basis. For the memorandum of agreement in which he undertakes to guard the interests of the Society, see ITAC, Jerusalem Local Committee Minutes Book, I, No. 88 (18 August 1863); *Jewish Missionary Intelligence* (September 1904), pp. 136–40.

29. Ibid. (June 1905), p. 84.

30. Ibid. (November 1905), p. 163.

31. *Works of Faith and Labours of Love*, XI (January 1908), pp. 72–4.

32. *Jewish Missionary Intelligence* (May 1907), p. 68.

33. Ibid. (December 1907), p. 188. The English institution did not halt in its development. In 1910 the London Society was granted a small tract of land adjacent to the hospital compound by the Jews of Safed as a sign of their appreciation of its medical enterprise in the city, and in the summer of 1912 an additional wing of two apartments was built for the use of the hospital nurses.

34. Bodleian, Dep. Cmj, d.25: report by Chaplin, 1899, p. 54.

35. *London Society for Promoting Christianity Amongst the Jews: Quarterly Notes*, 31 (August 1908), p. 2. Among other things, the expected contributions were earmarked also for a new building of the House of Industry, and for the renovation of the dining hall of the boys' school in Jerusalem.

36. Bodleian, Dep. Cmj, d.64: Friedmann to Denman, 19 May 1909, 29 May 1909, 10 July 1909, 7 August 1909; ibid.: Anderson to Denman, 18 August 1909; ibid.: Friedmann to Denman, 18 September 1909, 19 October 1909, 26 October 1909.

37. Ibid.: Beilharz to Friedmann, 14 June 1909; ibid.: Rogoff to Friedmann, 28 January 1910; ibid.: the Foreign Office in London to the secretary of the Society, 28 February 1910, 29 March 1910; ibid.: notification of the receipt of the *firman*, Foreign Office to the secretary of the society, 7 December 1910.

38. *Jewish Missionary Intelligence* (July 1914), p. 97. The article contained expressions of bitterness at the damage caused by passers-by to the building even while it was under construction. Special mention was made of the defacement of the frontal stone archway and the carving of names on the walls of the church.

39. In return for the transfer of the London Society institutions to the Scottish mission, the sum of £15,000 was received in London. Today the church in Safed on the slopes of Castle Hill is being used as a Jewish orthodox educational institution.

40. *Jewish Intelligence* (December 1872), p. 305: travel diary of James Neil.

41. *The Christian* (25 June 1908), pp. 17–18: article entitled 'The Excellency of Carmel'; *The Glory of Israel* (July–August 1904); Bodleian, Dep. Cmj, d.57: journal published by Joseph: *Mount Carmel, Messiah's Witness* (April 1897), p. 1; ibid.: detailed list of Joseph's property in Haifa, 25 October 1901. Today the building is used as a drug and alcohol rehabilitation centre under the management of the nearby Messianic Community.

42. Ibid., d.57: H.N. Moore in London to the secretary of the society, 30

November 1900; ibid.: Friedmann in Safed to Denman in London, 12 July 1901; ibid.: Joseph in London to the secretary of the society, 5 October 1901; ibid.: Thomas Chaplin to the secretary of the society, 25 October 1901. On 6 December 1901 Joseph signed the transfer documents and on 15 March 1902 the transaction was approved in the Land Registration Offices in Haifa. See ibid.: legal adviser W. Melmoth Walters (d. 1926) to Gidney, 24 June 1904.

43. Ibid., d.26: report by Crosby, 1902, pp. 7–10.
44. Ibid.: Joseph in Haifa to the London Committee, 7 November 1906; ibid.: Joseph in Haifa to Denman in London, 1 June 1909. On Schneider and the German 'Carmel Mission' Society, see Eisler, E.J. 'The History of the Carmel Mission 1904–1939' in Y. Ben-Artzi (ed.) *Haifa: Local History* (Haifa: 1998), pp. 51–62 (Hebrew).
45. Bodleian, Dep. Cmj, d.57: Friedmann in Safed to Denman in London, 13 August 1909; ibid.: Dr Anderson in Safed to Denman, 18 August 1909.
46. *Jewish Missionary Intelligence* (July 1919), p. 105.
47. *Ha'aretz*, 12 March 1992, p. 10a: article by Amos Ben-Vered (Hebrew).

# Conclusion

In 1809, a converted German Jew by the name of Christian Friedrich Frey founded a modest missionary society that wished to spread the Gospel among the Jews of east London. The initial conditions facing the energetic missionary did not predict a brilliant future, but reality proved the naysayers wrong. The London Society for Promoting Christianity Amongst the Jews grew at an extraordinary rate for three consecutive decades, extending its arms into the central cities of Europe, maintaining a foothold in Palestine and, for a while, turning its Jerusalem outpost into the centre of Protestant operations in the Holy Land.

During the years 1820–40, the London Society dispatched a dozen missionaries to Palestine, most of them of German nationality. Various obstacles prevented these missionaries from settling permanently in Jerusalem in the 1820s. The Ottoman regime, which did not allow any Protestant activity in its realm, is generally held responsible for this, and rightly so. However, even the conquest of Palestine by the Egyptians at the beginning of the 1830s and their rule during that decade – during which Cairo pursued a different policy and allowed the missionaries to establish a foothold in Jerusalem – failed to yield the anticipated missionary fruit.

It is safe to assume that by sending to Palestine a motley crew of foreign nationals, and refraining from sending qualified British missionaries available at the time, the London Society revealed its lack of confidence in its own ability to sustain a significant presence in Palestine. One of its emissaries, a Danish national, did indeed succeed in securing a foothold in Jerusalem and laying strong foundations for the future, but, able as he was, this was all he could accomplish. It took an external factor to transform the London Society's position in Palestine. It was only in the 1840s, and then only for a short while, that the society finally managed to begin to flourish and become the most significant foreign factor in Palestine. Ironically, this breakthrough resulted from the brainchild of another German. It was only then that British missionaries began to arrive and to thrive in Palestine.

Thanks to the London Society's footing in Jerusalem, the Queen of Britain and the King of Prussia decided to establish a joint Protestant bishopric in Palestine, appoint a society missionary as its head, and thus realise the hopes of the entire Protestant world. Despite the low expectations of the society in London, Berlin and Constantinople on the eve of its inception, the bishopric seems to have accomplished some of its goals. In any case, it did contribute considerably, both directly and indirectly, to the shift in the history of Palestine in the nineteenth century. In the early years of its existence, a complete identity between the Anglo-Prussian Protestant bishopric and the London Society was maintained. The joint entity laid the basis for the entire Christian activity in Palestine during that century. The legal status of Protestants in the Ottoman Empire improved, and the sentiment was that the time was finally ripe for raising Palestine from its ruins. Completely new Protestant communities were springing up. Health, education, charity and welfare institutions were established, attracting thousands of travellers, pilgrims, scholars and scientists to Palestine.

Like many other major events in history, the birth of the Anglo-Prussian bishopric in Jerusalem was rooted not in careful political planning, but rather in the personal motivations of one energetic individual. Certain aspects of the personal history of Christian Karl Josias von Bunsen, the Prussian ambassador in Bern, combined with his staunch belief in the idea of 'The Restoration of the Jews', have become determinant factors in the conjuncture that enabled the bishopric's establishment. The first and foremost motive for the creation of a Protestant entity, which would serve as a counter-weight to the presence of the Catholic Church in Palestine, was furnished by the insult and humiliation suffered by Bunsen when he served as the Prussian representative in the papal court at the Vatican. He found fellow travellers in England, a country he knew thoroughly through his marriage to an Englishwoman. In the many days he spent in London he befriended the London Society's leaders and became aware of its modest enterprise in Jerusalem. The actual implementation of the idea was driven by his good and devoted friend, Friedrich Wilhlem IV, King of Prussia, who cast his political weight in its favour and privately financed half of the institution's budget. After the decision to establish the bishopric was reached, another German, Michael Solomon Alexander, a converted rabbi and a London Society missionary, was appointed as its first bishop. Immediately upon arrival in Jerusalem, the new bishop began to develop and enhance the bishopric and pave the society's way by establishing joint institutions of the two entities and by strengthening their connection with the Jewish community.

Thus it so happened that living side by side in the London Society compound on Mount Zion, in addition to the first European missionary pioneers and the first Jewish converts in Palestine, were the British vice-consul, the first of the foreign consuls in Jerusalem and, above all, a member of the society, who served as the first Protestant bishop in the Ottoman Empire. The London Society lost no time in leveraging its reputation in Jerusalem to further its aims. It soon built the first hospital in the Holy Land and the first Western educational institutions in the country, and completed the building of the first Protestant church in the Orient.

The meteoric rise of the London Society in its first decades was made possible by a surge of faith that had inundated tens of millions of believers in the Protestant world, and especially in Britain, at that time. Their belief was that the return of the Jews to the land of Israel and their conversion to Christianity, followed by the millennium and the second coming of the Messiah, was closer than ever. This faith caught like wildfire, and in addition to gaining sweeping popular support it also touched the higher echelons of the British Crown, the heads of the Anglican Church, several members of the aristocracy and high-ranking state officials. These figures worked consistently and zealously towards the promotion of the London Society, which became a leading factor in the process of transforming the land of Israel from a forsaken desert land at the beginning of the nineteenth century, into a regenerating, repopulated country by its end.

The society was born at the peak of a religious wave that began at the end of the eighteenth century and held Europe in its thrall for about 50 years. The 'millennium' vision began fading in the early 1840s, just as the London Society was making its breakthrough in Palestine. It was the society's misfortune that it started to establish its position in Jerusalem just as the wave was ebbing, and with the death of the first Protestant bishop of the joint bishopric in Jerusalem, the society was seized by a weakness that continued during most of the second half of the nineteenth century. The first wave of Jewish immigration at the beginning of the 1880s did bring about a certain reawakening, but the vision that had fired the enthusiasm of believers until 1840 had long been extinguished.

The decline in the activities of the London Society in Palestine had certain local causes as well. Most of the change stemmed from the direction taken by the second bishop, Samuel Gobat, whereby the missionary focus was redirected at the Arab population of Palestine, a direction that inhibited the society's ability to develop properly. But it also seems worthwhile to examine the possibility that international power relations had an effect on this prolonged weakness. The British and the Germans were the most prominent Protestant forces in nineteenth-century Palestine, and the balance between these two superpowers was a determining factor in the success of their respective institutions in the country. At the beginning of the century, the London Society had been the first to settle in Jerusalem, with mainly Germans being sent as emissaries and representatives. For the founding of the joint bishopric in 1841, Prussia needed Britain's goodwill and cooperation. In the 1850s, when independent German institutions began to take hold, their missionaries were still earning their living at the service of the British missionary societies. It was only in the 1870s that the situation finally changed. Germany's international standing improved considerably following its unification in 1871, and so did the status of the German community in Palestine, especially after hundreds of Templars settled in the country. More than anything else, this decade was characterised by the London Society's feebleness. During these years the society failed to appoint to the leadership of its operations in Palestine even one single outstanding figure for a period longer than one year, employing no fewer than ten successive missionaries in that role. A similar pattern is not found in any of the society's stations in the British Isles or in Europe, nor was there was any shortage of money to account for the failure. Moreover, in 1875 the society's budget increased considerably. The decline in the status of the London Society in Jerusalem is perhaps associated with the expansion of the German community. The German missionaries were probably busy cultivating their nationalism in those days, and they opted to work under the German flag. A similar phenomenon occurred at the time among Catholic German missionaries in Palestine, who abandoned the traditional umbrella of the Vatican and began to work on behalf of the German interest. It was only Arthur Hastings Kelk, a brilliant administrator appointed as head of the mission in Jerusalem towards the end of the research period, who finally managed to resurrect the London Society's enterprise from its ruins, revitalise its stations in Palestine and prepare it for the influx of Jewish immigrants that flooded the country at the beginning of the 1880s.

The last two decades of the nineteenth century began with a great storm, when droves of Jewish refugees arrived in Palestine. This situation called for preparations that often stood in direct contradiction to the London Society's accepted norms of operation. In its previous dealings with Jewish communities in Europe, the society used to penetrate their neighbourhoods carefully, win their trust and engage in controlled attempts to convert individuals within the community. The hundreds of immigrants crowding voluntarily at the gates of the society's institutions in Jerusalem and Jaffa, without needing to be cajoled at all, required immediate action. The great potential for missionary activity among these people and the desire to exploit the unexpected event required the allocation of huge resources to the mission stations in Palestine, in order, among other purposes, to hand out money directly to the immigrants. The society was lucky to have, in Kelk, a highly capable representative in Jerusalem, who managed to prepare for and receive most of those wishing to take refuge under its wing; who, for the first time in its history, acted contrary to its policy, emptied its treasury and chose to walk the high wire, just a hairbreadth away from betraying the trust of his masters in London.

This period in the history of the society in Palestine was characterised by a great building momentum in Jerusalem and in Safed. The origin of most of the extant monumental edifices erected by the society across the country has long been forgotten. It is therefore interesting to investigate why only a fraction of the society's works left its mark on public awareness. A comparison with Germany, Britain's Protestant 'sister', is inevitable. The histories of both nations in Palestine are closely interwoven, but it seems that mostly German institutions, such the Talitha Kumi school, the Syrian orphanage, the Auguste Victoria hostel or the Dormition Church in Jerusalem, remain imprinted on the public memory. In our opinion, the roots of this phenomenon lie not necessarily in those who forgot, but rather in those who did not care to remind. Neither nation had political interest in Palestine, each for reasons of its own. But, towards the end of the nineteenth century, Germany began to express great interest in its nationals and their doings in the Holy Land, an interest that culminated in the visit of the German emperor, Wilhelm II, in Palestine in 1898. In contrast, with many of its nationals scattered across the globe, Britain invested less attention in the country. Unlike the German emperor, Queen Victoria never bothered to visit Palestine. Another reason for Britain to refrain from publicising the London Society's achievements in Palestine was the depreciation in the society's position in British public awareness. This was probably caused by the increased importance of the Jewish community in England, led by prominent public figures such as Moses Haim Montefiore and the Rothschilds. As the years went by, the Anglican Church, headed by the Archbishop of Canterbury, came to prefer maintaining a good relationship with the Jews in Britain to aligning itself with a missionary society involved in converting Jews to Christianity – a mission that was growing less and less popular in Britain. This process reached its climax in the formal revocation of the traditional endorsement conferred by the Anglican Church on the society from its inception and until 1992.

The mission's work in Palestine resulted in some 600 Jewish converts throughout the nineteenth century. The initial objective for which the London Society was founded, i.e., promoting Christianity among the Jews, has not been achieved.[1] But the missionaries assumed from the beginning that operations in Palestine would not be as easy and convenient as in England and Europe, and that the number of converts would naturally be lower. One of their first missionaries had already alerted them to this fact in the mid 1820s, stating that the society should not expect any openness towards the Christian faith from Palestinian Jews, unless 'he be prepared for actual martyrdom in consequence, or that he can fly the country, or find here a protector [from his brethren]'.[2] The majority of the Jewish public was perceived as coming to Palestine mainly to be buried, and hence as being firmly religious and poor prospects for conversion. At the same time, most of the Jewish community at the time was living on *haluka* (charity funds) and hence totally subordinated to an absolute obligation to its leaders and their doctrines. Converts would automatically lose their living allowance.

Aware of this situation, the heads of the London Society augmented their efforts and investments in the Palestinian mission, much beyond the relative anticipated success rate, and posted about a third of their global missionary force in Palestine.[3] Their basic assumption was the saying 'Cast thy bread upon the waters'. When missionaries had to find justification for their meagre achievements in Palestine, they often blamed the alienation that these Jewish converts suffered at the hands of their brethren, which drove them to leave Jerusalem and Palestine altogether and to be baptised at a mission station in another country. A plausible explanation was also furnished for the steep desertion rate among those who had joined the society and begun the conversion process. Although not all of them were actually baptised, the head of the Jerusalem mission nevertheless asserted that 'for every one that I baptise there are probably ten that leave us unbaptised, and yet having had the Gospel proclaimed to them'.

During the researched period, the London Society's endeavours came under sharp criticism from all directions. At times reservations were voiced even within the ranks of the Anglican Church itself, as evidenced by the following example from one of the Church's official organs towards the end of the century:

> It is absurd to suppose that a number of private irresponsible anonymous persons, meeting occasionally in a room in London, and calling themselves 'The London Society for Promoting Christianity Among the Jews', or by any other name, can represent the Church in her missionary character.[4]

However, most of the condemnations came from Catholic and Greek Orthodox officials in Palestine, who regarded the society's operations as an invasion of their territory and impeding their advancement, and naturally, from the leaders of the Jewish community, who saw the number of converts as a catastrophe and fiercely attacked the missionaries.

The antagonism that the London Society provoked in both these opponents was obviously the result of its activities, but more than that it was a consequence of its pioneering role. The fact that the society was the first among missionary communities in Palestine in establishing health, education, charity and welfare institutions had forced its opponents to stay alert and initiate similar projects if they wished to keep their flock. The chiefs of the Jewish congregation in Palestine and the Diaspora were obliged to establish hospitals, schools and many other organisations quickly to match the Society's institutions. The Catholic and the Greek Orthodox Churches, and the powers sponsoring them, France and Russia, were quick to follow suit, by stationing high-ranking parochial officials of their own and establishing many modern institutions.

Aware of their position as role models and trail blazers for others, the London Society leaders often stated:

> No honest Hebrew acquainted with the modern history of Palestine can fail to know very well, however little he may care to confess it, that the altogether new comforts and privileges he now enjoys are due in no small degree to the work, direct and indirect, of Protestant

missionaries, and more especially of the early missionaries to the Jews, if only as being the first in the field ... It was the missionaries who, according to the best of their abilities, at once commenced the work of liberal education, totally neglected before, and so carried it on as to compel the Jews themselves to follow in the same path. It was the missionaries, too, who used their utmost endeavours to raise the Hebrew women from that depth of degradation ... and who succeeded so far as to render it absolutely necessary for the most bigoted Jews in Jerusalem to open schools for girls, in order to keep the young people away from the missionary establishments. These messengers of the Gospel were the first to furnish duly trained and able medical men, and to found an excellent hospital, so as in this particular also 'to provoke the emulation' of the rabbis, whose medical institutions, subsequently founded in rivalry, are now also becoming very efficient, and no doubt a means of much temporal good to many.[5]

Thus a race was now under way in the Holy Land. All the factors participating in the struggle over their standing in the Palestinian arena eventually contributed to its development and progress. If nothing else, then for this alone, the land of Israel is greatly indebted to the London Society for Promoting Christianity Amongst the Jews.

### NOTES

1. At that time, the Protestant mission had converted 72,740 Jews around the world. To this the Catholics added 57,300 Jews, and the Orthodox Church 74,500. See Hastings, J. (ed.) *Encyclopedia of Religion and Ethics*, VIII (New York: 1955), p. 743, and additional sources mentioned there.
2. *Jewish Expositor*, 10 (1825), pp. 13–17.
3. In 1900, for instance, the total number of missionaries and wives was 210 persons, out of whom 66 missionaries were serving in the Land of Israel. See *Jewish Missionary Intelligence* (January 1900), p. 2.
4. *Westminster Review* (January 1886), p. 163.
5. Neil, J. *Palestine Re-Peopled; or Scattered Israel's Gathering. A Sign of the Times* (London: 1877), pp. 21–2.

# Bibliography

LIST OF ARCHIVES

BASLE – Archive of the Baslermission, Basle.

BODLEIAN – Archive of the LJS at the Bodleian Library, Department of Western Manuscripts, Oxford.

BONN – Archive of the German Foreign Office (Politisches Archiv des Auswrtigen Amtes), Bonn.

CHRISCHONA – Archive of the Basler Pilgermission, St Chrischona.

CHRIST-CHURCH – Archive of the LJS at Christ-Church, Jerusalem.

CMS – Archive of the Church Missionary Society, London.

CZA – Central Zionist Archives, Jerusalem.

FO – Archive of the British Foreign Office at the Public Record Office, London.

ISA – Israel State Archive, Jerusalem.

ITAC – Archive of the LJS at the Israeli Trust of the Anglican Church, Jerusalem.

JNUL – Jewish National and University Library Archives, Jerusalem.

KELLER – Archive of the Gottlieb Schumacher Institute at the Keller House, Haifa.

LAMBETH – Archive of the Anglican Church at Lambeth Palace Library, London.

PEF – Archive of the Palestine Exploration Fund, London.

ST ALBANS – Archive of the LJS (today the Church's Ministry Among the Jewish People), St Albans.


PERIODICALS

*Bread cast upon the Waters, being the missionary report of the London Society for Promoting Christianity Amongst the Jews*, London (1911– ).

*The Church Missionary Gleaner*, London (1874–1921).

*The Church Missionary Intelligencer*, a monthly journal of missionary information, London (1850–75).

*The Church Missionary Intelligencer and Record*, a monthly journal of missionary information, London (1876–1906).

*The Church of Scotland, Home & Foreign Missionary Record*, Edinburgh and others (1862–1900).

*The Church Quarterly Review*, London (1875/6–1968).

*Edinburgh Medical Missionary Society Quarterly Paper*, Edinburgh (1871– ).

*Haaretz*, Tel-Aviv (1919– ) (Hebrew).

*Hacefira*, Jerusalem (1874–1931) (Hebrew).

*Hamagid L'Israel*, Krakau (1856–1903) (Hebrew).

*Havazeleth*, Jerusalem (1863–64, 1870–1911) (Hebrew).

*Ha-Zevi*, Jerusalem (1884–1915) (Hebrew).

*Jerusalem Post*, Jerusalem (1948– ).

*Jewish Chronicle*, London (1841– ).

*The Jewish Era*, a Christian quarterly in behalf of Israel, Chicago, IL (1892–1903).

*Jewish Expositor and the Friends of Israel*, containing monthly communication respecting the Jews, and the proceedings of the London Society, London (1816–29).

*Jewish Intelligence*, monthly account of the proceedings of the London Society for Promoting Christianity Amongst the Jews, London (1835–76);

*Jewish Intelligence*, a monthly register of the London Society for Promoting Christianity Amongst the Jews, London (1877–84).

*The Jewish Intelligence, and monthly record of the London Society for Promoting Christianity Amongst the Jews*, London (1885–92).

*Jewish Missionary Intelligence*, the monthly record of the London Society for Promoting Christianity Amongst the Jews, London (1893–1910).

*Jewish Missionary Intelligence*, London (1911–62).

*Jewish Records*, chiefly for the use of collectors and small subscribers of the London Society for Promoting Christianity Amongst the Jews, London (1817–84).

*Jewish Repository and Monthly Communication Respecting the Jews, and the Proceedings of the London Society*, London (1813-1815).

*Jydske Tidende*, Kolding (1849– ).

*Jyllards Posten*, Copenhagen.

*The Missionary Herald*, American Board of Foreign Missions, Boston (1821–1934).

*The Missionary Record of the United Free Church of Scotland,* Edinburgh (1901–14).

*Monthly Intelligence of the Proceedings of the London Society for Promoting Christianity Amongst the Jews,* London (1830–34).

*Palestine Exploration Fund Quarterly Statement,* London (1869– ).

*Proceedings of the Church Missionary Society for Africa and the East,* London (1800–1921).

*London Society for Promoting Christianity Amongst the Jews, Quarterly Notes,* London (1901– ).

*The Report of the London Society for Promoting Christianity Amongst the Jews,* London (1809–1910).

*Tidings from Zion,* a monthly statement of the London Jews Society's work among the Jews of Palestine, Jerusalem (1882–85).

*Die Warte des Tempels,* Stuttgart (1845 – ), (in different names).

*Works of Faith and Labours of Love,* London (1900– ).

*Yated Neeman,* Bnei-Brak (1985– )(Hebrew).

*Zeitschrift des Deutsch Palästina-Vereins,* Leipzig (1878– ).

*The Zionist Bulletin,* London (1919–20).


BOOKS, JOURNALS, THESES


Abeken, H., *The Protestant Bishopric in Jerusalem; Its Origin and Progress. From the Official Documents Published by Command of His Majesty the King of Prussia and from other Authentic Sources* (London: 1847).

Abir, M., 'Local Leadership and Early Reform in Palestine. 1800–1834', in M. Ma'oz (ed.) *Studies on Palestine During the Ottoman Period* (Jerusalem: 1975), pp. 284–310.

Agnon, S.Y., *Tmol Shilshom* (16 ed.), (Tel-Aviv: 1979) (Hebrew).

Aiton, J., *The Lands of the Messiah, Mahomet and the Pope as Visited in 1851* (London: 1852).

Anderson, M.S., *The Eastern Question 1774–1923* (London: 1966).

Auerbach, E., *Pionier der Verwirklichung* (Jerusalem:1997) (Hebrew).

Ayerst, W., *The Jews of the Nineteenth Century. A Collection of Essays, Reviews, and Historical Notices* (London: 1848).

Bannister, J.T., *A Survey of the Holy Land; Its Geography, History, and Destiny. Designed to Elucidate the Imagery of Scripture, and Demonstrate the Fulfillment of Prophecy* (Bath/London: 1844).

Barclay, J.T., *The City of the Great King* (Philadelphia, PA: 1857).

Barclay, E.D., *Fredrick William IV and the Prussian Monarchy 1840–1861* (Oxford: 1995).

Bar-El, Y. and Levy, N., 'The Beginning of Modern Medical Practice in Galilean Towns, 1860–1900', *Cathedra*, 54 (1989), pp. 96–106 (Hebrew).

Bartal, I., 'The "Old" and the "New" Yishuv: Image and Reality', *Cathedra*, 2 (1977), pp. 3–19 (Hebrew).

Bartlett, W.H., *Jerusalem Revisited* (London: 1855).

Bar-Yosef, Y., *Ir Ksuma* (Tel-Aviv: 1958) (Hebrew).

Baumwol, Z., 'Acre in the Second Syrian War (1839–1840)', MA dissertation, University of Haifa, 1988 (Hebrew).

Ben-Arieh, Y., 'Pattern of Christian Activity and Dispersion in Nineteenth Century Jerusalem', *Journal of Historical Geography*, 2 (1976), pp. 49–69.

Ben-Arieh, Y., *A City Reflected in its Times. Jerusalem in the Nineteenth Century. The Old City* (Jerusalem: 1977) (Hebrew).

Ben-Arieh, Y., *A City Reflected in its Times. New Jerusalem: The Beginning* (Jerusalem: 1979) (Hebrew).

Ben-Arieh, Y., 'The Landscape of Palestine on the Eve of the Zionist Colonization', in I. Kolatt (ed.) *The History of the Jewish Community in Eretz-Israel since 1882. The Ottoman Period* (Jerusalem: 1989), pp. 75–141 (Hebrew).

Ben-Arieh Y. and Davis M. (eds) *Jerusalem in the Mind of the Western World, 1800–1948. With Eyes Toward Zion*, V. (Westport, CT: 1997).

Ben-Artzi, Y., 'Hartuv: A Forgotten Colony in the Judean Mountain', *Horizons: Studies in Geography* (1977), pp. 123–39 (Hebrew).

Ben-Artzi, Y., 'The Story of Hartuv', in Ely Schiller (ed.), *Zev Vilnay's Jubilee Volume* (Jerusalem: 1984), pp. 351–8 (Hebrew).

Ben-Artzi, Y., 'The Proselytes Colony: The Anglican Mission and the Establishment of a Jewish Village in Hartuv', *Tenth World Congress of Jewish Studies*, 10 (B1) (1989), pp. 312–18 (Hebrew).

Ben-Artzi, Y., Goren H. and Rogel, N., 'Medical Practice in Galilean Towns', *Cathedra*, 63 (1992), pp. 176–83 (Hebrew).

Ben-Zvi, I., *Eretz-Israel under Ottoman Rule. Four Centuries of History* (Jerusalem: 1968) (Hebrew).

Bessborough (Earl of), *A Place in the Forest, Being the Story of Stansted in Sussex* (London: 1958).

Biggs, C., *Six Months in Jerusalem, Impressions of the Work of England in and for the Holy City* (Oxford and London: 1896).

Blumberg, A., *A View from Jerusalem 1849–1858, The Consular Diary of James and Elizabeth Anne Finn* (Cranbury, NJ/London/Toronto: 1980).

Blyth, E., *When We Lived in Jerusalem* (London: 1927).

Bonar, A.A. and M'Cheyne, R.M., *Narrative of A Mission of Inquiry to the Jews from the Church of Scotland in 1839* (3rd edn), (Philadelphia, PA: 1845).

Bornstein-Makovetsky, L., 'Jewish Converts to Islam and Christianity in the Ottoman Empire during the Nineteenth Century', *Eleventh World Congress of Jewish Studies*, 11 (B2) (1993), pp. 130–4 (Hebrew).

Buchan, A., 'Remarks on the Climate of Jerusalem, from Observations made by Dr Thomas Chaplin', *Palestine Exploration Fund Quarterly Statement* (London: 1872), pp. 19–30.

Blov, A., *Hans Nikolajsen, og hans Mission I Jerusalem* (Copenhagen: 1900).

Bunsen, F., *A Memoir of Baron Bunsen, Drawn Chiefly from Family Papers by his Widow Frances Bunsen*, 2 Vols, 2nd edn (London: 1869).

Carmel, A., *Christen als Pioniere im Heiligen Land. Ein Beitrag zur Geschichte der Pilgermission und des Wiederaufbaus Palästinas im 19.Jahrhundert* (Basle: 1981).

Carmel, A., 'Conrad Schick's Road to Jerusalem', in Ely Schiller (ed.), *Zev Vilnay's Jubilee Volume* (Jerusalem: 1984), pp. 115–26 (Hebrew).

Carmel, A., 'Der Missionar Theodor Fliedner als Pionier deutscher Palästina Arbeit', in W. Grab (ed.), *Jahrbuch des Instituts für Deutsche Geschichte*, Vol. 14 (Tel-Aviv: 1985), pp. 191–220.

Carmel, A., 'The Activity of the European Powers in Palestine, 1878-1914', in I. Kolatt (ed.), *The History of the Jewish Community in Eretz-Israel since 1882. The Ottoman Period* (Jerusalem: 1989), pp. 143–213 (Hebrew).

Carmel, A., 'Palestine from the Beginning of the Nineteenth Century to the First World War', *Encyclopaedia Hebraica*, Vol. 6 (Tel-Aviv: 1993), pp. 684–99 (Hebrew).

Carmel, A., 'The Problem of the "Holy Land" in the International Policy (1799–1914)', *Encyclopaedia Hebraica*, Vol. 6 (Tel-Aviv: 1993), pp. 699–726 (Hebrew).

Carmel, A., *Die Siedlungen der Württembergischen Templer in Palästina 1868-1914*, 3rd edn (Stuttgart: 2000).

Carmel, A. and Eisler, J.E., *Der Kaiser reist ins Heilige Land. Die Palästinareise Wilhelms II, 1898* (Stuttgart: 1999).

Carmel, A., 'William Hechler: Herzls christlicher Verbündeter', in H. Haumann (ed.), *Der Erste Zionistenkongress von 1897: Ursachen, Bedeutung, Aktualität* (Basle: 1997), pp. 42–5.

Chamberlain, W., *The National Restoration and Conversion of the Twelve Tribes of Israel* (London: 1854).

Chaplin, T., 'Fevers of Jerusalem', *Lancet*, 2 (1864), pp. 263–5, 289–91.

Chaplin, T., 'The Site of Ebenezer', *Palestine Exploration Fund Quarterly Statement* (London: 1888), pp. 263–5.

Conder, C.R., *Tent Work in Palestine. A Record of Discovery and Adventure* (London: 1877).

Corey, M.W., *From Rabbi to Bishop: The Biography of the Right Reverend Michael Solomon Alexander, Bishop in Jerusalem* (London: [1956]).

*Correspondence Respecting the Condition of Protestants in Turkey, 1841–1851, Presented to the House of Commons in Pursuance of their Address of March 27, 1851* (London: 1851).

Crombie, K., *For the Love of Zion, Christian Witness and the Restoration of Israel* (London: 1991).

Crombie, K., 'A Real Son of Zion: Ben Zion Friedman and the Jewish Mission at Safed', *Mishkan. A Theological Forum of Jewish Evangelism*, 15 (1991), pp. 25–36.

Davis, M. and Ben-Arieh, Y. (eds) *With Eyes Toward Zion, Western Societies and the Holy Land*, Vol. 3 (New York: 1991).

Dawling, T.E., *The City of Safed: A Refugee of Judaism* (London: 1914).

De le Roi, J.F.A., *Die evangelische Christenheit und die Juden*, Vol. 3 (Berlin: 1892).

De le Roi, J.F.A., *Ferdinand Christian Ewald. Ein Lebensbild aus der neueren Judenmission* (Gütersloh: 1896).

De le Roi, J.F.A., *Michael Solomon Alexander der erste evangelische Bischof in Jerusalem. Ein Beitrag zur orientalischen Frage* (Gütersloh: 1897).

Douglas, J.D. (ed.), *The New International Dictionary of the Christian Church* (Grand Rapids, MI: 1974).

Egerton, F., *Journal of a Tour in the Holy Land, in May and June 1840* (London: 1841).

Eisler, J., *Der deutsche Beitrag zum Aufstieg Jaffas 1850–1914. Zur Geschichte Palästinas im 19. Jahrhundert* (Wiesbaden: 1997).

Eisler, E.J., 'The History of the Carmel Mission 1904–1939', in Y. Ben-Artzi (ed.), *Haifa. Local History* (Haifa: 1998), pp. 51–62 (Hebrew).

Eisler, E.J., *Peter Martin Metzler (1824–1907): Ein christlicher Missionar im Heiligen Land* (Haifa: 1999).

Eliav, M., *Eretz Israel and its Yishuv in the Nineteenth century, 1777–1917* (Jerusalem: 1978) (Hebrew).

Eliav, M., 'By Virtue of Women: The Role of Women in the Conversion Attempts by the British Mission', *Cathedra*, 76 (1995), pp. 96–115 (Hebrew).

Eliav, M., *Britain in the Holy Land 1838–1914: Selected Documents from the British Consulate in Jerusalem* (Jerusalem: 1997).

Eliav, M., 'Not a Jewish Proselyte but a Christian Convert', *Cathedra*, 59 (1991), pp. 191–3 (Hebrew).

Eliav, M., 'The Case of Shimon Rosenthal: Apostasy, Return to Judaism, and Relapse' *Cathedra*, 61 (1991), pp. 113–32 (Hebrew).

Ellern, H. and B., *Herzl, Hechler, the Grand Duke of Baden and the German Emperor 1896–1904: Documents Found by Hermann and Bessi Ellern* (Tel Aviv: 1961).

Ewald, F.C., *Journal of Missionary Labours in the City of Jerusalem during the Years 1842–3–4*, 2nd edn (London: 1846).

Finn, J., *Stirring Times or Records from Jerusalem Consular Chronicles of 1853 to 1856*, 2 Vols (London: 1878).

Fliedner, T., *Reisen in das heilige Land*, Part 1 (Düsseldorf: [1858]).

Frankel, L.A., *Nach Jerusalem! Reise in Griechenland, Kleinasien, Syrien, Palästina* (Vienna: 1860) (Hebrew).

Frey, J.S.C.F., *Judah and Israel or, the Restoration and Conversion of the Jews and the Ten Tribes*, 2nd edn (London: 1838).

Friedman, M.L., *The American Society for Meliorating the Condition of the Jews, and Joseph S.C.F. Frey its Missionary: A Study in American Jewish History* (Boston, MA: 1925).

Friedman, I., 'British Schemes for the Restoration of Jews to Palestine', *Cathedra*, 56 (1990), pp. 42–69 (Hebrew).

Friis, H.C., *Hans Nicolajsen, en dansk Jödemissionoer fra forrige Aarhundrede* (Copenhagen: 1949).

Frumkin, I.D., *Selected Writing of Israel Dov Frumkin* (Jerusalem: 1954) (Hebrew).

Fürst, A., *New Jerusalem*, Vol. 1 (Jerusalem: 1944) (Hebrew).

Gatt, B-Z., *The Jewish Yishuv in Eretz-Israel, 1840-1881* (Jerusalem: 1963) (Hebrew).

Gelber, N.M., 'The Question of Palestine during 1840–1842', *Measef Zion*, 4 (1930), pp. 44–64 (Hebrew).

Geldbach, E., *Der Gelehrte Diplomat* (Leiden: 1980).

Gibson, S. 'Conrad Schick and the Palestine Exploration Fund', in H. Goren (ed.), *For the Sake of Jerusalem, Conrad Schick* (*Ariel*, 130–1) (Jerusalem: 1998), pp. 64–8 (Hebrew).

Gidney, W.T., *Mission to the Jews, a Handbook of Reasons, Facts and Figures* (London: 1897).

Gidney, W.T. *Sites and Scenes: A Description of the Oriental Missions of the London Society for Promoting Christianity Amongst the Jews*, 2

Vols, 2nd edn (London: 1899).

Gidney, W.T., *At Home and Abroad. A Description of the English and Continental Missions of the London Society for Promoting Christianity Amongst the Jews* (London: 1900).

Gidney, W.T., *The History of the London Society for Promoting Christianity Amongst the Jews, from 1809 to 1908* (London:1908).

Gilbar, G.G. (ed.), *Ottoman Palestine 1800–1914: Studies in Economic and Social History* (Leiden: 1990).

Ginat, S., 'The Activity of the "London Society for Promoting Christianity Amongst the Jews" inside the Jewish Yishuv in Jerusalem (1825–1914)', MA dissertation, University of Haifa, 1986 (Hebrew).

Goodal, N., *A History of the London Missionary Society* (London: 1954).

Goren, H. (ed.), *For the sake of Jerusalem, Conrad Schick* (*Ariel*, 130–1), (Jerusalem: 1998) (Hebrew).

Goren, H. and Rubin R., 'Models and Maps of Jerusalem and its Buildings made by Conrad Schick', in H. Goren (ed.), *For the sake of Jerusalem, Conrad Schick* (*Ariel*, 130–1) (Jerusalem: 1998), pp. 79–92 (Hebrew).

Grabill, J.L., *Protestant Diplomacy and the Near East, Missionary Influence on American Policy, 1810–1927* (Minneapolis, IL: 1971).

Grajewski, P.B.-Z., *The Struggle of the Jews against the Mission from 1824 till our Times* (Jerusalem: 1935) (Hebrew).

Grajewski, P.B.-Z., *In Memory of the First Zionists* (Jerusalem: 1928) (Hebrew).

Grajewski, P.B.-Z., *In Memory of the First Zionists*, 2nd edn (Jerusalem: 1929).

Greaves, R.W., 'The Jerusalem Bishopric, 1841', *English Historical Review*, 64 (1949), pp. 328–52.

Hacohen, M.B-H., *My World*, Vol. 4 (Jerusalem: 1928) (Hebrew).

Halsted, T.D., *Our Mission: Being a History of the Principal Transactions of the London Society for Promoting Christianity Amongst the Jews from its Foundation in 1809 to the Present Year* (London: 1866).

Hanauer, J.E., *Walks About Jerusalem* (London: 1910).

Hanauer, J.E., *Walks in and Around Jerusalem* (London: 1926).

Hase, von K., *Kirchengeschichte auf der Grundlage akademischer Vorlesungen*, Part 3 (Leipzig: 1892).

Haslip, J., *Lady Hester Stanhope* (New York: 1934).

Hastings, J.E. (ed.), *Encyclopaedia of Religion and Ethics*, Vol. 8 (New York: 1955), pp. 713–45.

Hechler, W.H., *The Jerusalem Bishopric, 1841: Documents Chiefly Reprinted from a Copy of the Original German Account, 'Das Evangelische Bisthum in Jerusalem': Geschichtliche Darlegung mit Urkunden. Berlin 1842* (London: 1883).

Hodder, E., *The Life and Work of the Seventh Earl of Shaftesbury*, 3 Vols (London: 1886).

Holms, R.M., *The Forerunners* (Independence, MO: 1981).

Holtz, A. and Berger-Holtz, T., 'The Old Man of Jaffa: Moritz Hall', *Tarbiz. A Quarterly for Jewish Studies*, 49 (1990), pp. 215–28 (Hebrew).

Hopkins, H.E., *Sublime Vagabond: The Life of Joseph Wolff Missionary Extraordinary* (Worthing: 1984).

Horn, S.E., 'The Jerusalem Bishopric 1841', PhD dissertation, University of Minnesota, 1978.

Hummel, R., *Patterns of the Sacred: English Protestant and Russian Orthodox Pilgrims of the Nineteenth Century* (London: 1995).

Hurewitz, J.C., *Diplomacy in the Near and Middle East*, 2 Vols, 3rd edn (New York: 1972).

Hyamson, A.M., *The British Consulate in Jerusalem in Relation to the Jews of Palestine 1838–1914*, 2 vols (London: 1939–41).

Isaacs, A.A., *A Pictorial Tour in the Holy Land* (London: 1863).

Isaacs, A.A., *Biography of the Rev. Henry Aaron Stern, D.D.: For more than Forty Years a Missionary Amongst the Jews* (London: 1886).

Izhaki, R. 'The Ophthalmic Hospital of the Order of St John (1882–1948)', *Cathedra*, 67 (1993), pp. 114–-35 (Hebrew).

Jessup, H.H., *The Greek Church and Protestant Mission* (Beirut: 1891).

Jessup, H.H., *Fifty-Three Years in Syria* (New York: 1910).

Johns, J.W., *The Anglican Cathedral Church of Saint James, Mount Zion, Jerusalem* (London: 1844).

*Joseph Barclay, Third Anglican Bishop of Jerusalem. A Missionary Biography* (London: 1883).

Jowett, W., *Christian Researches in Syria and the Holy Land*, 2nd edn (London: 1826).

Kark, R. (ed.), *The Land that Became Israel: Studies in Historical Geography* (New Haven, CT: 1989).

Kedar, B.Z., *The Changing Land between the Jordan and the Sea* (Jerusalem: 1999).

Kedem, M., 'Mid-Nineteenth Century Anglican Eschatology on the Redemption of Israel', *Cathedra*, 19 (1981), pp. 55–71 (Hebrew).

Keith, A., *The Land of Israel According to the Covenant with Abraham, with Isaac and with Jacob* (Edinburgh: 1843).

Kersten, O., 'Das Klima von Jerusalem. Nach eigenen Beobachtungen dargestellt von Dr med. Thomas Chaplin', in Hermann Guthe (ed.), *Zeitschrift des Deutschen Palästina-Vereins* (Leipzig: 1891), pp. 93–112.

King, E.J., *The Knights of St John in the British Empire*, 3rd edn (London: 1934).

Klausner, J., *Awakening Nation: The First Aliya from Russia* (Jerusalem: 1962) (Hebrew).

Kobler, F., *The Vision Was There: A History of the British Movement for the Restoration of the Jews to Palestine* (London: 1956).

Kochav, S., 'Britain and the Holy Land. Prophecy, the Evangelical Movement and the Conversion and Restoration of the Jews 1790–1845', PhD dissertation, Oxford University, 1989.

Kochav, S., 'Beginning at Jerusalem: The Mission to the Jews and English Evangelical Eschatology', in Y. Ben-Arieh and M. Davis (eds), *Jerusalem in the Mind of the Western World, 1800–1948. With Eyes Toward Zion*, Vol. 5 (Westport, CT: 1997), pp. 91–107.

Kushner D. (ed.), *Palestine in the Late Ottoman Period. Political, Social and Economic Transformation* (Jerusalem: 1986).

Lambert, K.W., 'The London Society for Promoting Christianity Amongst the Jews 1809–1908. A Case Study of the Home Base Operations and Relationships', MA dissertation, Dallas Theological Seminary, 1976.

Lang, Y., 'The Struggle Against Missionary Activity at the Beginning of the First Aliya and its Reflection in the Jerusalem Press', *Cathedra*, 80 (1996), pp. 63–87 (Hebrew).

Latourette, K.S., *A History of the Expansion of Christianity*, Vol. 3, *Three Centuries of Advance* (New York/Evanston, IL/London: 1939).

Latourette, K.S., *A History of the Expansion of Christianity*, Vol. 4, *The Great Century* (New York/Evanston, IL: 1941).

Lees, G.R., *Jerusalem Illustrated* (Newcastle-on-Tyne/London: 1893).

Lieber, S., 'The Purchase of Land for "Christ Church" by John Nicolayson', *Cathedra*, 38 (1986), pp. 201–3 (Hebrew).

Lieber, S., *Mystics and Missionaries, the Jews in Palestine 1799–1840* (Salt Lake City, UT: 1992).

Livingstone, W.P., *A Galilee Doctor: Being a Sketch of the Career of Dr D.W. Torrance of Tiberias* (London: [1922]).

Lovell, R., *The History of the London Missionary Society*, 2 Vols (London: 1899).

Lückhoff, M., 'Prussia and Jerusalem: Political and Religious Controversies Surrounding the Foundation of the Jerusalem Bishopric', in Y. Ben-Arieh and M. Davis (eds), *Jerusalem in the*

*Mind of the Western World, 1800–1948: With Eyes Toward Zion*, Vol. 5 (Westport, CT: 1997), pp. 173–81.

Luntz, A.M., *Jerusalem: Literature Collection for the Research of the Holy Land*, Vol. 6 (1902) (Hebrew).

Macalister, S., 'Gleanings from the Minute-Book of the Jerusalem Literary Society', *Palestine Exploration Fund Quarterly Statement* (London: 1911), pp. 83–9.

McCaul, A., *The Old Path* (London: 1837).

McCaul, A., *Jerusalem: Its Bishop, its Missionaries and its Converts* (London: 1866).

Manna, A., 'The Sancak of Jerusalem Between Two Invasions (1798-1831). Administration and Society', PhD dissertation, Hebrew University, Jerusalem, 1986 (Hebrew).

Ma'oz, M., *Ottoman Reform in Syria and Palestine: The Impact of the Tanzimat on Politics and Society* (Oxford: 1968).

Ma'oz, M. (ed.), *Studies on Palestine During the Ottoman Period* (Jerusalem: 1975).

Margoliouth, M., *A Pilgrimage to the Land of My Fathers*, 2 Vols (London: 1850).

Marriott, J.A.R., *The Eastern Question: An Historical Study in European Diplomacy*, 4th edn (Oxford: 1940).

Mehnert, G., *Der englisch–deutsche Zionsfriedhof in Jerusalem* (Leiden: 1975).

Meyer, L., 'Joseph Samuel Christian Frederick Frey', *The Jewish Era*, 9 (1900), pp. 14–19.

Minor, C.S., *Meshullam! Or, Tidings from Jerusalem* (Philadelphia, PA: 1851).

Mirbach, von E.F. (ed.), *Das deutsche Kaiserpaar im Heiligen Lande im Herbst 1898* (Berlin: 1899).

Montagu, R., *Foreign Policy: England and the Eastern Question* (London: 1877).

Morgenstern, A., 'The First Jewish Hospital in Jerusalem', *Cathedra*, 33 (1984), pp. 107–24 (Hebrew).

Morgenstern, A., 'The Perushim, the London Missionary Society and the Opening of the British Consulate in Jerusalem', *Shalem* (1987), pp. 115–37 (Hebrew).

Müller, K. and Ustorf, W. (eds), *Einleitung in die Missionsgeschichte: Tradition, Situation und Dynamik des Christentums* (Stuttgart: 1995).

Neil, J., *Palestine Re-Peopled: Or Scattered Israel's Gathering. A Sign of the Times* (London: 1877).

Nicolayson, J., 'Mittheilungen für eine Skizze der Geschichte der englischen Mission und des evangelischen Bisthums zu

Jerusalem', *Zions-Bote*, 1 (1852), pp. 6–16.

Nini, Y., 'The Jewish Community in the Yemen in the Nineteenth Century and the Immigration to Palestine Until 1914', PhD dissertation, Tel-Aviv University, 1976 (Hebrew).

Norris, H.H., *The Origin, Progress and Existing Circumstances of the London Society for Promoting Christianity Amongst the Jews: An Historical Inquiry* (London: 1825).

Olin, S., *Travels in Egypt, Arabia Petraea, and the Holy Land*, 2 Vols (New York: 1843).

Oliphant, L., *The Land of Gilead* (Edinburgh/London: 1880).

Oliphant, M., *Memoir of the Life of Laurence Oliphant and of Alice Oliphant, His Wife* (Edinburgh/London: 1892).

Palmer, H.P., *Joseph Wolff: His Romantic Life and Travels* (London: 1935).

Penslar, D., *Zionism and Technocracy: The Engineering of Zionist Settlement in Palestine, 1870–1918* (Bloomington, IL/ Indianapolis, IL: 1991).

Perry, G.G., *A History of the Church of England* (New York: 1879).

Perry, Y, *Mount Hope. Deutsch-Amerikanische Siedlung in Palästina 1850–1858* (Haifa: 1995).

Perry, Y., 'The London Society for Promoting Christianity Amongst the Jews in Palestine: 1809–1841', MA dissertation, University of Haifa, 1996 (Hebrew).

Philippson, G., *Rabbi Samuel Halevi or the Blood Accusation of Damascus* (Warsaw: 1894) (Hebrew).

Pileggi. D., 'The Experiment at Artouf', *Mishkan: A Theological Forum of Jewish Evangelism*, 12 (1990), pp. 42–55.

Puryear, V.J., *International Economics and Diplomacy in the Near East: A Study of British Commercial Policy in the Levant 1834–1853* (Berkeley, CA: 1935).

Raheb, M., *Das refomatorische Erbe unter den Palästinensern: Zur Entstehung der Evangelisch-Lutherischen Kirche in Jordanien* (Gütersloh: 1990).

Rhodes, A., *Jerusalem As It Is* (London: 1865).

Richter, J., *A History of Protestant Missions in the Near East* (Edinburgh/London: 1910).

Rivlin, A.B., *Jerusalem, the History of the Jewish People in Nineteenth Century* (Tel-Aviv: 1966) (Hebrew).

Robinson, E., *Biblical Researches in Palestine and the Adjacent Region*, 3 Vols (London: 1856).

Rubin, R., 'History of the Colonization of Artass', in Ely Schiller (ed.), *Zev Vilnay's Jubilee Volume*, Jerusalem, 1984, pp. 325–30 (Hebrew).

Rustum, A.J., *The Royal Archives of Egypt and the Origins of the Egyptian Expedition to Syria, 1831–1841* (Beirut: 1936).

Sandel, T., 'Der Königl. Württemb. Baurat Dr C. Schick', *Die Warte des Tempels*, 15 (1902), p. 117.

Sapir, S., 'The Contribution of the Anglican Mission Societies to the Development of Jerusalem at the End of the Ottoman Rule', MA dissertation, Hebrew University, Jerusalem, 1979 (Hebrew).

Sapir, S., 'Historical Sources Relating to the Anglican Missionary Society Active in Jerusalem and Palestine toward the End of Ottoman Rule 1800–1914', *Cathedra*, 19 (1981), pp. 155–70 (Hebrew).

Sapir, S., 'Bishop Blyth and his Jerusalem Legacy: St George's College', *Cathedra*, 46 (1987), pp. 45–64 (Hebrew).

Sapir, S., 'The Anglican Church in Jerusalem', in Ely Schiller (ed.), *Zev Vilnay's Jubilee Volume*, Vol. 2 (Jerusalem: 1987), pp. 50–7 (Hebrew).

Sapir, S., 'Conrad Schick and his Activity with the British Mission in Jerusalem', in H. Goren (ed.), *For the Sake of Jerusalem, Conrad Schick* (*Ariel*, 130–1) (Jerusalem: 1998), pp. 73–8 (Hebrew).

Schama, S., *Two Rothschilds and the Land of Israel* (London: 1978).

Schick, C., 'Die Baugeschichte der Stadt Jerusalem in kurzen Umrissen von den ältesten Zeiten bis auf die Gegenwart dargestellt', *Zeitschrift des Deutschen Palästina-Vereins*, 17 (1894), pp. 251–76.

Schmidt-Clausen, K., *Vorweggenommene Einheit: Die Gründung des Bistums Jerusalem im Jahre 1841* (Berlin/Hamburg: 1965).

Schütz, C., 'Preussen in Jerusalem (1800–1861): Karl Friedrich Schinkels Entwurf der Grabeskirche und die Jerusalempälne Friedrich Wilhelms IV', PhD dissertation, Berlin, 1986.

Schütz, C., *Preussen in Jerusalem (1800-1861): Karl Friedrich Schinkels Entwurf der Grabeskirche und die Jerusalempälne Friedrich Wilhelms IV* (Berlin: 1988).

Schwake, N., *Die Entwicklung des Krankenhauswesens der Stadt Jerusalem vom Ende des 18. Bis zum Beginn des 20. Jahrhunderts*, 2 Vols (Herzogenrath: 1983).

Sengelmann, H., *Dr. Joseph Wolff. Ein Wanderleben* (Hamburg: 1863).

Shamir, S., 'Egyptian Rule (1832–1840) and the Beginning of the Modern Period in the History of Palestine', in A.Cohen and G.Baer (eds), *Egypt and Palestine* (Jerusalem: 1984), pp. 214–31.

Shirion, I., *Memoirs* (Jerusalem: 1943) (Hebrew).

Simeon, C., *Memoirs of the Life of the Rev. Charles Simeon*, W. Carus (ed.), 2nd edn (London: 1847).

Smith, H., *The Protestant Bishopric in Jerusalem* (London: 1847).

Smith, R.M., 'The London Jews' Society and Patterns of Jewish Conversion in England, 1801–1859', *Jewish Social Studies*, 43 (1981), pp. 275–90.

Sokolow, N., *History of Zionism, 1600–1918*, 2 Vols (London: 1919).

Spafford-Vester, B., *Our Jerusalem: An American Family in the Holy City 1881–1949* (London: 1951).

Spyridon, S.N., 'Annals of Palestine 1821–1841', *Journal of Palestine Oriental Society*, 18 (1938), pp. 63–152; in *Extracts from Annals of Palestine 1821–1841, Manuscript – Monk Neophitos of Cyprus* (Jerusalem: 1979).

Stern, H.A., *Wanderings among the Falashas in Abyssinia* (London: 1862).

Stock, E., *The History of the Church Missionary Society: Its Environment, its Men and its Work*, 3 Vols (London: 1899).

Strobel, A., *Conrad Schick: Ein Leben für Jerusalem* (Fürth in Bayern: 1988).

Taubenhaus, E., *One Man's Way: A Dreamer and Fighter in the City of the Kabbalists* (Haifa: 1959) (Hebrew).

Temperley, H.W.T., *England and the Near East. The Crimea* (London/New York/Toronto: 1964).

Temperley, H., *A Century of Diplomatic Blue Books, 1814–1914* (London: 1966).

Thiersch, H.W.J. and Gobat, S., *Samuel Gobat, Bishop of Jerusalem: His Life and Work* (London: 1884).

Thompson, A.E., *A Century of Jewish Mission* (Edinburgh: 1902).

Tibawi, A.L., *British Interests in Palestine 1800–1901: A Study of Religious and Educational Enterprise* (Oxford: 1961).

Tibawi, A.L., *American Interests in Syria 1800–1901: A Study of Educational, Literary and Religious Work* (Oxford: 1966).

Tibawi, A.L., 'The Letter Commendatory Relating to the Anglican Bishopric in Jerusalem', *The Muslim World*, 69, 1 (1979), pp. 1–7.

Tobler, T., *Topographie von Jerusalem und seinen Umgebungen*, Vol. 1, *Die heilige Stadt* (Berlin: 1853).

Tobler, T., *Nazareth in Palästina* (Berlin: 1868).

Tuchman, B.W., *Bible and Sword* (New York: 1956).

Valentiner, F., *Das heilige Land, 'wie es war' und 'wie es ist'. Für Kirche, Schule und Haus* (Kiel: 1868).

Vereté, M., 'Palmerston and the Levant Crisis 1832', *Journal of Modern History*, 24 (1952), pp. 143–51

Vereté, M., 'The Restoration of the Jews in the Protestant Thought in England during the Years 1790–1840', *Zion*, 33 (1968), pp. 145–79 (Hebrew).

Vereté, M., 'Why was a British Consulate Established in Jerusalem?', *The English Historical Review*, 85 (1970), pp. 316–45.

Way, L., *Reviewers Reviewed, or, Observations on Article II: Of the British Critic* (London: 1819).

Way, L., *A Letter Addressed to the Right Reverend the Lord Bishop of St David's*, 2nd edn (Dublin: 1820).

Webster, C., *The Foreign Policy of Palmerston, 1830-1841, Britain, the Liberal Movement and the Eastern Question*, 2 Vols (London: 1969).

Welch, P.J., 'Anglican Churchmen and the Establishment of the Jerusalem Bishopric', *The Journal of Ecclesiastical History*, 8 (1957), pp. 193–204.

Wilkinson, J., *The Courage Doctors: The History of the Edinburgh Medical Missionary Society 1841 to 1991* (Edinburgh: 1991).

Williams, G., *The Holy City: Historical, Topographical, and Antiquarian Notices of Jerusalem*, 2 Vols (London: 1849).

Wilson, C.W., 'Obituary of Dr Conrad Schick', *Palestine Exploration Fund Quarterly Statement* (1902), pp. 139–42.

Wolf [sic], J., *Missionary Journal and Memoir of the Rev. Joseph Wolf, Missionary to the Jews* (London: 1824).

Wolff, J., *Researches and Missionary Labours among the Jews, Mohammedans, and other Sects, By the Rev. Joseph Wolff* (London: 1835).

Wolff, J., *Journal of the Rev. Joseph Wolff, Missionary to the Jews, in A Series of Letters to Sir Thomas Baring* (London: 1839).

Wolff, J., *Travels and Adventures*, 2 Vols, 2nd edn (London: 1860).

Wolff, P., *Jerusalem nach eigener Umschauung und den neuesten Forschungen geschildert von Dr. Philipp Wolff* (Leipzig: 1862).

# Index